SURVIVING
THE MILLENNIUM

SURVIVING THE MILLENNIUM

American Global Strategy, the Collapse of the Soviet Empire, and the Question of Peace

Hall Gardner

PRAEGER

Westport, Connecticut
London

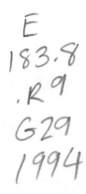

E
183.8
.R9
G29
1994

Library of Congress Cataloging-in-Publication Data

Gardner, Hall.
    Surviving the millennium : American global strategy, the collapse
of the Soviet Empire, and the question of peace / Hall Gardner.
      p. cm.
    Includes bibliographical references and index.
    ISBN 0–275–94754–8 (alk. paper)
    1. United States—Foreign relations—Russia. 2. Russia—Foreign
relations—United States.   3. United States—Foreign relations—
Soviet Union. 4. Soviet Union—Foreign relations—United States.
5. United States—Foreign relations—1989- I. Title.
E183.8.R9G29   1994
327.73047—dc20   93-23477

British Library Cataloguing in Publication Data is available.

Library of Congress Catalog Card Number: 93-23477
ISBN: 0-275-94754-8

First published in 1994

Praeger Publishers, 88 Post Road West, Westport, CT 06881
An imprint of Greenwood Publishing Group, Inc.

Printed in the United States of America

The paper used in this book complies with the
Permanent Paper Standard issued by the National
Information Standards Organization (Z39.48–1984).

10 9 8 7 6 5 4 3 2 1

For my family;
For Isabel, Celine, and Francesca;
For all those who supported this project
and for all those who did not.

Contents

Preface

Writing this book has been a bit like aiming at a bat in-flight. Not only has the present been darting back and forth (an earlier draft was completed just prior to the collapse of the Soviet empire), but the past has also been zigzagging almost as rapidly in the sense that new disclosures have uncovered previously clandestine aspects of the Cold War—and all has yet to be revealed. My purpose has accordingly been to incorporate as many of these newly disclosed facts as is possible into a broader theoretical perspective—one that I hope can help formulate an irenic global strategy for the post–Cold War era.

I would like to thank the libraries of the Johns Hopkins School of Advanced International Studies, the American University of Paris, and of the Fondation Nationale des Sciences Politique for their assistance in helping me obtain research materials. I would also like to thank the Cold War International History Project of the Woodrow Wilson International Center for Scholars for promptly sending me their studies based on archival research. The Lounsbery Foundation provided a small, but helpful, grant. Marc Glaeser helped to proofread; Radoslava Stefanova put in many extra hours in helping to produce the final manuscript.

I would also like to thank Richard J. Barnet, David P. Calleo, Charles F. Doran, Marcus Raskin, Robert W. Tucker, and I. William Zartman for their encouragement during the time this project has been in progress. Each has directly or indirectly influenced this work. Most of all, I thank George Liska for his crucial support—when it was most needed.

The views expressed—correct or incorrect—are, of course, my own responsibility.

Acronyms

ARRF	ACE Rapid Reaction Force
ABM	Anti-Ballistic Missile treaty
AFTA	Asian Free Trade Area
APEC	Asian Pacific Economic Caucus
BMD	Ballistic Missile Defense
CCP	Chinese Communist Party
CENTO	Central Treaty Organization
CFE	Conventional-Force-in-Europe talks
CJTF	Combined Joint Task Force
CIA	Central Intelligence Agency (U.S.)
CIS	Commonwealth of Independent States
CMEA	Soviet-East European Council for Mutual Economic Assistance
COCOM	Coordinating Committee for Export Controls
CSCE	Conference on Security and Cooperation in Europe
DPG	Defense Planning Guidance
EC	European Community (became European Union [EU] November 1993)
EEC	European Economic Community
EDC	European Defense Community
EFTA	European Free Trade Area
EBRD	European Bank for Reconstruction and Development
EUREKA	European Research Coordination Agency
ESDI	European Security Defense Identity
EU	European Union
EURATOM	European Atomic Community
FRG	Federal Republic of Germany
FSX	Advanced U.S.-Japanese fighter jet
G-5; G-7	Group of Five; Group of Seven (industrialized countries)

GATT	General Agreement on Tariffs and Trade
GDR	German Democratic Republic
GIUK	Greenland-Iceland-UK defense gap.
GPALS	Global Protection Against Limited Strikes
ICBM	Intercontinental Ballistic Missile
IAEA	International Atomic Energy Agency
IMF	International Monetary Fund
INF	Intermediate-Range Nuclear Forces
IRBM	Intermediate-Range Ballistic Missile
KGB	Soviet Intelligence Agency
KMT	Kuomintang (Chinese Nationalist Party)
MBFR	Mutual and Balanced Force Reduction Talks
MFN	Most-favored Nation status
MIRV	Multiple Independently Targetable Reentry Vehicle
MTCR	Missile Technology Control Regime
MX	Missile Experimental
NACC	North Atlantic Cooperation Council
NAFTA	North American Free Trade Agreement
NATO	North Atlantic Treaty Organization
NPT	Non-Proliferation Treaty
NSC	National Security Council (U.S.)
NSDD	National Security Decision Directive (U.S.)
OECD	Organization for Economic Cooperation and Development
OPEC	Organization of Petroleum Exporting Countries
PLA	People's Liberation Army (PRC)
PRC	People's Republic of China
PRM	Presidential Review Memorandum
REGT	Resurgent/Emergent Global Threat
SALT	Strategic Arms Limitation Talks
SDI	Strategic Defense Initiative
SSD	Safety, Security, and Disarmament talks
SII	Structural Impediments Initiative (U.S. and Japan)
SIOP	Single Integrated Operations Plan
SLBM	Submarine Launched Ballistic Missile
SLOC	Sea Lines of Communication
SS-18; SS-24	Surface-to-Surface MIRVed ICBMs (Russian)
START	Strategic Arms Reduction Talks
WEU	West European Union
UNCTAD	United Nations Conference on Trade and Development
UNRRA	United Nations Relief and Rehabilitation Administration
UK	United Kingdom
Visegrad group	Poland, Czech Republic, Slovakia, Hungary

SURVIVING
THE MILLENNIUM

Introduction:
U.S.-Soviet/Russian Relations
in the Twilight Zone

In contrast to essentially bipolar analyses of the Cold War and its aftermath, this book seeks to explore the complex interrelationships between the United States and Soviet Union, and between the United States and Russia, with the emerging core and semiperipheral powers and regional blocs. Much like a Cubist painting, the intent is to capture the historical dynamics of inter- and intra-state rivalry from multiple and interacting perspectives: the geostrategic, military-technological, political-economic, and sociocultural/ideological. The study examines foreign policy options involving threats of "encirclement" and "counter-encirclement" before, during, and after the Cold War with an emphasis on the causes and consequences of the Soviet implosion.

The book argues five fundamental points:

1. The post–1945 U.S.-Soviet/Russian relationship has been characterized by an ambivalent mix of discord and collaboration involving both the "containment" of the Soviet Union/Russia and a "containment" of emerging powers—a twilight zone somewhere between global peace and global war. This relationship has not merely involved the generally recognized "double containment"[1] of Germany and Japan after the decisive allied victory in World War II, but it also includes the initially collaborative U.S.-Soviet relationship in regard to emerging core and semiperipheral actors. The five dimensions of double containment (explained in Chapter 1) thus represent the historically evolving interplay between the United States and the Soviet Union/Russia in the effort to manage the burgeoning power capabilities of *potential* rivals and political-economic blocs.

2. American global strategy—as set forth by National Security Council Directive 68 (NSC 68)—did seek to undermine the Soviet empire, but at the risk of sacrificing Moscow's tacit role in checking or limiting the capabilities of American allies (as well as emerging third powers) for independent political-economic and military action. In essence, rather than seeking a *devolution* of Moscow's controls over Central and Eastern Europe through mutual compromise, U.S. national security managers chose a more military-oriented approach to containment involving the build-up of NATO forces, closer links to the U.S.-Japanese alliance (which consisted of a step-by-step merger of U.S. military might and consumerism with Japanese dual-use high technology and finance), a tenuous entente with the PRC, and supports for semiperipheral and peripheral anti-Soviet regimes and resistance groups. In particular, the not-entirely-reluctant U.S. acceptance of West German goals of unification helped to reinforce the political-economic and sociocultural/ideological undercurrents that ultimately worked to undermine the Soviet leadership. U.S. global strategy thus succeeded in breaking up the Soviet empire without provoking global conventional or thermonuclear war, but concurrently risked the destabilization of the Eurasian continent, as well as semiperipheral and peripheral states directly or indirectly affected by the U.S.-Soviet rivalry.

3. The inherent contradictions involved in the containment of both the Soviet Union *and* the burgeoning ambitions of U.S. allies also accounted for the *relative* decline of U.S. political-economic leadership vis-à-vis Germany/Europe, Japan, and potentially the PRC. (U.S. demands for "burden sharing," for example, were generally challenged by allied demands for "power sharing" and other concessions from the United States.) The collaborative aspects of the U.S.-Soviet/Russian relationship have been further undermined by the reluctance of Washington to draw Moscow into the world economy at an earlier date and by the ability of emerging powers to forge new geostrategic and political-economic blocs (an expanding European Union [EU], a potential Japanese "yen bloc," the PRC's absorption of Hong Kong in 1997), representing a significant transformation of the global equipoise. As a consequence, and in part as a means to stave off its own *relative* decline, the United States initiated its own hemispheric geoeconomic bloc, the North American Free Trade Agreement (NAFTA). In effect, in the not so inadvertent effort to destabilize the Soviet Union, the United States also fostered the burgeoning global/regional influence of U.S. allies and helped build the power capabilities of the PRC as well.

4. Tacit recognition of spheres of influence, formal agreements and cooperation on specific issues, instantaneous communication and the

reconnaissance revolution, plus essentially bipolar controls over nuclear weaponry were important, but not sufficient to prevent global conflict during the "long peace."[2] These factors were really secondary to the double containment of the evolving power capabilities of potential rivals. Accordingly, the more the Russian role in the five-dimensional double containment continues to unravel, the greater the danger that regional conflicts could escalate into global conflict. Rather than becoming "obsolete,"[3] global conflict has accordingly become even more plausible in the post–Cold War era.

From this perspective, it is dubious that the acquisition of genetically genocidal nuclear weapons by the emerging powers will necessarily deter regional or global conflict as suggested by the unit-veto theory.[4] As conventional weaponry becomes more accurate and deadly, and as the actual war-fighting utility of strategic nuclear weaponry declines, the dissuasive value of nuclear weapons will likewise continue to drop. War among nuclear powers of roughly equivalent military-technological capabilities could take place as an intermittent series of intense but generally *indecisive* conflicts involving conventional, not-so-conventional, and high-tech weaponry. The use of tactical nuclear weapons at earlier stages of conflict (particularly in peripheral regions) may not necessarily lead to an automatic usage of strategic nuclear weaponry. On the other hand, major nuclear weapons states could opt for preemptive strikes against the burgeoning nuclear capacity of emerging powers—assuming such actions are not considered too risky, drawing the major power into an undesired quagmire. At the same time, lesser powers could still threaten a major nuclear power—or its allies—with a relatively limited nuclear capacity, and concurrently engage in acts of regional imperialism. Moreover, much as Japan struck Port Arthur in 1904 and then Pearl Harbor in 1941, a surprise "all or nothing" nuclear strike by an isolated emerging power against a more powerful nuclear state cannot entirely be ruled out.[5]

Although the Korean War, the Berlin crises, the Cuban missile crisis, and the Arab-Israeli conflicts did come close to sparking global war, U.S.-Soviet conflict was generally indirect and limited to peripheral areas that did not affect "vital" security interests of the United States and Soviet Union. (The United States did, however, strike a Soviet air base at Vladivostok during the Korean War.) The post–Cold War era, however, has been characterized by the disintegration of both *external* and *internal* Russian spheres of influence and security. An overextended Soviet Union has been pushed back to Russia's seventeenth–century borders; regions vital to the survival of the Russian Federation itself have also demanded greater autonomy or independence.

The possibilities for global war have thus been exacerbated by the fact that the new Russia has been increasingly forced to relinquish its collaborative role in double-containing the emergence of the powers that might "threaten" its vital interests. As East Germany represented the keystone to Soviet external defenses, as well as to domination over Moscow's internal empire, German unification has raised Russian fears of isolation from Europe (pressing Russia closer to the PRC) and of potential fratricidal conflict with Slavic Ukraine. Turkish-Iranian rivalry for influence over Central Asia (and for influence over regions such as Tatarstan within the Russian Federation itself) may further alienate Moscow. Japanese pressure to regain the Kurile Islands (or northern territories) has put increasing pressure on the Russian Far East. Moscow's efforts to regain and sustain *primacy* (if not *hegemony*) over the former Soviet empire, including the retention of ties with former Communist elites, plus efforts to juggle the conflicting interests of Iran, India, and the PRC—if at all feasible—may concurrently prove provocative. Russian reluctance (or inability) to support strong sanctions against pan-Serb expansion plus military involvement in conflicts in Armenia/Azerbaijan, Georgia, Moldova, and Tajikistan have raised not unwarranted fears of a renewed Russian imperialism or *dominance*.

Moreover, as states attempt to gain political-military independence in a highly uneven polycentric global system (see Chapter 2), the emerging core and semiperipheral powers and blocs may well engage in provocative regional actions, or else forge new alliances that neither the United States nor the new Russia can effectively contain or manage. Interlinking alliance formations (and efforts to sustain the political-military allegiance of allies) could also draw emerging powers (not necessarily Russia) into conflicts in regions that are no longer part of clearly defined spheres of influence and security. Pan-nationalist demands to protect the Russian—and Russified—diaspora could spark conflict, but so could the regional ambitions of states other than Russia.

From this perspective, U.S.-Russian relations have still been characterized by games of encirclement and counter-encirclement. As long as there is no significant and mutual third party threat, it is dubious that Washington and Moscow can forge a long-term entente relationship despite the end of the Cold War and the apparent Russian ideological conversion to democratic liberalism. During the Cold War, despite tacit U.S.-Soviet collaboration, potential threats from Germany, Japan, Iran, and most pertinently China were not regarded as significant enough to impel Washington and Moscow to move beyond détente and toward a full-fledged entente.

5. Accordingly, without a perceived potential threat from a nuclear Ukraine in the post–Cold War era, it is dubious that the United States and Russia would have moved so rapidly to conclude the START II agreement and then, in January 1994, to forge a disarmament pact that is intended to dismantle the Ukrainian nuclear arsenal over a seven year period. From this perspective, in order to ameliorate tensions, a concerted irenic strategy that emphasizes "security with disarmament" should be implemented. Such a strategy would attempt to forge a U.S.-German/European-Russian-Japanese entente that would actively assist the amelioration of tensions between Russia and Ukraine, help double-contain the PRC, and minimize the dangers of Russo-Japanese, Sino-Japanese-Korean, or Indo-Pakistani-Chinese conflict, among other possibilities. This new concert would also work to avert the formation of new alliances which could possibly manipulate U.S. interests (Russia and the PRC; Germany/Europe with the PRC and/or Japan; Ukraine, Poland and/or the PRC, for example).

Such a strategy would involve the *grafting* of international security regimes, such as those of a significantly more effective and empowered Conference for Security and Cooperation in Europe (CSCE) and the United Nations (UN), onto previously existing security regimes, such as NATO and the U.S.-Japanese alliance. (President Bill Clinton's November 1993 Partnership for Peace initiative, for example, needs to be supplemented by the deployment of UN or CSCE preventive war forces in key strategic regions located throughout the former Soviet bloc.) A concerted strategy would accordingly grant the new Russia *legitimate* spheres of influence and security at the same time that it seeks to dampen the international and domestic sources of a revanchist backlash—a possibility that has appeared to gain credibility following the December 1993 Russian parliamentary elections but that is still not inevitable. Moreover, such a global strategy represents an alternative to that of tightening the belt of multilateral "encirclement" around Russia by means of expanding NATO and/or EU alliances into Central and Eastern Europe—that is, without simultaneously seeking joint U.S., German/European, and Russian security guarantees in such a venture.

There is a real danger, however, that the United States and the new Russia (along with the other major powers) will not be able to establish—and sustain—a more concerted relationship. Assuming that new systems of international security cannot be soon established, the United States and its remaining allies may then have to choose between interventionism and a not entirely risk free strategy of "appeasement" vis-à-vis Russia, the PRC, and/or other third powers depending upon the number and nature of "revisionist" or "revanchist" regimes.

In this study, Chapter 1 critiques U.S. global strategy as defined by NSC 68 and points to options that might have led to a more gradual *devolution* of Soviet power over Central and Eastern Europe—had these options been implemented during the Cold War. Chapter 2 examines the theoretical consequences of the end of the Cold War and questions whether contemporary U.S.-Russian relations have truly moved toward a "perpetual peace" involving the formation of democratic-liberal confederations in which the relationship between parliaments and their executive branches will necessarily inhibit war. Chapter 2 also looks at both the pre–World War I and pre–World War II analogies and discusses the question of appeasement. Chapter 3 first outlines relevant features of the pre-containment era in regard to tsarist Russian and then Soviet fears of encirclement and acts of counter-encirclement. The rest of Chapter 3, followed by Chapters 4–5, explores the dynamic forces of encirclement and counter-encirclement since 1945 that corroded the Soviet empire and that began to unravel the tacit Soviet role in the five-dimensional double containment of emerging powers and blocs. These chapters also point to lost opportunities in which a U.S.-Soviet entente could have been forged.

Aspects of "economic warfare" resulting in the collapse of the Soviet Union and the subsequent Weimar-like instability of Russia and Ukraine, the relative atrophy (and attempted revitalization) of U.S. political-economic capabilities, the global spread of dual-use high technology, and the emergence of Japan, Germany/Europe, and ultimately China as core political-economic actors within potential regional blocs are then examined in Chapter 6. The Soviet quest to achieve strategic-nuclear parity and the issues concerning U.S.-Russian parity and disarmament are raised in Chapter 7, as is the question of Ballistic Missile Defenses (BMD) and ostensible U.S.-Russian efforts to sustain the double containment over the missile and military-technological potential of the emerging powers. Chapter 8 sketches the basis of the new global equipoise in the U.S.-Russian "courtship" phase (1991–?) and analyses the efforts of the emerging powers to manipulate U.S. and Russian relations in a highly uneven polycentric international system. Chapter 9 argues for the concerted global strategy described above, but also outlines five pessimistic scenarios. If *homo geopoliticus* is to survive the millennium, U.S. national security managers must not commit errors similar to those committed by their British counterparts before World Wars I and II.

1

Five Dimensions of "Double Containment"

A CRITIQUE OF NSC 68

In the effort to formulate a global strategy designed to avert the real possibilities of major power war, a re-examination of the goals of National Security Council Directive 68 (NSC 68)—a document which continued to frame the essential contours of American national security policy throughout the Cold War—is imperative.

For the essential reasons that NSC 68 outlined in 1950, U.S. global strategy never sought to achieve a full-fledged entente with Moscow on the basis of political "parity" that might have truly ameliorated global tensions. U.S.-Soviet negotiations never fully addressed the key issues dividing both sides that would have permitted the two states to move beyond the twilight zone of confrontation and détente (a relaxing of tense relations between states) and toward entente (the development of actively cooperative relations). The next step is alliance (a formal or informal mutual defense pact).

NSC 68 argued that the Soviet Union would be unable to sustain the global competition with the United States and its allies in the long run. It thus ruled dogmatically—in part in an effort to galvanize the federal bureaucracy to support a radically new peace time policy of global engagement—that there was no necessity for any mutual compromise that would sacrifice American or allied interests. Accordingly, the United States refused to explore the nuances of potential entente or alliance offers by Nikita Khrushchev, Leonid Brezhnev, and Mikhail Gorbachev—*even if* such an entente or alliance could have been made open to other U.S. allies.

In what was truly a self-fulfilled prophecy, the overextended

Soviet empire did collapse, but NSC 68 made no thorough assessment as to what might occur if the Russian people did finally overthrow their Communist masters. On the one hand, failure to forge a U.S.-Soviet entente was in large part due to the fact that no immediate mutual threat impelled the two powers into closer relations. On the other hand, inability to forge a strong relationship also revealed a lack of foresight among the American elite in considering the long-term consequences of that failure: The dangers of general political and economic instability in a highly uneven polycentric global system, in which emerging powers could more easily assert their largely regional interests, including the fissiparous division of the Soviet Union into potentially rival republics.

In the period 1945–50, American national security managers determined not to explore the possibility of compromise with Moscow. Paul Nitze argued that the Soviet Union could only be contained through hard-line policies: NSC 68 extended the military dimension of the policy of containment as defined by George Kennan in 1948 in NSC 20/4. The stated purpose of NSC 68 was not to destabilize global affairs or roll back the Soviet Union by means of direct military force. Rather, the purpose was to sustain pressure upon the Soviet leadership to force it to relinquish its controls, using all aspects of "strategic leverage" (see Chapter 2) that the United States and its allies had at their disposal. Maintaining Germany and Japan within U.S.-led alliance systems in particular (and keeping France and Italy in tow) were key to sustaining the initial Anglo-American containment of the Soviet Union.

To cause the Soviet Union to implode from within, NSC 68 argued that Washington needed to sustain strategic nuclear, military-technological, and economic superiority "to keep [Moscow] off balance and force an increased expenditure of Soviet resources in counteraction."[1] The build-up of U.S. capabilities represented similar techniques to those used by Moscow, but the United States and its allies possessed greater resources. Such a policy would be dangerous, but less dangerous than "half measures" which "will be more costly and more dangerous, for they will be inadequate to prevent and may actually invite war."

Negotiations should be pursued, but these negotiations should only be used to expose the U.S. point of view and to draw the Soviet leadership closer to accepting that point of view, or else as a means to propagandize against Soviet intransigence to gain both allied and domestic U.S. support. Though minor agreements that sought to mitigate conflict should be pursued, the United States should not lose sight of its larger goal: A negotiated settlement could not take place until a vaguely defined "change . . . in the nature of the Soviet system" had taken place. But here NSC 68 made no clear statement as to whether Moscow *would* change in the direction that Washington believed it *should* change.[2]

The razing of the Berlin Wall in November 1989, at least initially, appeared to vindicate the "hawkish" hard-line Cold War strategy: A tough containment approach vis-à-vis Moscow did not bring global conventional or thermonuclear war. The essential contradiction of NSC 68 strategy, however, stemmed from its intent to bring about an internal revolution in the Soviet Union without concurrently resulting in global destabilization. In fact, NSC 68 had two interrelated and interacting goals: first, "a policy of attempting to develop a healthy international community"; and second, a "policy of 'containing' the Soviet system." The contradiction arose from the fact that as the Soviet Union moved from being an essentially continental Eurasian power to being a global amphibious power, its internal collapse would inexorably possess global ramifications—which would accordingly affect the political-economic stability of the international community.

NSC 68 did recognize the dangers of Soviet economic collapse; but it did not recognize how its hard-line strategy would actually exacerbate the very problems that it sought to avert. In effect, overall U.S. objectives did "not include unconditional surrender, the subjugation of Russian peoples, or a Russia shorn of its economic potential." The latter "would irrevocably unite the Russian people behind the regime which enslaves them." The United States did not seek to implement the first two objectives, but is in danger of actualizing the third. By not more gradually devolving Soviet controls thereby permitting the Soviet Union to enter the world trading system, for example, U.S. global strategy has risked a revanchist Russian backlash. It may have also risked the destabilization of the Eurasian continent—and much of the peripheral world directly or indirectly affected by U.S.-Soviet rivalry.

ALTERNATIVE STRATEGIES

There were numerous occasions when a "softer," more cooptive approach could have permitted a more gradual *devolution* of Soviet controls over Central and Eastern Europe and helped to draw the Soviet Union into the "community of nations" at an earlier stage. These alternatives cannot be dismissed as counter-factual: Many represent part of the historical record and were proposed as realistic options—even if they represented the positions that were not taken. In addition, the promises raised by these various alternative policies played an important role as aspects of the power-based bargaining process between Washington and Moscow. Moreover, even if these options were not actualized at the time they were proposed, some of these options were ultimately adopted, and others (or variations) may still be adopted in the new context of U.S.-Russian relations.

Initially, at the end of World War II, U.S. reluctance to move its armed forces into Berlin or Prague, concurrent with a prompt recognition of Soviet territorial claims, meant Soviet predominance over Central Europe. (Here, however, the desire to keep Moscow in the war with Tokyo resulted in an appeasement of Soviet demands in both Eastern Europe and Asia.) Chances for mutual diplomatic compromise were missed when Washington and Moscow failed to agree over the nature of the German state to be formed. By the 1950s, compromise was once again missed when it appeared that first Stalin (in March 1952), and then Khrushchev, were willing to offer a deal over Germany. In fact, the generally overlooked second version of the Rapacki disarmament plan, plus proposals by Nikolai Bulganin, promised both nuclear- and conventional-force reductions that were very similar to those later offered by Mikhail Gorbachev in 1989. In addition, Khrushchev proposed a NATO-Warsaw Pact nonaggression pact and appeared willing to consider formation of a confederal Germany.[3]

If pursued, an early compromise over the German question might have helped the Soviet Union gradually withdraw its grasp over Eastern Europe. Such a compromise would have looked to the creation of a loose Germanic confederation initially belonging to both NATO and the Warsaw Pact. A confederal approach to the German question would have subsequently mitigated claims to national self-determination among states in the Soviet bloc. Because it was feared that Germany might drift into neutrality, that the European economic recovery might be jeopardized, and that NATO might then be undermined, the chance for compromise was missed. In addition, neither the West nor East German leadership was eager to make these kind of changes in the status quo. Washington refused to press for possible openings for fear of alienating the West German leadership, and East Germany sought to impress Moscow with its importance as a strategic bulwark. (The likelihood that the East German Communist Party might have ultimately withered away in such a confederal state did not seem to influence U.S. or West German policymakers.)

Moreover, rather than framing the Truman Doctrine in such a way as to oppose Communism in general, the United States could have assisted Greece by working *with* the tacit support of Josef Stalin, as both Washington and Moscow had a common interest in seeking to contain Marshall Josip Tito's calls for a pan-Balkan alliance. The United States could have also supported Turkey (as it did) but in such a way as to reach a mutually acceptable compromise over Soviet naval and maritime access to the Mediterranean. Washington could have also been more sensitive to Soviet relations with Iran. Although the United States did not threaten the use of atomic weapons to force the withdrawal of Soviet troops from northern Iran (as President Truman later claimed),[4] Washington did not attempt to sustain a joint policy with Moscow once U.S. and British troops were withdrawn—in effect ending the Anglo-American-Soviet double containment over Iran. In retrospect, U.S. (and really Iranian) efforts to push Moscow out of the region ultimately proved counter-productive following the rise of anti-Western and anti-Soviet pan-Shi'ia and pan-Islamic movements.

A chance to limit or at least slow the spread of atomic weaponry was missed when Washington insisted on establishing an International Atomic Development Authority (IADA) with powers to control and own all atomic energy activities potentially dangerous to world security. As it was evident that Stalin intended to develop an atomic bomb, a more realistic policy might have been to accept a more limited option for control of atomic weaponry: Moscow's 1947 plan was nearly identical to the Nuclear Non-Proliferation Treaty (NPT) adopted almost twenty years later.[5] (NSC 68 did mention the possibility that, "contrary to our expectations," Moscow might accept agreements promising effective control of atomic energy and conventional arms, but "without any other changes in Soviet policies," such a change in Soviet policy would have to be considered very carefully before it could be accepted by Washington. Such a "problem" was dismissed as "unlikely."[6])

In Asia, the U.S. inability to bring Mao and Chiang Kai-shek together (and sustain a U.S.-Soviet alliance with the latter), plus the consequent inability to define its spheres of influence and security clearly, permitted both the Soviet Union and the PRC to press their claims. Having failed to prop up Chiang Kai-shek, the United States possessed few options. Washington at least initially attempted to turn Mao into a "Titoist"—by trying to turn him against Stalin. But this effort overlooked the significant geostrategic differences between the PRC and Yugoslavia and the fact that Maoist claims were of a higher order than those of Tito—and far more difficult to contain. Washington's temptation to support Mao raised Stalin's concerns that the PRC might upstage the Soviet Union for influence over the world Communist movement. A sustained joint U.S.-Soviet policy toward both Chinas and both Koreas, coupled with diplomatic recognition of the PRC and Taiwan as separate states, might have helped to ameliorate Korean tensions and contain the rival unification claims of the Chinese Communists (CCP) and Chinese Nationalists (KMT). It is clear, however, that once the Korean War broke out, both Washington and Moscow attempted to limit its consequences.

Following the Korean War, U.S. support for compromise over the Kurile Islands may have also reduced Soviet-Japanese tensions and may have helped to further enlist Soviet and Japanese support in the effort to contain the burgeoning power potential of the PRC. As the Sino-Soviet conflict intensified, the United States did not fully recognize the extent to which Beijing could threaten the global interests of both Moscow and Washington. Rather than moving toward U.S.-Soviet comanagement of the PRC (in the form of a NATO-Warsaw Pact, U.S.-Japanese-Soviet entente), the United States, by the Nixon administration, moved toward a rapprochement with China, intensifying Soviet perceptions of a "capitalist encirclement" which was linked to Chinese "capitalist roaders" and which supported East European independence movements.

Related to U.S. fears of a Sino-Soviet alliance, the reluctance of the United States to seek a negotiated settlement in Vietnam, either at the time of French withdrawal from Dien Bien Phu in 1954, or before the 1964 Gulf of Tonkin resolution, meant that Washington failed to forge a neutral Vietnam that would counterbalance China, and simultaneously help to limit Soviet influence through mutual compromise (as Hans Morgenthau argued at the time).[7] Washington also feared that Chinese counter-encirclement strategy (and links to Indonesia in the period 1962–65) were tacitly backed by Moscow. A Communist victory in Vietnam would then represent the fruits of Sino-Soviet collaboration and would lead Indochina to collapse like "dominoes." The U.S. preoccupation with Vietnam concurrently permitted Moscow to obtain central strategic nuclear parity with Washington, and to press its support for pro-Soviet national liberation movements (in part in rivalry with the PRC for control over international Communism). Accordingly, U.S. defeat in Vietnam, plus perceptions of Soviet expansionism, helped foster an anti-Soviet backlash by 1977–78, despite initial fears that Washington had already overextended its power capabilities during the Vietnam War. Ironically, however, it was Moscow which ultimately overextended its power capabilities once the Soviet Union collapsed in August 1991.

Additionally, from a domestic perspective, there was no effective American constituency that would back a compromise with the Soviet Union—in part due to the lack of significant U.S. investment in that country. With some exceptions (such as Henry Wallace, Robert Taft, Claude Pepper, and Walter Lippmann), the anti-Communist (and really anti-Soviet) bias of the U.S. foreign policy elite was influenced by anti-Soviet East European and Russian émigrés, and generally seconded by American liberals who feared McCarthyism. After the

McCarthy period, critics of U.S. foreign policy still feared American obloquy—well depicted by Alexis de Tocqueville. (McCarthyism had its historic roots after the Soviet revolution, the 1918 Spartacist revolt, and then the 1919 formation of the Comintern, resulting in the Palmer raids; these actions were ultimately followed by the "loss" of China and attacks on "pro-Soviet" China experts such as Owen Lattimore in the State Department; McCarthyism had a historical parallel in the anti-French Alien and Sedition Acts.) By the 1960s, American leftists tended to adopt anarchist, Titoist, Trotskyite, Maoist, or Third Worldist ideologies. From this perspective, a general ideological concordance *against* the Soviet Union among the "right," "center," and "left"—plus the lack of a clear and mutual third threat—prevented the formulation of an alternative, yet "realistic" global strategy.

The failure to resolve the foregoing questions, plus the failure to resolve the other key questions—such as those involving most-favored nation (MFN) status; dual-use high technology restrictions (defined by the Coordinating Committee for Export Controls [COCOM]); financial assistance and investment limitations; minimum Soviet participation in allied control councils in Japan and Italy; in addition to key strategic nuclear questions, such as whether or not to develop the hydrogen bomb, missiles with multiple warheads (MIRV), and the Strategic Defense Initiative (SDI)—all tended to exacerbate global tensions and cause a financially and ecologically disastrous nuclear and conventional arms rivalry. Failure to reach an earlier U.S.-Soviet accord likewise exacerbated tensions in regional hot spots in which Washington and Moscow often took sides with rival factions in an effort to exploit those regional rivalries rather than working jointly to reach political settlements. Joint U.S.-European-Soviet guarantees to Kuwait granted during the Iran-Iraq war in the 1980s might have checked Iraqi claims, for example; joint U.S.-European-Soviet pressure on Serbia in 1991 might have helped to further contain that conflict.

The Soviet elite consequently strained resources in an ultimately futile quest to obtain *parity* (see Chapter 2) with the United States and its allies—much as NSC 68 predicted. The combination of U.S. unwillingness to accept the Soviet quest for parity, fears of losing U.S. allies to a vaguely defined neutral status, the push of newly acquired U.S. allies for unification or revisionist claims against Soviet interests, lack of common values and *Weltanschauung* on the part of the American and Soviet leaderships, and most importantly, the lack of a clear and immediate mutual threat—all served to inhibit an alternative yet more flexible and "realistic" irenic diplomacy.

Because of the issues raised by the Soviet collapse, the concerns of a major critic of U.S. containment strategy, Walter Lippmann, have become more salient. It was Lippmann, more than George Kennan, who most emphasized the necessity for U.S.-Soviet collaboration, though both opposed NSC 68's efforts to deny Moscow nuclear strategic and political parity with the Washington. The key difference lies in the fact that Lippmann argued for the early establishment of a confederal Germany that might establish a basis for U.S.-Soviet collaboration.[8] Kennan, however, initially supported Bonn's claims to unification for fear that West Germany would be exposed to Communist subversion.

In his essay, *U.S. War Aims* (1944), Lippmann critiqued the use of Wilsonian "democracy" and "national self-determination" as a tool to undermine the Soviet empire. Lippmann emphasized the danger of implementing a strategy of "encirclement" against the Soviet Union and opposed the concept of a *cordon sanitaire*. America and Russia, he said, could have peace "if they use their alliances to stabilize the foreign policy of their allies"; but they would "have war if either of them reaches out for allies within the orbit of the other."[9] Lippmann went one step further to emphasize what other factors might generate a global conflict: "If the Atlantic Community, or any individual member of it, say Great Britain or France, made an alliance—*which was not open to the Soviet Union or made with its consent*—with Germany, or any state within the Russian orbit, say Poland, the event would be the certain sign that the structure of peace had been fatally broken [emphasis mine]."[10]

Here, of course, it can be argued that Lippmann was wrong. The incorporation of West Germany into NATO and of Japan into a bilateral U.S.-Japanese alliance did not bring war. It can also be argued that the collapse of the Soviet bloc in 1989–91 and Wilsonian support for the principle of national self-determination have not brought war either. But such a point of view misses the key difference between the largely bipolar world of the Cold War with its more clearly defined spheres of influence and security (a bipolarity forged *after* Lippmann wrote his analysis), and the more polycentric global system—that lacks clearly defined spheres of influence and security—which has begun to develop since the collapse of the Soviet empire. Lippmann's argument appears wrong—but only because Stalin moved into East Germany and Eastern Europe to preclude just such a possibility. Accordingly, it can be argued, the issues that Lippmann raised in 1944 really did not come to the forefront until the collapse of the Berlin Wall in 1989.

As not only the Warsaw Pact countries but also states within the former Soviet empire have obtained independence from Moscow, there is still a danger that a future formal or informal alliance might be formed by NATO with Poland, Hungary, the Czech Republic, Slovakia, and/or other states of the former Soviet empire, most provocatively, Ukraine. There is also a possibility that a *wider* European Union [EU] could forge a separate alliance with states "within the Russian orbit." Here, Finland—in addition to neutral Sweden and Austria—could enter the EU by 1995; the Czech Republic and Hungary also seek EU membership.

The initial February 1992 drafts of Pentagon Defense Planning Guidance (DPG) documents did consider "extend[ing] to East and Central European nations security commitments similar to those extended to Saudi Arabia, Kuwait, and other Gulf states."[11] The February document also warned of the possibility of a "resurgent/emergent global threat" (REGT), should a revanchist Russia (perhaps linked in alliance to other states, such as the PRC) come to the forefront around the year 2001. REGT could become a self-fulfilled prophecy if Russian fears of encirclement are actualized. This could happen if Ukraine threatens to move out of its rather tenuous "union" with Russia in the Commonwealth of Independent States (CIS) and looks for support from Germany/Europe, the United States, or, increasingly likely, the PRC. Ukrainian efforts to forge closer defense ties with Poland, Hungary, and the Baltic states have been denounced by Moscow; Kiev, in turn, denounced efforts to forge a Russian version of the Monroe Doctrine. Russian efforts to forge a close entente with the PRC have also been, in part, designed to head off a Ukrainian-PRC alignment. Encirclement may also be actualized if Turkey continues to press its claims in rivalry with Iran, or if the United States and Japan refuse to reach a compromise with Russia.

The later Pentagon May 1992 DPG draft toned down the language of the original draft (Japan, Germany, and India were no longer deemed potential military threats); it called for a "democratic partnership" with the new Russia. The earlier draft, however, still raised suspicions as to Washington's ultimate intent. Total Pentagon allocations demanded remained at $1.5 trillion over the 1992–97 period. Despite efforts to cut costs through a Bottom-Up Review, this fact indicated that demands for U.S. war-fighting capabilities against potential Russian and regional threats had not changed significantly, and raised questions as to whether the U.S. military-industrial complex had truly become permanent. By November 1993 Russia formulated its own controversial military and strategic doctrine (see Chapter 7).[12]

On the one hand, NATO has not overtly threatened to "encircle" the new Russia; it has welcomed former Warsaw Pact and Soviet republics to its new North Atlantic Cooperation Council (NACC) to discuss confidence- and security-building measures. In addition, the Bush administration insisted that Moscow retain sole command and control over former Soviet nuclear weapons. More emphatically, the June 1992

Bush/Yeltsin summit and the December 1992 signing of the START II agreement promised to move toward a new U.S.-Russian entente. The rush to sign the START II agreement was to a large extent intended to forestall Ukrainian efforts (as well as those of Belarus and Kazakhstan) to retain their nuclear arsenals. President Clinton then sought to strengthen the U.S.-Russian relationship through military cooperation and renewed G-7 "strategic investment."

On the other hand, it is not clear how long Washington will continue to grant Moscow the role of "first among equals" in the newly formed CIS. In effect, post–Cold War American foreign policy has been afflicted by the precarious effort to "balance" Wilsonian ideological support for national self-determination against support for Russian primacy/hegemony over the former Soviet republics and East European states. President Clinton's Partnership for Peace proposal of November 1993 was intended to counterbalance rival interests among states of the former Soviet bloc; at the same time, it permits Washington to hold its options open, and not necessarily include or exclude NATO membership for any one state, including Russia. The latter stated its intent to join the Partnership in March 1994—but could still pose some "basic conditions."

From the point of view of those who seek to limit Western commitments and liabilities, it is feared that premature admission to NATO could permit politically and economically instable Central and East European states to not so inadvertently drag NATO or the EU into regional conflicts (not necessarily those with Russia). Instable states could also change leaderships, shift allegiances, and expose NATO military capabilities and secrets. Moreover, NATO membership for these states could overextend NATO capabilities, particularly if Moscow takes counter-measures (see Chapter 7). And finally, NATO's inability to act in the former Yugoslavia (despite air strikes in early 1994) does not portend well for a defense of Central or Eastern Europe—in case Western resolve should be tested.

From the opposite viewpoint, Henry Kissinger, for example, has argued that NATO membership for Central European states may actually help to discredit a Russian revanchist movement by showing Western resolve. Moreover, he has argued that Central European state membership in NATO is largely inevitable, as these states will ultimately be drawn into the EU, and hence, indirectly into NATO. There has accordingly been a push (encouraged by Bonn) to incorporate Central European states into NATO *prior* to the development of a full-fledged Russian partnership with NATO. Before the January 1994 NATO summit, Poland and Lithuania pressed for a precise timetable for NATO membership; Poland threatened an alliance with a nuclear

Ukraine if membership in NATO was not soon granted. Secretary of State Warren Christopher responded that "swift expansion of NATO eastward could make a neo-imperialist Russia a self-fulfilling prophecy." But he also warned that ". . . if there's a reversal, if they're a revanchist country, then . . . NATO would have to consider the erection of a security barrier of the kind we had in the past."[13]

In regard to Kiev, certain foreign policy analysts have urged "tilting" toward Ukraine—despite its precarious instability.[14] This approach, however, appears myopic. While Washington should try to mediate between Kiev and Moscow, lack of foresight could lead Washington to play the Ukrainian card much as it played the China card. If permitted to retain its nuclear arsenal, for example, Kiev could seek to implement a neo-Gaullist nuclear strategy in which it would either point nuclear weapons in all directions or, more likely, seek to "trigger" a nuclear linkage with the United States and the EU in case of confrontation with Russia. Moreover, continued tensions between Moscow and Kiev over nuclear weapons could jeopardize the nuclear reductions promised by START II, and lead Washington to put strategic nuclear forces on a high state of alert—against both Kiev and Moscow. Thus rather than support Kiev's claims to nuclear independence, the Bush and Clinton administrations moved to work with Moscow in pressuring Kiev to dismantle its nuclear arsenal. In effect, the January 1994 executive agreement between the United States, Russia, and Ukraine seeks to dismantle all Ukrainian nuclear weaponry over a seven year period.

Having thus worked to forge a U.S.-Russian disarmament pact in regard to Ukraine, it seems necessary to continue in the same direction in regard to other East European states. Accordingly, if the latter are brought into NATO *without Russian cooperation involving joint U.S.-Russian security guarantees or assurances*, or if the January 1994 disarmament pact with Ukraine should break down, or if the United States, the new Russia, and other major states cannot formulate concerted strategies in regard to emerging "new" powers in general, the structure of peace may well be "fatally broken"[15] in Walter Lippmann's words.

THE SOUND OF ONE HAND CLAPPING

Ironically, the collapse of the Soviet Union and the essentially bipolar global order has thus worked to exacerbate global U.S. security concerns. In effect, U.S. global strategy has been affected by the "sound of one hand clapping": U.S. military power has been drawn into the Persian Gulf and toward the Horn of Africa and the former Yugoslavia, in part because there is no longer a Soviet countervailing power in the region that could check Chinese, pan-Serb, pan-Islamic, or other regional power influences. Despite efforts to act under UN auspices, U.S. actions raise concern that Washington is attempting to assert global predominance. Some observers have thus argued that Soviet collapse has resulted in a *de facto* Pax Americana, or "unipolar" world.[16] But it is still not at all clear that Washington can sustain its military and economic primacy/hegemony indefinitely, or more to the point, whether it can, in all circumstances, assert its interests in an unilateral fashion without alienating its allies or provoking conflict with its rivals.

Contrary to the warnings of NSC 68 (which did recognize that foreign economic policy, if improperly implemented, could "do actual harm to our national interests"), U.S. containment policy worked to distort the American political economy. The U.S. transformation into a net debtor nation by 1986–87—in part because of excessive defense expenditure to meet the Soviet "threat"—raised questions about the efficacy of U.S. global strategy and its indirect domestic consequences. Despite its continued military predominance and its large market, the extent of U.S. relative technological/financial atrophy leads one to question whether the U.S. can sustain its position of political-economic and military-technological primacy/hegemony indefinitely into the future. While the United States has remained in the position of "first among equals"[17] among its allies, the general loss of confidence in U.S. economic leadership, radical fluctuations in the global monetary and trade system (largely beyond the control of any one territorial state), plus the collapse of the Soviet empire (leading states to seize new opportunities for political-economic influence) have opened possibilities for rival core and semiperipheral states and blocs to move up the ranks of political-economic and military-technological power status.

Relative U.S. political-economic atrophy—relative to Germany and Japan whose economic and technological potential the United States itself originally helped to build as a means to contain the Soviet Union—has made it increasingly difficult for Washington to take the lead in helping to stabilize the post–Cold War order. U.S. efforts to revitalize its capabilities through the North American Free Trade Agreement (NAFTA) and the General Agreement on Tariffs and Trade (GATT) may prove successful in the long term; but in the meantime it is dubious whether the United States can assert enough leverage to contain (by itself) the demands of the newly emerging powers. In addition to financial difficulties involved in helping to stabilize former Soviet bloc states, Washington has also had trouble convincing its own allies to take concerted actions, particularly since U.S. allies have been engaged in political-economic and geostrategic friction with the United States. In regard to West Germany since *Ostpolitik*, and in regard to Japan since the 1980s, Washington has tended to follow, rather than lead, its allies. This is particularly true since Washington has relied upon West German and increasingly Japanese finance to float its budget deficits through international investment in the United States and through the purchase of U.S. government bonds.

Relations among the Western Allies may accordingly become more two-faced; how well the Allies coordinate their policies will depend on the intensity of their economic disputes, the nature of the G-7 relationship with Russia, Ukraine, and China, and on the depth of their divergence regarding perceptions of regional threats. It has been argued that shifting trade and financial interests could break up U.S. alliances; yet it appears dubious that Germany/Europe and Japan will make a clean break with the United States.[18] Despite ostensibly complementary economic interests, China and Japan eye each other with suspicion over the two Koreas and the South China Sea (if not Mongolia and Siberia); at the same time, both may *threaten* a pan-Asian alliance to pressure both the United States and Russia. Both Germany and Russia continue to face off over Central and Eastern Europe; but both could still *threaten* a Russo-German pact. Both Japan and Germany can thus *threaten* not to support U.S. policy on geostrategic, political-economic, and military-technological levels in order to gain U.S. concessions, even if they remain formal members of American alliances. These states can also forge new defense agreements with third states: Britain, France, and Germany have increasingly looked to Japan for defense ties; France and Germany have also looked to Eastern Europe for potential allies.

At the same time, Washington will attempt to use its increasingly limited strategic leverage to pull these states back in closer alignment with U.S. interests to prevent them from making good on their threats—and hence sustain a double containment. One rationale for drawing Poland, the Czech Republic, and Hungary into NATO, for example, is to prevent a German-Russian condominium over these states. Another possibility is that Washington could acquiesce in the efforts of Tokyo or Bonn to obtain nuclear weapons on the condition that they remain within U.S.-led regimes—a decision that could potentially alienate Russia, the PRC, or other states. The dilemma is that Bonn's flirtation with Moscow and that of Tokyo with Beijing, combined with inter-allied foreign policy and trade disputes, *does* raise fears of a breakup of U.S. alliances. The *threat* to shift sides in order to press for concessions and advantages—the quintessential aspect of strategic leveraging—could represent the underlying cause of a global war.

From a domestic perspective, relative U.S. political-economic atrophy could mean the end of the bipartisan consensus that had been established when the Soviet Union represented a clear "threat" (despite Moscow's tacit collaborative role) and result in a more isolationist stance. Here, for example, Congress did not permit President Bush to take initiatives not judged in the immediate national interest, but that could have helped guarantee global security in the long term: Congress did not back Freedom Support Legislation, nor did it work to rapidly extend sufficient funds to stabilize the Russian ruble. The Bush administration itself—taking an essentially minimalist approach—did not stress the importance of aid for Russia.[19]

President Clinton's April 1993 promises of $1.8 billion of U.S. aid above the $1.6 billion already promised at the emergency G-7 meeting in Tokyo in April 1993 (coupled with promises of roughly $43 billion depending on the success of Russian reforms), raised questions as to where such money was to be found at a time of radical budget cuts and when foreign aid—particularly to one's former antagonist—was not a popular concern. President Clinton, as he attempts to balance domestic and international priorities, may not be able to manage the domestic-oriented demands of the U.S. Congress (or his own Democratic party) after the failure to provide a promised "peace dividend" and middle-class tax reprieve after sacrifices (Korea, Vietnam, and heavy defense spending) that American citizens made during the Cold War.

Accordingly, should the United States move into greater isolation—or follow a myopic protectionist policy based upon its alleged economic interests—emerging powers could attempt to take advantage of the apparent lack of U.S. or Russian interest to assert their regional interests. On the other hand, if a concerted global strategy cannot be established soon, the United States—or a resurgent Russia—could opt for provocative and demagogic unilateral intervention in a belated effort to preclude the total collapse of the former largely bipolar global "order."

THE UNRAVELING OF THE SOVIET ROLE IN THE FIVE-DIMENSIONAL DOUBLE CONTAINMENT

From this perspective, there was absolutely no discussion in NSC 68 as to what might happen to the positive and collaborative side of the U.S.-Soviet relationship vis-à-vis the major powers of West Germany, Japan, and China, as well as in regard to significant emerging powers, once the Soviet Union did collapse. The domestic weaknesses of the Soviet Union (which were purposely exacerbated by a hard-line U.S.

containment policy) thus helped to undermine the collaborative Soviet role in the five-dimensional double containment.

My concept of double containment takes that of Wolfram F. Hanrieder a bit further.[20] My definition includes tacit structural elements of U.S.-Soviet collaboration in containing the potentially independent political-military capabilities of both American (and Soviet) allies. Five-dimensional double containment thus involves a tacit Soviet role despite U.S. efforts to "encircle" the Soviet Union, and concurrent Soviet efforts to "counter-encircle" the United States—at the same time that both sides tested each other's intentions and explored the possibilities of forging a deeper entente or alliance through power-based bargaining and strategic leveraging.

In the generally recognized double containment of Germany, both Washington and Moscow attempted to sustain political and military controls over West and East Germany; each side concurrently built up rival alliance systems in an effort to counterbalance the military capabilities of the other. The U.S.-Soviet relationship also involved the double containment of West European states under a liberal American primacy/hegemony; concurrently, from the Soviet perspective, the relationship involved the containment of Central and East European states and nationalities under the fist of Soviet/Russian domination. (Former Soviet bloc states are not only suspicious of Russia, but also of the United States. Kiev, for example, has regarded the Bush and Clinton administrations as supporting Russian hegemony. See below.)

Second, there was also a double containment of Japan. The United States accepted Soviet military pressures on the north of Japan (agreed to at Yalta) and saw the need to place limits on Japanese military-nuclear capabilities through constitutional limitations. Although the United States refused to partition Japan in much the same way as Germany and Korea, Washington agreed with the Soviet Union to limit or contain Japanese military capabilities by sustaining the U.S. military presence in Japan, and by building Japanese self-defense forces within prescribed limits. In addition, U.S. efforts to sustain a first-strike potential and forward strategy were not merely intended to contain the Soviet Union, but also to help reassure—and indirectly double contain—U.S. allies, Germany and Japan, by reducing pressure to develop independent political-military and nuclear capabilities.

Third, there has been a U.S.-Soviet effort to sustain a double containment of China and prevent its unification with Taiwan. Both the United States and the Soviet Union did attempt to swing China to their respective side before the Korean War, largely by appearing to promise support for Chinese unification; Moscow was more successful in the short run. By 1960, however, in tacit cooperation with Washington, Moscow abruptly dropped its support for China's nuclear program. The Nixon administration then withdrew tacit U.S. collaboration with Moscow against Beijing: As Nixon sought to play upon Sino-Soviet tensions, Beijing looked to the United States for support. This continued until 1981, when China adopted a more independent stance vis-à-vis the so-called superpowers. By 1987–93, Beijing took a more decisive tilt toward Moscow, forging a "Rapallo pact" with the new Russia (see Chapter 2).

Fourth, there has been a double containment of secondary rimland states—such as Turkey, Iran, India, Taiwan, and the two Koreas. With the breakup of the Soviet Union, Poland, Ukraine, Belarus, Kazakhstan, and Mongolia also fall into this category. In effect, as East Germany represented the keystone that held together the internal Soviet/Russian empire, the historical steps toward German unification helped break down Soviet political-military and ideological controls over not just Central and Eastern Europe, but Belarus, Ukraine, plus the Baltic and Central Asian states as well.

And lastly, there has been a fifth dimension of double containment over much of the developing world. Although Washington and Moscow did provide military, economic, and technological support to opposing sides in different regional conflicts, there was generally a tacit agreement on the part of both powers to at least attempt to maintain a relative equipoise of power capabilities among rival regional states. (The United States generally attempted to give its allies a leading military-technological edge.) In political-economic terms, Washington chose not to aid the forces of global development in part to prevent the rise of new competitors. The U.S. refusal in 1950 to implement the Havana Charter meant that GATT became the world's trading organization by default. The latter chiefly reflected U.S. and European agricultural interests (at the expense of agricultural interests in the developing world) and did not provide for economic development assistance, for example. Only by the 1960s, following Soviet expansion into peripheral regions, did Washington begin to concern itself with global development issues.[21] In military-technological terms, both Washington and Moscow worked (albeit not necessarily successfully) to deter the rise of new nuclear weapons states by signing the Partial Test Ban treaty in 1963 and the admittedly weak Non-Proliferation Treaty (NPT) in 1967. New efforts to sustain the double containment of the emerging powers include the 1987 Missile Technology Control Regime (MTCR); the Bush administration's promise of U.S.-Russian cooperation in the development of Ballistic Missile Defenses (BMD); and the January 1994 U.S.-Russian-Ukrainian disarmament pact.

The concept of double containment, however, does not preclude efforts by the contained powers to break out of that containment. The effectiveness of the five-dimensional double containment has thus been further mitigated by the two-faced nature of the U.S.-Soviet competitive/cooperative relationship in regard to the rise of third powers, as well as the ability of third states themselves to play East against West and West against West. In particular, cooperative U.S.-Soviet actions tended to alienate both U.S. and Soviet allies, leading the latter to seek out new options. The efforts by the United States to sustain détente with the former Soviet Union, for example, weakened U.S. efforts to reassure its allies that it would protect their interests.

In addition to playing upon Soviet political-economic weaknesses, Bonn was able to play upon contradictory U.S. policies to seek out reunification under Bonn's own initiative. It was precisely the tension between containing the Soviet Union and containing Germany, and between the difficulties of simultaneously deterring the Soviet Union, and those of reassuring U.S. allies while cooperating with the Soviet Union—particularly once the Soviet Union gained strategic nuclear parity—that helped to unravel the double containment of Germany. In effect, using aspects of strategic leveraging, Bonn utilized Western idèological support for the aims of unification, intra-German trade, NATO's commitment to a forward defense of West Germany, plus promises of aid, technological assistance, and diplomatic supports for both Berlin and Moscow, to obtain unification. German unification did not altogether terminate the double containment, but it substantially weakened Four Power controls—despite limitations set on German armed forces including the renunciation of nuclear, chemical, and biological weaponry on German territory. Neither Russia nor the United States can be certain of its ability to influence German policy in the long term.

In regard to Japan, the Nixon "shock" (the opening to China, plus the surcharge on Japanese exports) created a dilemma of reassurance. At the same time, however, throughout the U.S.-Japanese relationship, Tokyo has attempted to quietly play upon American fears of either a Soviet-Japanese or, more pertinently, a Sino-Japanese alliance to assert its interests. In addition, yen "diplomacy" has helped spread Japanese political-economic influence globally: Using its economic capabilities, Tokyo has set the framework for a foreign and economic policy more independent of the United States.

In regard to the PRC, Nixon's efforts to play the PRC against the Soviet Union led the PRC to use its newly found geostrategic position vis-à-vis the United States, the Soviet Union, Europe, and Japan, in part to pressure Taiwan in the hope of ultimate reunification under Beijing's aegis. Since the 1970s, China has used its pivotal geostrategic position and promises of a large market to play East against West and West against West. By 1992, the United States appeared (at least temporarily) to tilt back into support of Taiwan—not merely in order to expand arms sales, but also to counterbalance Chinese pressures and the "threat" of a Sino-Russian alliance with a much more powerful PRC.

In regard to the fourth dimension of double containment, emerging semiperipheral rimland powers often sought to play U.S. against Soviet interests. In order to prevent a U.S.-Soviet deal over East Germany, East Berlin sought to enhance its position vis-à-vis Moscow. Before the Soviet collapse, "national-communists" in Kiev sought concessions from Moscow (such as the Donbass, Bukovina, and the Crimea) in order to enhance their relative position of power within the Soviet Union; after the Soviet collapse, Kiev threatened to retain nuclear weapons and attempted to play the interests of the United States, Germany/Europe, Russia, and China against each other. Moreover, as a means to pressure NATO and the EU into accepting its claims to membership, Poland threatened closer defense and economic ties with a nuclear Ukraine. Belarus and Kazakhstan initially threatened to retain nuclear weapons; and Mongolia has looked to the PRC and Japan for support.

During the Cold War, Turkey threatened to leave NATO in an effort to gain U.S. support so as to counterbalance Greece and obtain concessions for its economic interests; after the Cold War, Turkey began to assert its interests in the Balkans, the Caucasus, Central Asia, and Middle East. During the Cold War, India—largely out of fear of China—played its own Soviet card in order to attract U.S. support; after the Cold War, India sought out high technology from the United States and continued to develop its own ballistic missile capability. (Here, Soviet/Russian efforts to relax tensions with China after 1982 resulted in the feared loss of tacit Soviet nuclear supports for India.)

The relinquishment of the British, American, and Russian condominium over Teheran after World War II, for example, raised the long-term prospects of a more independent Iranian policy. Once Soviet troops had left northern Iran (but maintaining a double containment of Azerbaijan), Teheran tended to play U.S. and Soviet interests against one another, but also turned to Beijing for support. Nixon's "blank check" to the Shah (in part a result of the Shah's threat to turn to Moscow, in addition to Iranian oil wealth) enhanced Iranian power capabilities. U.S. arms sales and supports, however, did not work to stabilize the regime against pan-Shi'ia Islamic revolution.

The two Koreas have also played the major powers against each other: The Korean War was, in part, provoked by both North and South Korean fears of a U.S.-Soviet double containment. By the 1970s, both North and South Korea used the threat to develop nuclear weapons as a means to obtain greater security guarantees (if not diplomatic recognition) from the United States, Soviet Union, and/or PRC.

Furthermore, as states, such as France, Germany, and Japan, began to assert their own interests vis-à-vis the United States, emerging powers were consequently able to play upon intra-Western rivalries to enhance their own power capabilities and pursue their own regional interests. By threatening to trade with one power or the other, rising states could gain political and economic concessions, as well as access to dual-use and military technology. As the "loose" bipolar system continued to break down, the United States and the Soviet Union no longer represented the sole suppliers of "security," particularly as European states or China could fill in orders.

The key dilemma for the post–Cold War era is thus as follows: Efforts of rising powers or regional blocs to break out of the five-dimensional double containment may generate considerable friction between the United States and Russia if Washington and Moscow both seek to forestall an emerging third power from siding with the other. The new Russia has begun to reassert its interests in part to preclude a greater loss of former Soviet spheres of influence and security. Moscow has supported the interests of states such as India, Iran, and to a certain extent, Serbia, and has warned Central and East European states against joining NATO or the WEU. Moscow has sought to anchor relations with the PRC and attempted to check the rise of Ukraine, and to block the development of Poland-Ukraine and Ukraine-PRC axes. Moscow may also hope to draw Germany closer to Russian interests.

Washington, on the other hand, may seek to keep Bonn and Tokyo double-contained within pro-Western regimes so as to prevent the two from venturing into political military independence, at the same time that Washington consents to their foreign policy goals—in potential conflict with those of Moscow and/or Beijing. (As was the case with France, the United States could acquiesce to the development of German and/or Japanese nuclear weapons. But here, the French nuclear *force de frappe* was less controversial, as a nuclear France was not hostile to the Soviet Union and as France played a role in the double containment of Germany.) Yet should Germany and/or Japan obtain nuclear weaponry, such an occurrence could represent the final rupture of the Russian (and American) role in the double containment. Moreover, if emerging powers, such as Ukraine, either tilt toward U.S. or European interests or gain political-military independence relative to the United

States and Russia, and if the United States, Russia, Germany/Europe, and Japan cannot forge a new more concerted relationship, the original collaborative aspects of the five-dimensional double containment risk being absolutely undermined (see Chapter 9 for scenarios).

PHASES OF ENCIRCLEMENT AND COUNTER-ENCIRCLEMENT

After the pre-containment era (1803–1941)—in which U.S.-tsarist Russian relations began to sour in the 1890s after the Sino-Japanese War and U.S. Open Door policy *prior* to the Bolshevik revolution—six distinct phases of U.S.-Soviet "encirclement" and "counter-encirclement" (which include power-based efforts to forge an entente or alliance) can be identified. Phase I (1941–45) involved U.S.-Soviet suspicions held over from the pre-containment era, but which were largely suppressed in the allied effort to defeat the Axis powers. In essence, the wartime alliance represented a marriage of convenience: Washington "appeased" Soviet claims in Central and Eastern Europe and in Asia to keep Moscow in the war against Germany and then against Japan. Phase II (1945–53) followed the Potsdam Conference and the use of the atomic bomb to defeat Japan and contain Russia. Cold War imprecations resulted from U.S.-Soviet competition to obtain the political allegiance of the two Germanys, plus rival claims to former spheres of influence of the Axis powers, as well as rival efforts to attract the political-military allegiance of the PRC. Phase III (1953–67) *appeared* to represent a consolidation of the U.S.-Soviet double containment and recognition of mutual spheres of influence and security after the Korean War. Phase IV (1968–77) represented an intensification of Soviet counter-encirclement strategy—designed to impel the United States into an entente—and the concurrent U.S. effort to build up the power capabilities of the PRC, Japan, West Germany, as well as states such as Iran—despite the aura of détente. Phase V (1978–84/87) represented the intensification of U.S. encirclement strategy in which the tacit Soviet role in the five dimensional double containment continued to unravel. Phase VI (1988–91) appeared to represent steps toward a formation of a new U.S.-Soviet détente, but actually represented the final blows of a technical knock-out, particularly following German unification. Each of these periods possesses significant ramifications for contemporary U.S.-Russian relations, as the seventh phase (1991–?) is likewise characterized by games of encirclement and counter-encirclement (plus power-based bargaining and strategic leveraging) despite the aura of the end of the Cold War.

2

Geohistorical Analogies and the Question of Perpetual Peace

STRATEGIC LEVERAGING

Is the global system moving toward a new relationship of "perpetual peace"—in which the "democratic liberalization" of the former Soviet bloc will result in a new global concert? Or is it moving toward another "twenty-years crisis"?[1] This chapter will first define the concept of "strategic leveraging"; it will deal with theoretical issues (such as the quest for *parity/superiority* and the question of *legitimacy*) inherent to inter-state rivalries. It will also examine sociocultural/ideological concerns raised by the "end of history" debate. Next, it will look at geohistorical analogies for what clues history may provide to better understand the post–Cold War international system. It will conclude by discussing the question of "appeasement."

States utilize aspects of "strategic leverage" in an effort to expand, sustain, or even retract their position of *relative power and sovereignty within the global and regional equipoise of power capabilities, perceived political intent, and international norms (the latter often supervised or enforced by international regimes)*. Strategic leverage is the dynamic process by which rival powers gain influence or control over other states and actors by means of alliances and military supports, political-economic policies, diplomatic, and cultural contact. Historically conditioned techniques of strategic leveraging include both rewards and sanctions, plus the threat and actual use of force, including the "threat" posed by military-technological rivalries, as well as political-economic conflict and sociocultural/ideological subversion. Aspects of encirclement and counter-encirclement—best described by Kautilya in the *Arthasastra* (circa 300 B.C.)—include efforts to build alliances and deny opponents the fruits of those alliances.

In essence, U.S. insular-core encirclement strategy was designed to check Soviet power potential and slow Moscow's efforts to move from essentially semiperipheral to core economic status, and from continental to amphibious geostrategic status.[2] Moscow's continental and then amphibious counter-encirclement strategy was designed to pressure weak points such as West Berlin and Cuba in an effort to overstrain Western resources and breakup Western alliances—that is, if a U.S.-Soviet entente that recognized Soviet *parity* and the *legitimacy* of Soviet spheres of influence and security could not be formed.

Soviet expansion was essentially "defensive" in nature as Moscow sought to move from semiperipheral and amphibious status so as to counter predominant U.S. and allied core and insular status. Moscow judged the potential political-economic and sociocultural/ideological "threat" from the emerging powers (Germany, Japan, and China) to be more imminent than did Washington, particularly as these powers bordered the Soviet empire. Hence, as an essentially insular power, the United States was not as immediately affected by a potential "encirclement" as was the case for the former Soviet Union. In essence, Moscow possessed a more heightened sensibility to the link between potential external and internal threats to its control. Following the collapse of the amphibious Soviet empire, the new Russia has become a predominantly land-locked continental semiperipheral power, with some remaining core capabilities. (The breakup of NATO or of the U.S.-Japanese alliance, however, could raise U.S. fears of Russian counter-encirclement.)

Systems of alliances can force a rival power to respond by straining resources to build up its military capabilities to counter any potential threat; aspects of strategic leveraging thus also include the continual innovation of technology for dual-use "peaceful" or "military" purposes. In addition to being an instrument for war, an arms race can serve as a "political power factor" that may be intended to pressure an opponent to forge an overall entente, to force compromise over a particular unresolved issue, to gain a state's diplomatic recognition and respect, and to make a state's leadership think twice about engaging in hostile actions. How a rival state reacts to that arms race may determine whether two powers join in alliance or continue to perceive each other as potential threats. In this sense, nuclear weapons played a key symbolic role in pressuring the rival state's policy and helping to strain its intrinsic resources—in addition to playing a role of dissuasion.

Military build-ups and costly standing armies can weaken a state's political and social coherence, as well as a state's technological and economic capabilities in the long term, if the rival is not resilient enough to compete on all levels, particularly as "encirclement" implies barriers to trade, technology transfer, and control of trade routes. Encircling or counter-encircling alliances help assure that an allied power's military, technological, and economic capabilities (including finance, resources, and markets) will be used to support only members of that particular alliance and thus be denied to the rival or its allies. And finally, support for an ally may give overt or tacit support to that ally's own irredentist or revisionist claims, which likewise may help to undermine the legitimacy and political support for the rival regime.

Geostrategic aspects of strategic leveraging also include utilization of key pressure points—or support for peripheral states and/or revolutionary movements—that can disrupt alliances or be used for "strategic denial." The Soviets utilized states such as North Korea, Egypt, Cuba, and North Vietnam to pressure Western interests; the United States utilized states such as South Korea, Israel, South Vietnam, Zaire, and South Africa to check Soviet and/or Chinese advances. Chinese counter-encirclement strategy utilized support for North Korea, North Vietnam, the Khmer Rouge, and for Indonesia in the 1960s, among others. On the other hand, buffer states such as Finland, Sweden, Austria, and Mongolia helped mitigate tensions between the rival powers. The subsequent collapse of key buffer states— Tibet, Cambodia, Afghanistan, the former Yugoslavia—then raised the prospects of renewed tensions. A divided Korea has also played a role as buffer between the Soviet Union, the PRC, and Japan, as has Taiwan between the PRC and Japan. If not well-managed, the potential unification of these latter buffer states could destabilize the regional and global equipoise of power capabilities and perceived political intent. In addition, how will Russia perceive the possible incorporation of formerly neutral states such as Finland, Sweden, and Austria in the EU—if Russia itelf does not become an EU member?

States cannot (absolutely) control capital movements and global market forces. Because of the transient nature of global market forces, states cannot entirely control shifts in the location of centers of production or of trade and exchange, and the subsequent shifts from semiperipheral to core status or vice-versa. But states can attempt to *channel* global finance, trade, and investment in ways that are more or less beneficial to that particular state and its entrepreneurs or state owned companies.[3] Economic aspects of strategic leveraging thus include positive supports—arms and high technology sales, direct investment, subsidized loans, granting of most-favored-nation (MFN) status, technical assistance, and so on. Coercive or negative policies include systems of preferential tariffs and quotas, technology denial, boycotts, freezing of assets, and monetary manipulation. States can also permit or seek to deny the entrance of rivals into international and multilateral regimes as a means to influence a rival's policy or behavior. In addition to military-technological assistance to NATO members, NSC 68 listed these examples of strategic leveraging: Marshall Plan aid, grant assistance to Japan and South Korea, loans by the Export-Import Bank, restrictions on East-West trade, purchasing and stockpiling of strategic raw materials, efforts to reestablish an international economy based on multilateral trade, declining trade barriers, convertible currencies, plus efforts to resolve the U.S. balance-of-payments problem!

Short of the effective international management of capital, trade, and investment (efforts entertained by the GATT negotiations), the attempt to build regional economic and potentially (but not necessarily) protectionist and trade diverting "blocs" also represents another economic form of strategic leveraging. The expansion of the United States, ultimately incorporating fifty states, and steps to forge NAFTA with Canada, Mexico, and potentially other Latin American states; the expansion of the EC/EU from six to twelve members, and potentially to fifteen or more in the near future; the formation of a Asian free trade zone (AFTA) possibly linked to a Japanese "Yen bloc"; China's steps to absorb Hong Kong and possibly Taiwan; Russia's efforts to forge an integrated CIS—all are aspects of strategic leveraging that help reduce the political-economic and military-technological dependence on outside states or blocs and stave off relative or absolute decline.

Maintaining close relations with key "oasis" states as core or semiperipheral financial centers—Japan, West Germany, South Korea, Kuwait, Saudi Arabia, Taiwan, Bahrein, Brunei—represents another way to stave off relative decline. But here, even financial relations may prove secondary to geostrategic relations: U.S. ties with Taiwan were initially downgraded in favor of the PRC, for example; U.S. ties with West Germany deteriorated with the collapse of détente. On the other hand, the Soviet Union under Gorbachev began to downgrade ties with East Bloc states in effort to curry favor from states such as West Germany and South Korea. Moscow also reduced links to Cuba in order to favor more affluent Latin American states.

The expropriation of industry (or refusal to pay foreign debts) was a tool used by Communist states during the Cold War, but was not exclusive to Communist regimes alone. After the American Revolution, U.S. state legislatures expropriated the estates of British loyalists. Moreover, U.S. reaction to states refusing adequate compensation was not a determinant feature of the Cold War. U.S. reaction differed in accord with the importance of the particular state in the strategic nexus. U.S.

recognition of Stalinist Russia in 1933, and U.S. actions vis-à-vis Mexico in the 1930s, Egypt and Iran in the 1950s, Peru in the 1960s, and Chile in the 1970s differed according to American calculations of global and regional strategic interests.[4] (At the same time, Soviet abolition of private property and lack of standard legal codes weakened prospects for closer U.S.-Soviet collaboration on a political-economic level and hindered plausible steps to bring about market-oriented reforms.)

During the Cold War Washington generally overstated Moscow's military, technological, and economic prowess as well as its political intent. In many ways, power assessments were as much subjective as objective (based on close observation), as so-called objective analysis incorporated subjective perceptions of both actual and estimated potential capabilities, as well as perceptions of political intent. In general, policymakers often overemphasized military/nuclear power as a central category and overlooked the importance of political intent, common interests, and the willingness of states to bargain with each other in response to both domestic and foreign policy considerations, regardless of their estimated relative power capabilities (and conflicting ideologies). In addition, U.S. policy was never absolutely consistent: Intrabureaucratic rivalry revolved around differing interpretations of Soviet intent as well as the specific nature of a bureaucracy's mission. The National Security Council (NSC) tended to shape the grand contours of U.S. global strategy—although its policy was often challenged by the more diplomatically-oriented State Department. In addition, the Commerce Department, whose general mission was to advance high-tech and dual-use technology sales, was at times at odds with both the NSC and the State Department.

Through strategic leveraging, the elite of the major powers may seek geopolitical parity (isothymia—the desire to be recognized as an equal) or superiority (megalothymia—the desire to be recognized as a superior)[5] in relationship to third states. From this perspective, state elites are often concerned with recognition as much as power; and successful diplomacy can recognize their legitimate right to global "coequal" decision-making power and help avoid conflict. Here, the question whether a state can seek parity or superiority depends precisely on the interaction between the two states: The final estimation depends on whether the one power (from a position of strength) accepts the rival's quest to be recognized as coequal; or whether it permits the latter to obtain superiority because of its relative weakness. Whether states will strive to obtain superiority, or whether they will find a modus vivendi or else a firm entente on the basis of political-military parity, will thus be determined by the nature of their power-based bargaining, political intent, intrinsic capabilities, and the extent of their common security and economic interests vis-à-vis third powers.

During the Cold War, the United States tended to view Moscow's actions as a quest for *megalothymia*, not *isothymia*. Moscow did achieve central strategic nuclear weapons parity and threatened superiority by the 1970s to counter both the actual and potential capabilities of the United States and its allies, but Moscow never achieved, nor was it granted, political parity—or recognition as a legitimate coequal decision-making power. Soviet efforts to *impel* the United States into an entente relationship on the basis of parity failed.

Furthermore, despite Soviet boasts, and much as NSC 68 predicted, Moscow could not permanently commit its intrinsic power capabilities to sustain its efforts to achieve parity with Washington. The Soviet Union saw itself under constant threat precisely because it could not sustain the military-technological, political-economic, and sociocultural/ideological aspects of competition with the United States *and* its allies (such as West Germany) over the long term. This fact challenged the view that, theoretically at any rate, had made "internal balancing more efficient than external balancing."[6] Once Moscow's intrinsic power capabilities plummeted, the bipolar equipoise could not be sustained. Not only did the bipolar equipoise collapse, but Soviet relationship of dominance over its external and internal empire also collapsed. The new Russia then sought to sustain either *primacy* or *hegemony* over former Soviet bloc states, if not *dominance* over lesser states that resist its position as "first among equals."[7]

In general, American theorists and policymakers tended to view the world through "bipolar glasses"; Soviet policymakers, however, tended to view the world from a more polycentric framework—the global "correlation of forces." Yet by focusing almost exclusively on the bipolar U.S.-Soviet relationship, U.S. policymakers subsequently tended to overlook new challenges—including those to the United States itself—coming from China, Japan, and West Germany/Europe, among other emerging powers. The fundamental methodological issue raised here was the general failure to examine the Hegelian interaction of the "whole" (dominated by the bipolar U.S.-Soviet relationship) with the "parts" (the emerging powers as they interacted with the bipolar whole). With the consequent breakdown of the structural aspects of bipolar U.S.-Soviet interaction, the changing dynamics of the global equilibrium—*the global and regional equipoise of power capabilities, perceived political intent, and international norms*—led to the formation of an "uneven polycentric" global system.

On the one hand, the actual number of major powers is less

significant than the nature of the *perceived* political intent of those actors and the nature of their alliance formations. If all the major actors share limited goals and possess mutual interests, and do not solidify into rival alliances, then there is a greater chance that irenic diplomacy can succeed in preventing regional conflicts from becoming global. (Here, for example, the pre–World War I Franco-Russian Dual Alliance limited Britain's ability to form an entente with Imperial Germany.)[8] Moreover, a cooperative relationship or concert can exist among two or more major powers with divergent ideologies, *particularly if these states possess mutual interests in containing or countering a rival or potential rival(s).* On the other hand, an "uneven polycentric" system may be more unstable than a truly multipolar system in which power is more evenly distributed. Disequilibrium tends to be more endemic in conditions of an uneven polycentrism because states possess very different actual *and* potential power capabilities. The equipoise is more precarious.

PLAYING BARBARIAN AGAINST BARBARIAN

Imperial China's geostrategist, Wei Yuan, urged China to learn from barbarians, at the same time that it used "barbarians against barbarians." Emerging states can exert a significant challenge to the status quo powers, particularly if those powers hope to draw a third state to their side. Major powers may use strategic leveraging to "contain" lesser powers; lesser powers can play upon divisions and weaknesses of the major powers to assert their interests through techniques of strategic leveraging. Even if a rising state is not necessarily close to "parity" with the major powers, it can still influence the decision-making process of nuclear powers, particularly if such a state is willing to threaten and/or take action to assert its interests in its particular region and "geostrategic nexus" or if a lesser state threatens to shift allegiance so that the major state must accede to its demands. In such a way, even a relatively less powerful state can play a role as a significant "center of power." Under the U.S.-Soviet "duopoly" (economic aspects of double containment), states were largely dependent upon either the United States or the Soviet Union to supply both security and techno-economic assistance. Yet, as a more polycentric global system developed, lesser states could play rival multinational or state-controlled firms against one another to gain advantages through the purchase of dual-use technology.

In general, states threatened by internal collapse or by foreign powers may seek varying forms of external supports or enlargement in an effort to forestall their feared decline or to reduce dependency upon third powers. The process of enlargement may take defensive, economic, and ideological forms. Alliances such as NATO were linked economically by GATT and bilateral agreements; the former Warsaw Pact was linked to the Council for Mutual Economic Assistance (CMEA). Ideologically, as a show of solidarity during the Cold War, states tended to adopt either Wilsonian or Leninist internationalism. Enlargement can also take the form of political-economic integration, such as the EU (based upon a Franco-German axis), or NAFTA, and so on. In these examples, states accept some limitations on sovereignty in the hope of reaping greater mutual benefits. At the same time, however, states (if not coerced) generally reserve the right to opt out of such arrangements through "vital interest" or "national emergency" clauses. Title V of the Maastricht Treaty, which outlines provisions for a common EU foreign and security policy, specifies, for example, that "in cases of imperative need" members may take "necessary measures . . . having regard to general objectives of joint action."[9]

In addition, states—or really pan-movements—can seek new linkages through forceful expansion based on actual *or* invented ethnic/cultural/linguistic/ideological/religious and/or economic common denominators. In order to reduce dependency upon third powers, pan-movements may pressure several governments simultaneously or use one state as a home base; they may also seek to impose their strategic or economic interests (diverting trade routes, for example) upon reluctant states. (States or regions claimed by pan-movements may actually prefer autonomy or national self-determination over forced integration, as was the case for the Sudetenland or the Austrian Tyrol in relation to Nazi pan-Germanism.) At the same time, the goals of such movements may not be consistent; each faction may base itself on a differing value or goal. (Pan-movements based on religion, for example, may possess different goals than those based on ethnic or linguistic backrounds.[10])

In regard to Russia, the pan-Slav messianism of Nikolai Danilevsky could resurrect itself in the twenty–first century (or sooner) in a *revanchist* form—under the actual or pretended aims to protect Russian—or Russified—populations. Such a movement could result in fratricidal conflict with Ukraine, which has attempted to defect from the original "Slavic Union" of Russia, Belarus, and Ukraine formed after the Soviet collapse. Here, Kiev is under pressure from Russian irredentist claims in the east and pro-Polish claims to the west. Pro-Polish irredentist movements also claim parts of Belarus (which in turn has claims to Lithuania). A pan-Slav, National Bolshevik, and greater Russian coalition might accordingly seek to preclude perceived pan-

Polish, pan-German, or pan-European expansion. (The pan-European movement has, in effect, attempted to contain pan-Germanism through expansion into Central Europe.) A Russian revanchist movement might also seek to preclude the rise of pan-Shi'ia or pan-Turk Islamic movements. Russia, for example, fears that a unified Azerbaijan might undermine Moscow's controls over Central Asia and over the Russian Federation itself. Concurrently, Turkey has opposed a greater Armenia (supported by Russia) and a unified Kurdistan. (The latter is also opposed by Iran and Iraq.) Conflicting pan-Turk interests also collide with Greek pan-Hellenic aspirations. Varying pan-Arab and pan-Islamic movements have collided with Zionism and Eretz Israel.

China seeks to repress the rise of pan-Turk and pan-Mongolian movements (a factor bringing Beijing toward cooperation with New Delhi and Moscow). At the same time, Han chauvinism has asserted its claims to "Chinese" Taiwan in part to forestall all possible secessionist movements within the PRC. Hindu chauvinism has likewise begun to react to internal and external fears of pan-Turk and pan-Islamic encirclement—in fear of India's own disaggregation. On the other hand, Russian fears of pan-Asianism (perceived anti-Russian collaboration between Central Asian states, Japan, and China) may impel Russia closer to the West—as the nineteenth-century Russian philosopher Vladimir Soloviev believed was possible.

But the possibility of a Russian-Western entente still depends upon perceived global interests of pan-North Americanism and pan-Europeanism, as well as the *actual* global geostrategic interests and interactions of states, and not those *pretended* or *idealized* by pan-movements. In order to obtain a deeper legitimacy than that provided by more secular ideologies, pan-movements often claim to represent the "lost" or "true" values of previous civilizations or religions. Rival (and internally conflictual) pan-movements, however, do not necessarily portend a "clash of civilizations." (Nor will such a clash purify the world of "evil" as millennial expectations claim.) As pan-movements are often recurrent, they represent an *end of millennium crisis* involving a process of reequilibriation following the collapse of a previous global order.

THE QUESTION OF LEGITIMACY

Major political crises that are not dealt resiliently can lead to questions among both the elite and general population as to the legitimacy (the generally perceived right to rule) of the leadership in power. Such crises may also lead to questions about the perceived legitimacy of the international order itself (i.e., the established international norms, which have been historically enforced by the major powers generally after global wars).

In distinction to traditional definitions of legitimacy as "power whose exercise is morally or legally justified,"[11] legitimacy is best depicted as the self-propagated right of an elite to rule, or to possess dominion, over a particular territory or territories (or over spheres of influence and security). An elite attempts to preserve its right to rule by basing its regime upon varying myths, values, and propaganda, as well as claims of security and economic well-being, in addition to claims of international "legality" and "morality." Claims to legitimacy are not based upon domestic constituencies and consensus alone, but are also linked to demands for recognition and claims of geostrategic and military parity with significant rival states, and the ability of the state leadership to provide adequate security. Among the major powers, efforts to sustain a rough equipoise of actual and potential power capabilities and geostrategic outreach, plus "equal" or "proportional" participation in global decision-making, are prerequisites for gaining *parity*, and hence for the acceptance and recognition of a major state as a legitimate global power in the eyes of both the international community and the domestic constituency. In this perspective, legitimacy can be established through foreign assistance in opposition (in the Nietzschean sense) to alternative leaderships which are, ironically, often perceived as backed by alien interests that do not serve the "national interest."

This definition applies to both the Soviet and the American revolutions. The U.S. Revolution was actively backed by only about one-third of the population: George Washington only succeeded against Britain following French intervention. American principles of legitimacy—northern-inspired democratic liberalism and federalism— were then reimposed following the U.S. Civil War. V. I. Lenin received diplomatic and significant financial support from Imperial Germany and imposed Soviet legitimacy after the Russian Civil War. Moreover, the legitimacy of the post–World War II German and Japanese leaderships was largely *constructed* by the United States against the threats of communism and/or revanche. (The United States did not necessarily support German "social-democratic" aims, for example.) Chinese Communists used their anti-Japanese record to undermine Chiang Kai-shek and help build their legitimacy (despite the fact that the 1941 Soviet-Japanese neutrality pact compromised their aims). Fledgling states, have attempted to construct their legitimacy by developing national ideologies and seeking external security supports and diplomatic recognition. Ukraine, in particular, has sought to build its identity *against* that of Moscow: Initially Kiev spoke of removing itself from former Soviet power structures in order to ostensibly reforge a new relationship with Russia on the basis of "parity" at a later date.

As so-called sovereign states (states possess only *relative* sovereignty) depend upon external as well as internal supports, state elites are both inward—and outward—looking. In general, elites seek to implement foreign policies that will best suit their domestic agendas and attempt to strike trade-offs between conflicting domestic and international interests which are simultaneously intended to sustain that leadership and/or its supporters in power. Conversely, rival elites may use cultural/ideological aspects of strategic leveraging to undermine the legitimacy of a state's leadership and/or its alliances— if not the nature of the global order itself. These latter factions may or may not be able to undermine a particular elite's claims to legitimacy, depending upon the resiliency of the leadership in dealing with foreign and domestic challengers, and the extent to which foreign powers assist domestic opponents. The elite in power accordingly seeks to sustain its legitimacy through the threatened use of force, cooptation, or compromise, and the skillful use of ideology.

As Gorbachev was no longer able to coopt domestic groups into following the mandates of the Communist leadership, former Communist leaders began to adopt a democratic/nationalist veneer to attract supporters. Since the crackdown in Tiananmen Square in 1989, the Chinese Communist elite used a mix of repression, "defense education," campaigns against bourgeois liberalization, combined with a cooptation of "moderates"—plus claims to Taiwan and fears of foreign intervention—in order to break up the Chinese democratic movement and rebuild CCP legitimacy. Not so ironically, the ruling parties in both Beijing and Taipei have appealed to claims for unification to sustain legitimacy. Both have opposed Taiwanese independence.

On the international level, an elite seeks to perpetuate its legitimacy through power-based bargaining, the forging of ententes and alliances, as well as the manipulation of ideology and propaganda. The 25 April 1993 Russian referendum (given support by emergency G-7 assistance) represented an attempt to build Yeltsin's legitimacy, even if the results were not absolutely decisive. Tensions between the president and parliament were, at their root, one of legitimacy: Prior to Boris Yeltsin's crackdown on the first Russian parliament in September– October 1993, both the parliament and the Russian president attempted to enlist outside powers (Washington and Kiev!) as well as domestic constituencies, such as the Russian military, to support their respective side. Concurrently, former Communists in Russia and Eastern Europe have begun to rebuild their legitimacy in new forms.

Violent and nonviolent means of cultural, linguistic, religious, and ideological dissemination are all used in an effort to influence elite or popular opinion, to gain supporters, or to start insurgencies. Western images of religious and individual freedoms and culture had a powerfully subversive effect on the East, as did support for "democracy" and "national self-determination" through the Voice of America and Radio Free Europe. The Soviet Cominform, Soviet-supported "peace" groups, plus lip-service in support of black American and Native American rights, represented a much less successful propaganda.

Cold War ideology has been characterized by "nationalistic universalism"[12] that tended to reify national goals into universal ones. On a deeper level, and showing the linkage between domestic and foreign relations, Aristotle's characterization of ideological rivalry in *The Politics* appears to apply to the Cold War. Elites seek to preserve their power and influence by creating fears that their constitutions (freedoms) might be subverted by enemies at home or abroad: "the distant fear must be brought home." In the conflict of "democracy" against "communism," nationalistic universalism, combined with efforts to bring the distant fear home, worked to sustain tensions during the Cold War and helped fend off criticism that could either undermine the legitimacy of a particular elite or political party to rule, or that could challenge the appropriateness of specific foreign and/or domestic policies.

INNOVATION AND THE QUESTION OF PERPETUAL PEACE

Coping with social, political, economic, and technological "innovation" is fundamental to a state's survival as a sovereign or relatively independent actor. Innovation can threaten the power capabilities of those states which cannot maintain their resiliency vis-à-vis their rivals; it can also threaten the relative status of specific factions or interest groups within a society. In many ways, the issue of innovation really precedes the more concrete security concerns raised by the production of armaments. Innovation can thus potentially create the socio-political preconditions for war or revolution—much as Thucydides and Karl Marx argued. More contemporarily, Joseph Schumpeter raised similar points from a democratic-liberal perspective.[13]

For Thucydides, the threat of Athenian innovation raised fears in Sparta—initiating the Peloponnesian Wars. In Karl Marx's depiction, adaptation to the "ever revolutionizing means of production" requires—on the pain of extinction, reaction, or revolution—profound readjustments in the domestic sociopolitical, military-technological, and global equipoise. Where railroads and oil played a key role in transport and energy infrastructure in the nineteenth and early twentieth century, today, dual-use strategic-economic infrastructure such as nuclear power plants, as well as emerging technologies, such as microelectronics, have played key roles in military-industrial innovations, energy, as well as in production for consumer goods. In today's circumstances, Marx's analysis—extended by Joseph Schumpeter—best applies to the effects of the new technological revolutions upon the outmoded industrial and decapitalized infrastructure of so-called Communist states. At the same time, the capitalist world is not immune to socio-political instabilities caused by revolutionary technology, shifting markets, and so on.

Adopting epoch-making innovations and emerging technologies, however, is not the only issue. Karl Polanyi showed the link between high finance, the gold standard, and constitutionalism in the nineteenth and early twentieth centuries, and argued that the instable nature of the global market transformations worked to undermine the global and regional equipoise in those periods.[14] Today, a linkage between private and government finance, monetary convertibility, and "democracy" can be studied in the reform process taking place in the former Soviet Union and Eastern Europe—if not in the PRC since the U.S. rapprochement. In this view, the forces pressing for "democracy" and "liberalization" cannot be viewed as separate, but rather form two sides of the same coin. In other words, though capitalism as a dynamic system can function (but not very effectively in an autocratic or one-party system without freedom of information, movement, or property rights), it still brings with it seeds of sociopolitical change, if not instability.

The apparent "victory" of democracy and liberalism over Soviet communism has resulted in the belief that "democratic-liberal" ideology has gained global predominance: "What is emerging victorious is . . . not so much liberal practice, as the liberal *idea*."[15] Here, Francis Fukuyama recognizes that democratic-liberal ideas have not necessarily been put in practice; he only states that it is the *idea* of democratic liberalism that has gained ascendancy. In this view, the end of history argument cannot be ruled invalid if nondemocratic regimes eventually emerge, because these regimes will be judged in contrast to the still predominant democratic ideals and practices.

Democratic-liberal theorists recognize that democratic-liberal states must be "constitutionally secure" so as "not to engage in war with one another."[16] Such theorists also recognize that democratic states have not necessarily been willing, or able to, assist other fledgling "democratic" states, such as Weimar Germany or Japan's interwar Taisho democracy. Michael Doyle, for example, recognizes that the *relative* decline of U.S. hegemonic leadership may pose dangers, not so much because economic rivalry will spiral into war, but because the liberal societies "will no longer be able to provide the mutual assistance they might require to sustain liberal domestic orders in the face of mounting economic crises."[17] (Doyle himself does not anticipate the advent of perpetual peace until the twenty–second century—though the recent spread of "democratic-liberal" states following the Soviet collapse could alter his calculations.)

But not only have democratic-liberal states been guilty of not sufficiently aiding fledgling democracies; they have not necessarily been forthcoming in providing security guarantees to full-fledged democracies (as was the case in 1919 when an Anglo-French-American security pact never materialized or in 1921–22 when the United States rejected a three-way security treaty with Japan and Britain once the Washington Naval Conference had scrapped the 1911 Anglo-Japanese alliance).[18] Because of traditional fears of "entangling alliances," the United States has only reluctantly engaged in an entente or alliance relationship with third countries, whether democratic or nondemocratic. This fact has made the prospects of forging a long-term cooperative security pact with the new Russia and/or Ukraine—democratic or not—highly dubious.

A careful reading of Immanuel Kant indicates that democratic-liberal theorists should not lay all the blame on nonliberal states in case of war. U.S. Cold War strategy violated several of Kant's preliminary articles to establish *Perpetual Peace* among states. Kant would have opposed many of the "acts of hostility" engaged in by both the United States and Soviet Union during the Cold War. Assassinations and breeches of agreement, for example, might make mutual confidence impossible during a future time of peace. Kant also opposed the use of the national debt and a system of credit as a tool of foreign policy and "as an instrument of aggression" which shows "the power of money in its most dangerous form" and which can result in inevitable bankruptcy among several states "in the long run." Kant warned of the dangers of foreign economic policy if it went beyond "some subjective latitude." (This is a danger likewise pointed out by NSC 68.) In addition, Kant was careful to distinguish between a "truce" (a suspension of hostilities) and "perpetual peace." Accordingly, as the Cold War was not fought according to Kant's preliminary rules, the danger is that the "end of the Cold War" may represent a mere truce, and not lead to the establishment of a secure "federation of free peoples" leading to global peace.[19]

From this perspective, continued sociopolitical instability and deep depression, most reminiscent of the interwar years, could threaten to overturn the present mix of democratic/nationalist leadership in Russia, Ukraine, or other states. Much as Jean-Jacques Rousseau argued, elites whose power and status are threatened may be in "perpetual need of war" (even if it ruins the state) "as a price of keeping their own office . . . as a means of oppressing the people on the plea of national necessity . . . [and] of rigging the market and setting up a thousand odious monopolies."[20] Moreover, much as Hegel argued in *The Philosophy of Right* against Kant, a Kantian alliance of democratic-liberal states could well be matched by a countervailing alliance of "absolutist" states—each asserting its own interests or else acting in concert.

The contemporary democratic-liberal perspective of Richard Ullman outlines the declining utility of territory, natural boundaries, mineral resources, and agricultural production. He thus argues that the traditional rationale for war has no objective basis. Ullman's viewpoint could be valid if all states were willing to accept the risks and highly uneven vulnerabilities of liberal interdependence; but such an approach may not appear convincing to a leadership striving to sustain itself in power (and particularly if liberal states themselves continue to deny the sale of advanced technology to non-liberal states!). Ullman's argument that the realization that "real power" is "human capital" and "knowledge"[21] does not necessarily enhance the prospects of global cooperation (nor prevent industrial espionage). Rather than plead for cooperation, an elite may go to war for more territory (which also includes "human capital") on the calculated risk that technology and "knowledge" will be ultimately forthcoming once its brutal actions have been accepted as a *fait accompli*.

Moreover, Ullman's contention that "the West would be unlikely to feel directly the impact of even tumultuous conflicts—including full-scale civil warfare—between Moscow and its once subservient provinces"[22] ignores the fact that U.S. allies might be unable to stay out of conflict if the present truce between Ukraine and Russia comes to an end, for example, or that the United States would have to sustain a high level of nuclear alert during such a conflict. On a deeper level, Ullman's statement unfortunately appears representative of a general Western insensitivity to the dangers of conflict within former Soviet spheres of influence and security—an insensitivity which lies at the root of the crisis in U.S.-Soviet/Russian relations. It was the very inability or unwillingness of the West to "feel" or "empathize" with Moscow's external *and* internal security dilemma that initially prevented the implementation of policies designed to *devolve* Soviet controls.

But let us assume, for the moment, that Russia and Ukraine, among other states, do develop stable and secure constitutions and economies. The critical question then is whether all societies can accept similar definitions of democracy and whether differing "democratic" systems are necessarily compatible. Much as schisms occurred *within* both Christianity and Islam, and more relevantly *within* Russian Marxism (between Georgi Plekhanov, who sought a pro-capitalist "parliamentary dictatorship" on the English model, and V. I. Lenin, who sought a personal/party dictatorship), schisms in the world democratic movement are not implausible. The United States itself saw the makings of a democratic schism in the federalist versus anti-federalist debates—debates which are somewhat similar to those of contemporary Russia, though the latter are complicated by the largely artificial division of Russia into ethno-territorial units, republics, and regions. American, European, Russian, Japanese, Chinese, and Ukrainian definitions of political, social, and economic "democracy," for example, may all diverge significantly, both in theory and practice.

During the Cold War, the U.S. Congress refused to ratify the SALT and START treaties until Moscow had made greater concessions; Congress refused to grant MFN status to the Soviet Union unless Moscow changed its emigration practices; Congress has also threatened to take MFN status away from the PRC. Congress also demanded greater "burden sharing" from democratic allies. All these factors raised tensions during the Cold War, particularly as the U.S. executive branch either failed to gain Congressional support for policies that might ameliorate tensions, or else the president used threats made by Congress to force greater concessions from Soviet Union, the PRC, or even U.S. allies (in regard to "burden sharing," for example).

Will the parliaments of Russia (the Duma) and of the Ukraine (the Rada) necessarily sign treaties agreed to by their executive branch? Or will post–Cold War states deliberately forge executive agreements in the effort to avoid parliamentary involvement? Or will unstable democracies dissolve recalcitrant parliaments? In the post–Cold War era, executive branches have begun to play the demands of their legislatures against third parties. The Ukrainian parliament's decision in 1993 to postpone ratification of START I (later ratified with thirteen "strings" attached) and the Non-Proliferation treaty (NPT), as well as the Russian parliament's protest against START II, raised tensions, as did the first Russian parliament's claims to the Crimea and support for pan-Serbian expansionism (prior to that parliament's dissolution). Furthermore, Boris Yeltsin's September 1993 decision to dissolve the predominantly former Communist parliament established under Mikhail Gorbachev did not produce a new parliament that will necessarily support a pro-Western policy. Objective issues—the pace of economic reforms, the threat of high employment, decisions affecting Russian domestic and international security, Russia's role in the world, the quality of the Russian president's leadership—will continue to affect the Russian parliament's rulings and pro- or anti-Western orientation. Moreover, Russian "liberalism" could metamorphose into black-market "libertarianism" if parliamentary special interest groups are able to block executive branch controls on aerospace, arms exports, and dual-use technologies—once again raising global tensions. From this perspective, "democratic" checks and balances on executive power may raise, rather than lower, the possibilities of war—*but only if an entente or alliance guaranteeing mutual security is not firmly established.*

GEOHISTORICAL ANALOGIES

U.S. global strategy in regard to the former Soviet Union tended to mimic British policy toward both tsarist Russia and Imperial Germany. Here, the Soviet Union was like Imperial Germany in the sense that it was a global amphibious power with regional allies; but it was also like tsarist Russia in the sense that the Soviet Union was a Eurasian power with specifically Russian strengths and weaknesses. From this perspective, the United States implemented a global strategy, particularly in the 1970s, very much like that of Britain in regard to tsarist Russia, particularly in the period between 1884 and 1902–07. Following the Soviet collapse, however, the United States has attempted to reach an entente with the new Russia, much as Britain tried to reach an entente with tsarist Russia in the period 1902–07, but in circumstances that are reminiscent of both the collapse of the tsarist empire and the *indecisive* defeat of Imperial Germany.

Prior to the reluctant Soviet invasion of Afghanistan, the United States, along with its European allies, looked to an alliance with China as an "active strategic counterweight" to the Soviet Union, and likewise tightened its alliance relationship with Japan in 1978. Not too dissimilarly, less than a hundred years earlier, after tsarist Russian threats to "buffer Afghanistan," Great Britain looked first to an apparently rising China during its period of "self-strengthening" for an alliance in 1884; then, after the defeat of China in the Sino-Japanese War in 1895, Great Britain was able to forge an alliance with Japan by 1902. Much as Great Britain considered any Russian threat to "buffer

Afghanistan" as a *casus belli*, and built up its rimland defenses in Persia and India, the Carter Doctrine also declared any threat to Pakistan or Iran as a *casus belli*. The United States concurrently built up Pakistan to check Soviet pressures, but its efforts to build up Iran collapsed following the pan-Shi'ia Islamic revolution. Then as Beijing's policy moved into greater "independence" in the 1980s, the United States sought to strengthen its alliance with Japan—the geohistorical parallel to the 1902 Anglo-Japanese entente.

Despite tensions between Britain and Russia throughout the nineteenth century, Britain was able to reverse alliances in the period 1902–14—largely in response to Imperial Germany's naval threat. Britain thus attempted to draw tsarist Russia into the Anglo-French entente against Imperial Germany, coming to terms with Russia over Tibet, Afghanistan, and Persia. (London concurrently claimed that its alliances with Paris and St. Petersburg were intended to resolve regional disputes; they were thus defensive and not directed *against* Imperial Germany.) Tsarist Russia's defeat in the 1904–05 Russo-Japanese War, combined with steps toward constitutional liberalism, opened the door to an alliance with Britain, much as Soviet defeat in Afghanistan and steps towards democratic liberalism opened the door to closer U.S.-Soviet/Russian relations.

Britain and tsarist Russia were accordingly able to forge an entente relationship against a mutual foe, but the previous Imperial German-Japanese "encirclement" of Russia had already set in motion the external and internal forces of destabilization, resulting in the Russian revolution, secessionist movements in Ukraine, Belarus, the Caucasus, and the Far East. Ultimately, after the Leninist coup, Soviet Russia was forced to accept a separate peace with Imperial Germany at Brest-Litovsk. The Russian Civil War resulted in Great Power intervention, the Russo-Polish War, and indirectly influenced the Chinese revolution.

The collapse of the Soviet empire has accordingly resulted in a situation that parallels the collapse of both Imperial Germany and tsarist Russia. Much like that of tsarist Russia, Soviet collapse can be traced to "dual" or "multiple" sovereignty—the rise of national, regional, and local administrations beneath the noses of the central Kremlin government. Political-economic instability led to the rise of Lenin and then Stalin after a few months of "democratic" government; the collapse of Imperial Germany led to a longer-lasting Weimar democracy, 1918–33. In many ways, the failed August 1991 putsch and the September–October 1993 *pronunciamento* of General Alexandr Rutskoi can be compared to and contrasted with the Weimar German Kapp putsch or either the failed Bolshevik Petrograd or the Kornilov coup before the October Revolution. The September 1993 dissolution of Russian parliament can also be compared and contrasted with Tsar's dissolution of the Duma—the Russian parliament of that time. At the same time, Yeltsin's threats to "rule by decree" do not appear too dissimilar to presidential disputes with the Weimar German Reichstag. The Russian constitution of December 1993 possesses a resemblance to that of the Weimar Republic due to the strong authoritarian powers given the executive branch combined with the instable nature of coalitions within Russia's new parliamentary system.

Perhaps more like Weimar Germany than tsarist Russia, the new Russia has been confronted with the dangers of hyperinflation and "great depression." Russia is faced with instability caused by the "lost generation" of a demobilized army, high unemployment, lost savings, and lack of social mobility. Such a depression is as much "material" as "spiritual"—as Communist ideology has lost most of whatever legitimacy it once possessed. Here, democratic-liberal propaganda may have actually inflated expectations of radical change, setting the stage for a revanchist backlash if such expectations are not fulfilled.

After the defeat of Imperial Germany, the great landed estates (including those of the kaiser) were not parceled out; and industrial cartels and monopolies were not broken up. Perhaps not too dissimilarly, Communist Party property has yet to be parceled out, and the former Soviet *nomenklatura* have resisted the breakup of former Soviet conglomerates into more competitive units. Moreover, much like the trial of Imperial German leadership at the Reich Supreme Court in 1921 (which largely vindicated the Imperial German leadership's role in the World War I), the trial of the Communist Party proved inconclusive and compromised. Here, the trial of Mikhail Gorbachev and Communist Party activities possessed a double barrel which is representative of the rivalry among factions trying to build a new legitimacy: Russian democrats sought revenge for disastrous totalitarian misrule; "national patriots" sought a scapegoat for the collapse of the Soviet empire.

Despite the more stringent demands of the Versailles *Diktat*, Imperial Germany was not defeated decisively; likewise, the new Russia still remains a power capable of taking military action against regional (and indigenous domestic) actors if deemed "necessary" to sustain Russian primacy/hegemony and to defend the Russian—and Russified—"diaspora" and "near abroad" outside the largely land-locked Russian federation. There also remains the danger that the newly politicized Russian army, which has organized to oppose efforts to divide its integrated forces, may well become—much like that of Weimar Germany—a "state within a state." Boris Yeltsin has thus far appeared to walk a tightrope between Russian democrats and pan-nationalists—much as Weimar leader Gustav Stresemann had to deal with General Hans von Seecht. Like Weimar elites, Russian elites have viewed former Soviet states as transitional *Saisonsstaaten*. Both before *and* after the dissolution of parliament in September–October 1993, the Russian leadership has been pressured by demands to assert hegemony over former Soviet states—possibly repeating the "politics of the diagonal" characteristic of both Imperial and Weimar Germany.

The 1989–93 debates appear reminiscent of debates as to whether or not to aid tsarist or Soviet Russia, with or without political strings attached. In 1917, U.S. aid advanced to Russia was lost; at the same time U.S. policy did little to help sustain the fledgling Russian "democracy" before the Bolsheviks seized power. Between 1944 and 1947, massive aid proposals and loans to Russia (such as the Morgenthau plan) were ruled out. In contemporary circumstances, fears of instability and of wasting relatively limited resources, as well as fears of assisting a potential enemy, have thus far limited G-7 financial assistance. In fact, G-7 aid appears more reminiscent of the Dawes plan for Weimar Germany than a "Marshall Plan" or other aid promised Russia in the past. The Dawes plan represented a U.S. sponsored and financed effort to stabilize the collapsed German and European economy, in part to counter the threat of Soviet-inspired communism. The Dawes plan helped bring Germany out of its depression (temporarily) and helped underwrite Germany's reparations to France and Britain, involving the "merry-go-round" of debt. The 1929 global depression and Wall Street crash cut off U.S. funding, however. Accordingly, the Dawes plan, plus the Locarno Pact, were intended to stabilize economies and borders in Europe.[23] (In today's circumstances it has ironically been Germany, and not the United States, which has borne the brunt of aid to the former Soviet Union.)

In addition to allied divisions over economic issues, other parallels with the interwar period are also striking. The thus far largely impotent Conference on Security and Cooperation in Europe (CSCE) has paralleled the League of Nations: Both organizations insisted on the "principle of unanimity"—except for states directly involved in disputes—to reach decisions. The UN itself has not formulated a concerted strategy: Lack of a concerted policy in regard to war in the former Yugoslavia appears to parallel the lack of a concerted policy in regard to the Spanish Civil War, for example. Furthermore, although the new Russia took the Soviet position on the UN Security Council—thus giving Russia a more privileged position than Weimar Germany obtained from the League of Nations—Moscow's membership on the Security Council may not necessarily prevent its isolation. In addition, the two-plus-four treaty, and treaties guaranteeing Polish and Czech borders with Germany have paralleled the Locarno Pact that resulted in the consequently over-optimistic "spirit of Locarno." The demilitarization of the former East Germany can be contrasted with demilitarization of the Rhineland, for example. An eastern Locarno—the 1934 plan of French Foreign Minister Jean Louis Barthou—has yet to be formulated to resolve the conflicting territorial claims throughout Eurasia. (The EU has promised to address the latter region in mid-1994.)

Much like interwar disarmament talks, such as the 1922 Washington Naval Conference, disputes regarding the "proportion" of nuclear/conventional forces allocated to states of divergent geostrategic interests *and* potential capabilities, and the nature of "security guarantees" granted lesser states, are likely to plague negotiations. Efforts to draw the former Soviet republics (among other states) into the NPT, the missile technology control regime (MTCR), the START I and II agreements, and/or the Conventional Force in Europe (CFE) II treaty, may prove difficult to implement. The January 1994 U.S.-Russian disarmament pact with Ukraine may also prove difficult to sustain.

From this perspective, the contemporary global situation is no longer best compared to that of the pre–World War I era alone in which the Soviet Union, Eastern Europe, and India played a role similar to Imperial Germany, Austria-Hungary, and Italy.[24] Rather, today's geohistorical constellation of powers is more like the interwar period, in which the implosion of the Soviet Union plays a role similar to the indecisive defeat of Imperial Germany—though once again without the Versailles *Diktat*. The new Russia thus cannot be compared to Weimar Germany alone, but is best depicted as a crossbreed of Weimar Germany and of tsarist Russia in 1917. Significant differences result from the fact that Germany represented a Central European power, while Russia represents a Eurasian power. At the same time, however, the United States has not yet moved into isolation as in the interwar period; its relationship with Germany/Europe and Japan is thus far more reminiscent of Britain's relationship with France and Japan before World War I—prior to the breakup of the Anglo-French and Anglo-Japanese alliances.

Moreover, much as in the period before and immediately after World War I, Western-inspired democratic liberalism has initially gained the upper-hand. The collapse of Communist legitimacy in the Soviet Union, Eastern Europe, and to some extent in the PRC, has paralleled the collapse of monarchist legitimacy in Prussia/Germany, Austria-Hungary, and tsarist Russia (as well as in Imperial China). Much as monarchist legitimacy had been challenged by "national self-determination," so too has Communist legitimacy, opening the door to new sociocultural/ideological rivalries.

During the Cold War, Moscow represented an *initial* amphibious challenger whose quest for parity and legitimacy as a coequal decision-making power was most reminiscent of Imperial Germany's *initial* amphibious quest for *Gleichberechtigung* (or parity). Both Imperial Germany and the late Soviet Union sought to achieve *parity* from a position of relative military strength. Yet unlike Imperial Germany, both tsarist Russia and the Soviet Union tended to use tactics of self-abnegation (retrenchment, retreat, and radical disarmament proposals) to cover their military-technological and economic weaknesses and to offset their rivals. In contemporary conditions, the essentially land-locked Russia has hoped to sustain not too great a "disparity" with the United States, which is most reminiscent of land-locked Weimar Germany's efforts to sustain not too great a "disparity" with Britain.

After World War I, Weimar Germany thus sought to forge an entente with Britain and France; similarly, after the Cold War, Russia has sought to establish an entente with the United States and the EU. The Weimar leadership sought *primacy/hegemony* over Poland and *Anschluss* with Austria; not too dissimilarly, the Russian leadership has demanded a stronger political-economic union with Ukraine and/or the return of the Crimea to Russian control, plus primacy over former Warsaw Pact states. Concurrently, after Versailles, factions within Weimar Germany continued to press for revanche; likewise, factions in Russia have pressed for revanche after the Cold War.

With German unification, the rise of the PRC, and the breakup of the Soviet Union, the geostrategic constellation has changed radically. The systemic U.S.-German/European-Russian-PRC-Indian-Japanese interrelationship (plus Ukraine and Kazakhstan) has begun to parallel the systemic interwar Anglo-French-Weimar German-Stalinist Russian-Italian-American interrelationship (plus Poland and Turkey). The breakup or erosion of the Soviet alliances with Eastern Europe, India, and the Central Asian republics has thus possessed many parallels with the breakup of Imperial Germany's alliance with the Austro-Hungarian empire, Italy, and the Ottoman Empire. Here, India, in relation to the Indian Ocean, plays the role of interwar Italy in relation to the Mediterranean and Adriatic. The PRC plays the flanking role of Stalinist Russia. The new Russia and the PRC have, in effect, formed a Sino-Russian "Rapallo pact," in part to prevent the other from siding with an encircling U.S.-EU-Japanese alliance—as well as to press both Chinese and Russian interests against the latter states.

In addition, much as Weimar Germany feared a Franco-Polish

"encirclement" potentially linked to Britain and Stalinist Russia, the new Russia has feared the possibility that Ukraine may align with Poland and/or the EU linked to the U.S.-Japanese alliance. (Kiev could also align with Beijing.) Or, alternatively, much as tsarist Russia was confronted with an "encirclement" of Imperial Germany linked to Ukraine, Japan, and Turkey, so too has the new Russia been faced with the prospects of "encirclement" by a unified Germany, Ukraine, Turkey, and Japan—linked to the United States.

Much as was the case in 1919, questions have been raised as to whether the United States will sustain a close defense relationship with Europe, and whether NATO can function effectively without a clear enemy and in out-of-area conflicts in which U.S. and EU interests may not prove "complementary" (such as the former Yugoslavia). On the one hand, the EU could move toward a more "complementary" position vis-à-vis the United States; on the other hand, the EU could move toward greater political-military independence, or else look to East European states for support. Germany/Europe could also look to the PRC and/or Japan (an EU-Japanese "plutonium alliance") for support, if the United States cannot reassure European and Japanese security. As long as Germany remains double-contained within NATO and the EU, it is dubious that Bonn will move toward greater political-military independence or that it will move too close to Moscow, as German-Russian relations involve Janus-faced cooperation and mutual suspicions.

Thus far, Japanese actions are *superficially* reminiscent of its former East Asian co-prosperity sphere. The U.S.-Japanese alliance is so far like that of the 1902 Anglo-Japanese alliance. On the other hand, Tokyo could split from the United States as it did from Britain after the 1921–22 Washington Naval Conference, if its security and economic interests are not reassured—potentially developing a nuclear capability. Whereas Japan took an aggressive posture in the years before World Wars I and II, it is contemporary China that has taken a more assertive military policy—in an effort not to repeat the mistakes of the Dowager Empress (but perhaps repeating them).

During the Cold War, the "no-man's-land" (also called the arc of crisis) primarily included North Africa, the Middle East, Central Asia, and the Far Eastern littoral. Today's no-man's-land has now expanded to incorporate the Baltics, Eastern Europe, and the Caucasus; moreover, it runs even deeper into the Central Asian underbelly of the former Soviet Union. In regard to Central and Eastern Europe, Western support for "national self-determination," combined with the Chernobyl-like meltdown of the Iron Curtain, has helped to unleash a critical mass of rival irredentist ethnic and pan-national claims from

Stettin in the Baltic, Varna in the Black Sea, and Trieste in the Adriatic. The possible formation of a Ukraine, Central Europe, and Baltic state alliance might represent a contemporary Little Entente. (In many ways, post–1945 West Germany has—by peaceful means—riddled the Iron Curtain, obtaining late Imperial German war aims first actualized at the 1918 Treaty of Brest-Litovsk.)

Moreover, the collapse of the Soviet Union as a countervailing force (checking U.S. influence and double-containing the rise of regional powers) has, in part, been responsible for the further extension of U.S. interests into these new zones of regional security. Much as Britain attempted to reassert controls over its global empire in the 1920s, so too has the United States tried to reassert its global interests. U.S. links to Kuwait and Saudi Arabia, plus pressure on Iraq, and tenuous intervention on the Horn of Africa have tended to parallel British efforts to protect Egypt and control the Suez Canal—despite Egyptian resistance. U.S. "gunboat diplomacy" has evolved into "cruise missile diplomacy."

Parallels and contrasts can also be made with a loss of Imperial German colonies and Soviet overseas spheres of influence and security. Much as Imperial Germany pressured France in Morocco, so did the Soviet Union pressure Europe in Algeria and Libya. The collapse of Soviet supports for Algeria has indirectly opened the door to pan-Islamic subversion in North Africa. Imperial Germany's North Sea Fleet threatened Britain from Helgoland; the Soviet nuclear fleet and access to Cuba likewise threatened the United States. The collapse of Soviet support for Fidel Castro could accordingly permit the United States to reenter Cuba. After World War I, Britain, France, and Japan all moved to fill in former German spheres of influence; similarly, by the 1960s, Moscow tended to move into peripheral states under former British, Italian, Spanish, Portuguese, or French colonial controls. Today, core, semiperipheral states, and pan-national movements have all been vying for influence within former Soviet spheres of influence and security.

Whereas the relatively isolated former Soviet bloc appears to be moving toward an interwar–type depression; the United States, the EU, and Japan seem to be moving toward a relatively less severe depression, perhaps more like that of 1873–93 (which not so accidentally followed Italian, German and American political-economic integration), with an upturn expected in the late 1990s. Here, G-7 assistance and debt rescheduling to the former Soviet Union can be regarded as modern versions of the Dawes/Young plans intended to "buy" the peace between Germany and Russia, and sustain a pro-Western government in power. (Here, mark and yen "diplomacy" have largely supplanted dollar "diplomacy"—though Tokyo has remained reluctant to assist Moscow.) At the same time, much as Weimar Germany saw the Dawes/Young plans as a means to revise the Versailles Treaty, restore its international influence, regain military "parity" with its neighbors, regain some of its colonies and eastern borderlands, the new Russia may also intend to use G-7 assistance to revise international treaties and reassert its primacy/hegemony—if not dominance—over CIS states and over former Soviet spheres of influence and security.

THE QUESTION OF APPEASEMENT

In a geohistorical perspective, much as British, French, and American strategies had been split in the interwar period as to how to handle Weimar Germany, Stalinist Russia, Fascist Italy, Imperial Japan, and problems posed by national self-determination such as the rise of Poland and Turkey, contemporary American, German/European, and Japanese strategies may also split as to how to handle the new Russia, the PRC, India, as well as the rise of Ukraine, Kazakhstan, and states, such as Serbia, Croatia, and North Korea.

Unwilling to dismember Germany (as France demanded), the United States and Britain hoped to rebuild the Weimar Republic as a bulwark against Soviet influence; at the same time, however, the United States and Britain were reluctant to appease Weimar Germany's demands for political-economic primacy/hegemony over Poland and Austria, for example—leading Adolf Hitler to conclude that a pan-German nation could only be built by force. After failing to prevent the collapse the Weimar Republic, the British elite were thus confronted with the imperialism of Hitler (who sought a *globally* revanchist goal of reestablishing Germany as a major power) and that of Stalin (who sought an essentially *regionally* revanchist goal of establishing Soviet/Russian controls over Poland and the Baltic states) in addition to that of Benito Mussolini and Emperor Hirohito. With the collapse of the Molotov-Ribbentrop pact, the West then appeased Stalin's claims in the effort to keep Moscow in the war against the Axis powers (despite Stalin's own actions in Finland, the Baltic states, and in Poland).

In 1945–46, U.S. policy shifted from "appeasement" to that of "containment." The Cold War was accordingly characterized by the Western refusal to formally accept Soviet defined spheres of influence and security. By the late 1960s, the United States reluctantly accepted the apparent necessity of "appeasing" Chinese interests (relative to professed Western support for human rights and for Taiwan) as a counterpoise to Soviet political-military power and Japanese economic influence. The post–Cold War era has subsequently been characterized by a choice between appeasing, containing, or rolling back a number of actors. Such a divisive policy split involving geostrategic and political-ethical dilemmas can be observed in the way the United States sought to roll back Iraq (but appeased Syria, and, to some extent, Iran) in 1990–91 vis-à-vis the largely hands-off American policy toward Serbia and Croatia in 1991–93. Unless more concerted steps are taken, the latter policy has tended to parallel the refusal to intervene in the Spanish Civil War. (Russian diplomatic support for Serbia thus far differs from more overt German-Italian support for Francisco Franco's Spain. But both served to test allied resolve.)

Whereas Iraq, Syria, Serbia, and Croatia represent relatively minor peripheral actors, there is still a danger of more extensive pan-national expansion, "ethnic cleansing," and human rights abuses on an even more horrible scale if revanchist Russian, militant Hindu-Indian, or, among others, Chinese chauvinist movements, for example, come to power. (Chinese *laogai* prison labor camps, for example, are presently more extensive than those of the former Soviet Gulag.) The political-ethical implications of dealing with revanchist states may thus be similar to the dilemmas of having to deal with fascist and Communist regimes in the interwar period.[25] These implications possess major repercussions for Western policymakers: Maintaining peace becomes particularly problematic when self-defined collective entities declare themselves as nations in conflict with either sovereign states or with other self-defined nations and if each collective entity possesses "legitimate" claims to a particular territory or power over a particular nation or people.[26] Furthermore, another fundamental question is whether states do possess the right to call in allies to their assistance to resist overt aggression—even at the risk of sparking a more generalized or global war.[27]

Moreover, although long-term socio-economic cycles do exacerbate the chances for global war as argued by "long-wave" theorists (who have predicted the increasing likelihood of global war in the early twenty-first century following the next economic upswing),[28] global conflict can still be averted. Here, both "long-cycle" theorists and neo-Kantians have tended to overlook the argument that the possibility of a future global war really depends upon the international policy responses to revisionist powers and the nature of alliance linkages formed among major and emerging powers. This is true as the political decision-making process is *relatively* autonomous; apparent socioeconomic "cycles" and political lobbying groups may *influence* or help *precondition* political decision-making behavior, but these pressures do not necessarily *determine* those policy decisions. *Political-economic and sociocultural/ideological factors related indirectly to war causation can be superseded if states possess common geostrategic interests (particularly in containing third powers), or else adopt irenic policies of compromise, retrenchment, or appeasement.*

As there are still significant differences between the interwar period and now, the failure of appeasement before World War II does not necessarily foreordain the failure of the future application of a similar (but hopefully better managed) policy in contemporary circumstances—depending upon the systemic circumstances of how many powers are to be appeased and the long-term geopolitical intent of those powers.[29] Appeasement does not mean capitulation: A concerted policy can manage demands for expansion by states without necessarily opening the floodgates to all revisionist movements. Thus, to avert global war, it is necessary to prevent the isolation of a significant power from decision-making processes of the other major powers. A concerted global strategy may temporarily tilt against the interests of one or more major and minor powers, but it must not alienate a significant power altogether. (If, however, a major state does feel pressured by decisions antagonistic to its perceived vital interests, then the chances of global conflict will be greatly exacerbated.) The dilemma is that when confronted with a major challenger, the traditional encirclement (or pseudo-balance of power reaction) has been to side with lesser powers against the major challenger, rather than seeking to cooperate with—if not appease—that challenger through diplomatic engagement.

If the new Russia cannot ultimately be drawn into a more concerted defense and economic community of nations, the option of appeasement may become the only available strategy to that of attempting to draw Central Europe, Ukraine, and the PRC into a pro-Western "encirclement" of Russia. Moreover, much as it was dubious that Stalinist Russia could be drawn into an alliance without appeasing Stalin's interests in Eastern Europe, it is dubious that the United States can draw China as an "active strategic counterweight" against a potentially revanchist Russia. Any such effort to bring the PRC back toward the West could result in an appeasement of Chinese claims vis-à-vis the South China Sea and Taiwan—in potential conflict with Japan.

Assuming that Russian claims themselves cannot be mitigated by irenic diplomacy designed to dampen a Russian revanchist backlash (see Chapter 9), any future strategy may thus be impelled to appease Russian claims in the effort to contain those of the PRC (on the assumption that Russia itself would accept such Western demands). While the NATO-Japan-PRC encirclement of the Soviet Union did not bring global conflict, an encirclement of Russia (even if Russia does forge closer ties with the PRC) could well result in global war—particularly if the Russian elite believe that they must forestall the disaggregation of Russian Federation itself through an expansionist and preclusive strategy.

From an optimistic perspective, however, assuming efforts to bring a nonrevanchist Russia into a concerted defense and economic community of nations and to treat the new Russia as a legitimate coequal of the other major powers do succeed, these actions *could* aid in the maintenance of global peace, and secondarily in the sustenance of democratic confederations globally. Should the new Russian democracy be sustained, it may then be possible that a U.S.-Russian-EU-Japanese concert could ultimately help China and other states move toward democratic-liberal reforms—as China itself did in the early twentieth century prior to its civil war.[30] This could be true as long as each of these states can sustain a cooperative defense and economic relationship, and assuming that new federal arrangements (including aspects of autonomy) can be forged internally in both Russia and China; and assuming other states do not move into a revanchist phase and that schisms among democratic-liberal states themselves do not begin to fester.

This being said, the key dilemma—as recognized by Niccolò Machiavelli in the *Discourses*—is that even major states with an apparently firm alliance commitment may be drawn into conflict because of the nature of their criss-crossing allegiances to minor powers in conflict. The very *threat* of a significant ally to develop more independent political-military capabilities and possibly threaten to take sides in order to press for concessions and advantages, or to support a regional actor against its rival—the quintessential aspect of strategic leveraging—represents one of the fundamental causes of global war. It is thus possible, even in circumstances of a renewed détente moving toward entente, that the new Russia and United States could still be drawn to the support of conflicting allies on opposing sides as these emerging regional powers expand their regional spheres of influence and security (and concurrently fear the loss of either U.S. or Russian security guarantees as Washington and Moscow move to form a closer entente).

On the other hand, it is also plausible that Russia and the United States could join forces to block the rise of third parties—assuming that both perceive that third state as a mutual threat and that both seek to prove their alliance commitment. If the apparently burgeoning regional conflicts of the late twentieth century are not to become generalized, the major powers must either remain neutral or resolve issues by concerted action so that the push-pull nature of major and minor power interactions does not explode into global conflict.

3

Origins and Dynamics of the U.S.-Soviet Antagonism

THE RELEVANCE OF THE PRE-CONTAINMENT ERA (1803–1941)

The roots of the Cold War cannot be understood without examination of the U.S.-Russian/Soviet relationship before the Bolshevik revolution and throughout the interwar period, and without reference to the expectations raised by the 1907 Anglo-Russian entente and by the 1941 Anglo-American-Soviet wartime alliance.

Until the late nineteenth century, Russian-American relations were more positive than negative. Catherine the Great's refusal to assist the British in suppressing the American colonists was perceived (right or wrong) as a statement of Russian support for the American Revolution. Tsar Alexandr I's efforts to secure the release of the crew of a U.S. frigate taken hostage by Tripolitan pirates helped to initiate Russo-American friendship in 1803—prior to tsarist recognition in 1809. This latter effort paralleled Mikhail Gorbachev's efforts to help release U.S. citizens taken hostage in Lebanon in the 1980s—an action which helped break the ice of the Cold War.

Following the Napoleonic Wars, tsarist Russia began to expand into Central Asia and the Far East. It supported Greek independence against Turkey; established economic relations with Brazil; and sought to use Haiti as a potential entrepôt for its state trading company. Yet despite interests in Alaska, the Oregon territories, and northern California, as well as efforts to turn the Pacific into a "Russian lake," tsarist Russia retracted rather than oppose U.S. expansion over North America. In effect, Russia respected U.S. "spheres of influence" as announced by the 1823 Monroe Doctrine. Russia also tended to side with the Union against South Carolina's threats to secede; the U.S. government tended to *look through* Russia's 1830 crackdown on Poland—as well as the 1849 crackdown on Hungary—despite the American public outcry. The fact that Commodore Perry beat out a Russian squadron on its way from the Baltic, and then forced limited concessions on Japan in the 1854 Treaty of Kanawaga, did not alienate Russia. St. Petersburg, London, and Paris followed suit: The U.S. treaty was not exclusive. (Commodore Perry's actions—what the Japanese call the "Day of Black Ships"—can be seen as a precursor to U.S. efforts to beat out the Soviet Union over control of Japan at the end of World War II.)

Following the Crimean War (in which the United States profited from trade with Russia and signed an accord for the protection of neutral shipping), St. Petersburg preferred to see Alaska controlled by the United States rather than by Britain; and Hawaii controlled by the United States rather than by Britain or Japan. Americans did show animosity to the Russification of Poland in the 1860s and the subsequent Russification of Poland, the Baltics, and Ukraine in the 1880s under Tsar Alexandr III. At the same time, the State Department downplayed Russian actions. Both the United States and Russia could claim common ideological interests in the "freeing" of the serfs in the aftermath of the Crimean War and the "freeing" of the slaves after the American Civil War. U.S. conquest of Indian and Spanish/Mexican America could be regarded as parallel to tsarist efforts to conquer Turkish-Persian Central Asia.[1] In essence, tsarist Russia used its links to the United States, plus pressure in Central Asia and the Far East, to counter British global outreach and, ultimately, to pressure Britain into an entente; the United States concurrently used its links to Russia to counter European influence.

The turning point in U.S.-Russian relations came after Tsar Nikolai II came to the throne and the Sino-Japanese War, followed by the Spanish-American War, in which the United States seized the Philippines. Here, Washington recognized Tokyo's suzereignty over Korea in order to gain Japanese recognition over the U.S. hold over the Philippines. Coupled with British overtures for an Anglo-German-U.S. alliance against Russia in 1898, one intention of the Open Door Policy in 1899 was to check Russian expansion in Asia. On the one hand, Russia sought to monopolize trade in Manchuria and Korea—the latter controlled Russian communication lines from Port Arthur to Vladivostok; on the other hand, it sought to counter Japan after the 1894–95 Sino-Japanese War. U.S.-Russian economic rivalry had begun to intensify after the 1870s; and by 1901–05, a major trade war arose out of disputes over oil concessions, Russian purchases of rail lines, sugar subsidies, and sales of U.S. agricultural equipment which ironically helped to augment Russian wheat production in competition with U.S. farmers.

Combined with burgeoning economic tensions, American mediation to help end the Russo-Japanese War of 1904–05 also caused resentment. Foreshadowing Leninist ideology, Russian elites claimed that "American trusts" had precipitated the war to drive Russia out of Manchuria. U.S. mediation at the "hasty" Peace of Portsmouth was regarded as preventing Russia from rebuilding its fleet in order to ultimately defeat Japan, whose capabilities had been stretched to the limit by the war. Teddy Roosevelt, on the contrary, argued that Japan could have driven Russia out of all of Siberia and as far west as Lake Baikal (a dubious proposition at that time). Thus, despite the fact that Russia was forced to give up claims to Korea, Port Arthur, and south Sakhalin, the United States saw itself as restraining Japanese demands—ironically, also alienating Japan—which had designs to annex southern Manchuria.[2]

Tsar Alexandr II's "revolution from above" had introduced democratic reforms on the local and provincial levels. Tsar Nikolai II's steps toward economic liberalism, encouragement of foreign investment (not without pitfalls) and adoptation of the gold standard in 1897 under Finance Minister Sergei Witte (1892–1903) preceded tsarist political liberalism. Following the Russo-Japanese War, and the 1905 revolution, the Tsar's *October Manifesto* established the Duma—the new Russian parliament. But in seeking to establish absolute control over the use of military force, and to limit the Duma's power of the purse, Tsar Nikolai II dissolved the first two Dumas (1906 and 1907) and sought to increase the participation of the wealthy landed classes in the third (1907–12) and fourth (1912–16). The reduction of Polish representation in the third Duma additionally exacerbated demands for Polish independence. Despite the Tsar's efforts to change its constituency, the Duma continued to attack tsarist incompetence—at the same time that revolutionaries accused members of the Duma of being tsarist lackeys. The establishment of the Duma was also accompanied by the pro-capitalist agrarian reforms of Prime Minister Petr Arkadievich Stolypin (1906–10).

Surprising the world, Britain moved to forge an entente with Russia in the period 1902–07, reaching political settlements in Afghanistan, Tibet, and Persia—establishing a condominium over the latter despite its steps toward constitutional reforms. In effect, the rise of Imperial Germany as a naval threat impelled Britain to move closer to the United States, Japan, France, as well as Russia: The market-oriented and "constitutional" reforms taken in Russia at that time made British overtures easier. The United States, on the other hand, was not impressed: Congressional outrage over the persecution of the Jewish population (combined with increased Jewish emigration) led to the 1911 termination of the 1832 Russo-American trade agreement. The U.S. State Department argued that the severing of U.S.-Russian economic relations would weaken the U.S. position in dealing with Russia in the Near and Far East, and make things more difficult for those persecuted. (These actions—supported by presidential candidate Woodrow Wilson to win the election—thus represented the historical precedent to the 1974 Jackson-Vanik and Stevenson amendments. Not too dissimilarly, Richard Nixon claimed that refusal to grant MFN status and other concessions would weaken U.S. leverage over Russian behavior. In addition, much as British and German firms began to take the tsarist Russian market away from American firms, European and Japanese firms moved into the former Soviet market.)

With the advent of World War I—in part sparked as a result of Russian support for pan-Serb goals against Austro-German penetration of the Balkans and Turkey—U.S. trade with Russia began to pick up; and yet, isolationist American hopes to stay out of the war were foiled by Russian collapse. The United States initially greeted the Russian revolution in March 1917 with optimism, and hoped the new Russia would continue the war effort. The U.S. decision to intervene in the "war to end all wars" was made in April 1917, however, once it was clear that Russia would not continue to fight. As George Kennan pointed out, Allied and U.S. demands crudely expressed by Elihu Root, U.S. emissary to Russia, as "no fight, no loans," may have helped weaken an already fragile Provisional Government. The demand to keep Russia in the war conflicted with the other major aim of U.S. policy—to ensure the survival of the Provisional Government and its experiment in democracy.[3] (Here, it should be noted that London promised both Tsar Nikolai II and the provisional Russian government the reward of Constantinople if Russia would sustain its war effort.)

Contrary to French interests, and indicating that ideological conflict was not necessarily inevitable, Woodrow Wilson did consider the possibility of working with the Bolsheviks in an effort to keep Russia in the war following the collapse of the Provisional Government. But unlike Trotsky, Lenin was opposed to continuing the war effort with Western assistance. Lenin expected Germany's war efforts to collapse, and revolution in Germany was to follow after the war. Lenin did not want to get caught in a two-front war against both Germany (which threatened to support Ukraine, Turkey, and Persia) and Japan.[4] The dual blows—defeat in the Russo-Japanese War, and then defeat by Imperial Germany in World War I—led to collapse of the tsarist regime, civil war, and Leninist revolution—the latter in part financed by Imperial German General Erich von Ludendorff since 1915. But despite initial German support, it was Berlin's threat to continue warfare into Ukraine that finally brought Lenin to capitulation at the Treaty of Brest-Litovsk (1918). Soviet Russia was forced to give up the Baltic states and Poland to Germany, recognize Finland, and lose large areas of Byelorussia, Ukraine, and part of the Transcaucasus.

Allied intervention in Russia in April 1918 was largely intended to prevent military supplies from being transported to Imperial Germany; it was likewise intended to assist resistance to Germany. Concurrently, Allied actions were also intended to help restrain Japanese intervention in the Far East and prevent Japan from absorbing Russian territory in Siberia (the Russian Far East had also declared itself independent). In Central Asia, London was more concerned with pressuring Turkey and containing pan-Islamic and pan-Turk movements that might cause instability in India and Afghanistan than in supporting movements against the Bolsheviks.

In supporting the White armies, the U.S. intention was not to support separatist movements but to sustain the integrity of the Russian empire. The United States did, at least initially, consider covert support (through the British and French) to aid Ukraine and the Don cossacks to resist both the Germans and the Bolsheviks. But Washington, unlike Paris, refused to recognize Ukraine prior to the German takeover of Kiev. Washington thus resisted French pressures (Marshall Ferdinand Foch's "crusade") to crush the Bolsheviks; Paris and White forces accordingly rejected Woodrow Wilson's 1919 proposal for a peace conference. The United States refused to recognize the breakaway republics, which had claimed "sovereignty over a portion of the territory of the nation" until there was "evidence of the possession of a right to exercise sovereignty over all Russia."[5] (Yet even Paris was reluctant to support separatist forces that might break up its traditional Russian ally and counterweight to Germany, as states of a dismembered Russian empire could ultimately turn to Germany for alliance.)

Involved in an undeclared war, U.S. troops were withdrawn from the west in July 1919 and from Siberia in 1920. The Bolshevik victory resulted in the reabsorption of Byelorussia and much of Ukraine—except for the extensive western regions taken by Poland after the Russo-Polish War (1919–20) at the Treaty of Riga. Lenin's promises of national self-determination to Armenia, Georgia, and Central Asian states were not granted; movements independent of Bolshevik control were soon crushed. The Red Army was able to retain control of much of the former Russian territory except Finland, Poland, and the Baltic states. Moscow then began to reassert its Eurasian interests by 1921, forging treaties with Turkey, Persia, Afghanistan. Moscow also pressured British interests in China by supporting both the KMT and CCP against Manchu rule.

Even prior to the formation of the Comintern in 1919, U.S. foreign policy moved to "contain" the Bolshevik threat. An instable Weimar Germany used the specter of Sparticist revolution to gain U.S. financial support for its reconstruction in 1918. As German collapse threatened European recovery (and global markets), the United States willingly built up Germany.[6] On the other hand, even though Washington refused to accept the Soviet Union in the 1921–22 Washington Conference, the United States did seek to ease Japan out of Siberia and held off recognizing the newly independent Baltic states until the Soviet Union did so—in deference to Soviet interests.

U.S.-Soviet relations remained tense as the 1922 Genoa Conference failed to reach an agreement over the costs of Soviet nationalization of Western property against reparations due to the Soviet Union from Allied intervention in the Civil War. Whereas Britain, France, and Italy (and Weimar Germany through the Rapallo agreement involving secret military assistance) moved toward de facto recognition of the Soviet Union by 1922–23 (and lifted the Allied blockade), the United States did not recognize the Soviet government until 1933. With the transfer of financial hegemony to the United States from Britain, the Americans increasingly managed Europe's economic concerns but largely followed British pro-German and anti-Soviet geopolitical interests (over the objections of France, which sought both to dismember Germany and to contain the Soviet Union). Both Washington and London sought to stabilize Berlin: The Locarno treaties and the 1924 Dawes plan were intended to guarantee borders, open new markets and investment outlets in Europe, avert a German revanchist backlash or revolutionary movement, and counterbalance Soviet influence. At the same time, however, Berlin was not permitted political-economic reintegration with Vienna, for example. (Today, the two-plus-four talks—coupled with German recognition of Polish and Czech borders—represent a new Locarno treaty; but G-7 assistance represents a Dawes plan for Russia—not Germany.)

Initially, Roosevelt's efforts in the 1930s to recognize the Soviet Union were based more on the threat posed by Japan than that posed by Adolf Hitler. The Japanese Kwantung army had violated Chinese territorial integrity and sought monopolistic control over Manchuria contrary to the U.S. Open Door Policy. The United States accordingly hoped to pressure Japan with a U.S.-Soviet entente. Arguments against recognition of the Soviet Union in 1933 (U.S. businesses claimed losses of

$300 million, Soviet support for "world revolution," the world reaction to collectivization in 1928–33, and the abolishment of religion and private property) failed to hold weight. U.S. diplomatic recognition helped Moscow strengthen its position vis-à-vis both Germany and Japan. Moscow also shifted from a position supporting general disarmament to support for the French position that "security must precede disarmament." Hence Stalin encouraged collective intervention against Benito Mussolini and Hitler; yet after the failure of the 1934 Barthou Plan to forge an eastern Locarno, alliance talks with Moscow broke down.

Having previously forbidden Weimar Germany to expand its political-economic influence more gradually, London and Paris (backed by Washington) opted for "appeasement" at Munich (while simultaneously seeking to coopt Rome in addition to Berlin). This action destroyed the French alliance with the Little Entente and isolated Russia. Concurrently, as Hitler (unlike Neville Chamberlain and Edouard Daladier) could promise a partition of Poland and the Baltic states, Stalin forged a separate peace with Hitler to avert an Anglo-French-German-Italian coalition against the Soviet Union. To contain Hitler, it would have been necessary to accept the movement of Russian troops through Romania or Poland (opposed by the Poles, who had forged a nonaggression pact with Hitler in 1934); it was also feared that an alliance with Moscow would swing East European states toward Berlin (a possibility that could have been countered by a strong Anglo-French alliance with these same states). Most importantly, however, Russian forces were not prepared for conflict because of the Soviet-Japanese War and purges in the Red Army. Much as Lenin had been haunted by the threat of a two-front war against Germany and Japan during the Russian Civil War, a similar fear of a two-front war against Germany and Japan likewise haunted Stalin. Rather than fight Germany, Stalin began a rapprochement with Hitler in the summer of 1938. Hitler's invasion of Poland brought both Britain and France into the war against Germany; but the West chose not to go to war with both dictators over the Polish question in the hope that Stalin would not side overtly with Hitler. Accordingly, Roosevelt maintained relations with the "Communist devil." It was hoped that Stalin would continue to keep Japanese forces tied down, at the same time that Roosevelt and Stalin supported the Chinese nationalists (KMT)—although Stalin also tried to play the Chinese Communists (CCP) and KMT against each other.

After the unexpected collapse of France, Stalin seized all three Baltic states (having already moved into Finland), even though the Hitler-Stalin pact had assigned Lithuania to Hitler. Stalin's efforts to hold onto Bessarabia and Bukovina (the latter seen by Soviet Foreign Minister Vyacheslav Molotov as "demanded" by Ukraine to achieve its unification) had also angered Hitler, who opposed Stalin's additional demands for control over the Balkans and Dardanelles. Stalin then made peace with Japan in April 1941, having received reports of Hitler's attack since August 1940, and ended support for Chiang Kai-shek. Once again, Stalin avoided a two-front war and only offered Soviet support against Japan once Hitler was defeated. Prior to Operation Barbarossa in June 1941, the Soviet-Japanese neutrality agreement initially angered Washington which froze Russian (and Japanese) assets. The end of the Soviet-Japanese War permitted Japanese expansion southward—ultimately resulting in Pearl Harbor.

ATOMIC DOUBLE CONTAINMENT (ENCIRCLEMENT AND COUNTER-ENCIRCLEMENT: PHASE I, 1941–45)

Differences in war strategy between the United States and the Soviet Union were manifest as early as the 1941 Atlantic Charter. In essence, Stalin sought to revise the 1921 Treaty of Riga and the 1895 Treaty of Portsmouth; at the same time, Stalin was not adverse to pressing Soviet interests beyond former tsarist territories if the opportunity arose; yet he still hoped to press the United States into a full-fledged entente relationship if possible.

In July 1941, Stalin asked the Allies to open a second front in France (a request not to be granted until D-Day 1944). By December 1941, Stalin insisted on retaining Estonia, Latvia, Finland, Bessarabia, and eastern Poland (the Curzon line) seized during the 1939 Molotov-Ribbentrop pact. Stalin initially considered detaching the Rhineland, and possibly Bavaria, from Germany (demands later reversed in an effort to appeal to German nationalism). He sought bases in Romania and Finland with a guarantee of exits from the Baltic, but accepted British bases in Denmark and Norway. (After 1945 Stalin withdrew his forces from the latter despite the importance of northern Norway's warm water ports.) At the Teheran Conference, Stalin argued the fact that Poland and the Baltic states had been under tsarist rule did not prevent the formation of the 1907 Anglo-American alliance with tsarist Russia; likewise Soviet control over these same states should not prevent an Anglo-American alliance with the Soviet Union.[7] (Washington, however, was only an indirect party to 1907 Anglo-Russian entente.)

By 1944, Soviet forces obtained German Königsberg (now Kaliningrad), Romanian Bukovina, Czech Uzhgorod, Polish Lvov, and

Hungarian Mukachev, as well as the Japanese Kuriles (or northern territories) and south Sakhalin Island (the latter two were regarded as part of the Yalta accords). On one side, Stalin's absorption of both Poland and East Germany can be seen as strategic: to divide Germany and create a defensive buffer against all potential corridors of invasion. The overextension of Soviet controls also helped to obtain new bargaining chips for deals with the Allies after the war. On the other side, Stalin's efforts can be seen as an attempt to dominate his internal empire and prevent the East European and Slavic republics from reaching out for foreign support. The granting of East German territory to Poland (the Oder-Neise line) was intended to force Poland into a permanent alliance with the Soviet Union against Germany. The division of Polish territory (the Rukh) between Ukraine and Byelorussia was intended to coopt Ukrainian and Byelorussian nationalist sentiment. Here, Ukraine was granted Polish Lvov, for example. (Lenin had previously granted the industrial basin of the Donbass to Ukraine as a "reward" for service in the civil war.) Here, Stalin used aspects of both cooptation and repression (Nikita Khrushchev's 1946 purge in Ukraine) to assure Ukrainian and Byelorussian compliance with Russia as the Slavic "big brother" and to check German influence. Stalin hoped to forestall the kind of events that took place in 1917–18 and again in 1989–91.

Washington's failure was twofold. First, there was a reluctance to move into Berlin and Prague. Second, the United States did not concurrently recognize the legitimacy of newly acquired Soviet spheres of influence and security that Western armed forces could not reach, so as not to raise long-term Soviet suspicions.[8] These two failures led to inevitable Soviet predominance over Central Europe; but they were not failures that can be attributed to a naïve trust in Stalin's aims. The strategic dilemma was to make certain that Moscow would remain in the struggle against Hitler, who was on the verge of developing atomic weapons, and to avert a separate Soviet-German peace. To attack Germany through the Balkans and Eastern Europe (as Churchill had argued) might alienate Russia. (In addition, General George Marshall opposed Churchill's position because of the logistical nightmare of dealing with guerrilla warfare in Balkan terrain.) Once in Germany, General Dwight Eisenhower sought a clear line of demarcation so as to prevent U.S. and Soviet troops from accidentally clashing over Czechoslovakia where there was no conclusive political agreement.

Prior to the certain "success" of the atomic bomb, it was additionally believed at the time of the Yalta Conference that Stalin's assistance would be needed to fight Japanese resistance in Manchuria, Korea, and north China, and to maintain close U.S.-Soviet relations after the war. With British, U.S., and Soviet forces dividing up Europe, the shift away from the "four policemen" concept toward a *quid pro quo* approach before Roosevelt's death has been well told.[9] The July–August 1945 Potsdam Conference (which created the Council of Foreign Ministers) revealed the open rift between the two sides over Poland, Soviet rule in Bulgaria and Romania, war reparations, Tito's demands for Trieste, the Allied administration over Germany, and Soviet expansion in Asia. The United States likewise refused to include Soviet interests in the formulation of reconstruction policies over fascist Italy.

As the atomic bomb had been tested the day before the Potsdam Conference, efforts to revise suddenly the Yalta agreement and stall Sino-Soviet talks over the fate of northern China largely failed to further contain Soviet advances in the Far East.[10] Stalin had been aware of the atomic bomb (because of agent Klaus Fuchs plus anonymous secret agent "Perseus") and awaited its use before attacking Japan, having warned Japan that it was violating the 1941 Soviet-Japanese neutrality pact several months before. It was thus not the atomic bomb itself that stopped Stalin from advancing to Hokkaido: Stalin respected U.S. interests in Japan (only promising assistance in accord with British and U.S. demands) and moved into North Korea in accord with the Potsdam agreement—though he could have taken the whole peninsula.

ANGLO-AMERICAN ENCIRCLEMENT AND BURDEN SHARING: PHASE II, 1945–53

Churchill's "Iron Curtain" speech of March 1946—warning of Communist domination from Stettin in the Baltic to Trieste in the Adriatic—reconfirmed Stalin's fears of an Anglo-American "capitalist encirclement." As the speech contradicted Winston Churchill's 1944 "percentages agreement" that promised Stalin a sphere of influence and security in Eastern Europe, it indicated that a weak Britain had moved to strengthen its ties with its primary core ally, the United States. London would no longer act as a mediator between Moscow and Washington. Then, at the same time that Washington accused Moscow of violating Yalta in regard to free elections in Eastern Europe, and of forging monopolistic economic pacts with East European states, as well as supporting Communist parties in France and Italy (the latter a key to control of the Mediterranean/Adriatic), Moscow counter-accused the West of reneging on its agreement to contain the potential rise of West German "revanche" and Japanese "militarism" through Marshall aid and the Dodge plan. Stalin believed that Bonn would be able to recover in twelve to fifteen years and forewarned that the West would not be able to "absorb the export capacities of Japan and West Germany."[11]

On the U.S. side, in the process of consolidating Allied rule (and creating a self-sustaining political-economic recovery) at the same time that it engaged in de-Nazification, the United States permitted concessions to West German leaders in order to forestall the rise of Communist, extreme nationalist, or even "neutralist" movements. Allied forces' needed to build the legitimacy of the new West German "democratic" political leadership—and likewise counter Soviet propaganda supporting a united, yet Sovietized, Germany. The need to reconcile Christian Democratic leader Konrad Adenauer with Social Democratic leader Kurt Schumacher meant that the United States had to show that West European integration did not mean an end to hopes for unification. (By 1949 President Truman and Secretary of State Dean Acheson supported Adenauer; British Prime Minister Clement Attlee, however, favored Schumacher.) Thus in September 1946, to counter Molotov's opposition to the separation of the Ruhr and Rhineland, U.S. Secretary of State James Byrnes renounced the Oder-Neise line agreed to at Potsdam, siding with claims to Germany's 1937 borders and looked to the economic integration of western zones of occupation.[12] Concurrently, U.S. support for Warsaw's claims to its 1939 boundaries tended to push Kiev closer to Moscow. Claims to German unification were ultimately formalized in the 1949 Constitution, which was considered provisional so as to prevent perceptions of a permanent division of Germany.

Almost immediately after German defeat, U.S. and Soviet commissioners had disagreed over the question of German war reparations and the German ability to repay. From the summer of 1945, the United States began to tilt away from a "corrective" peace and toward a "constructive" peace. In effect, the United States saw itself as subsidizing German war reparations (owed to Russia) because of the burden of occupation costs; and it opposed French efforts to detach the Ruhr and the Rhineland (as Paris had in the interwar period). Primacy given to German "burden sharing" was particularly supported by the U.S. War Department over the State Department: The latter had supported a more balanced restoration of the German and European economies. Marshall aid hence sought to remedy the dangers of political-economic instability; aid was also in part based on the conviction that an imminent Communist victory in China would mean the necessity to build up West European power capabilities.

Unable to compromise on an appropriate format for German confederation or unification, Moscow and Washington began to compete for Germany's political allegiance by supporting different unification formulas.[13] Moscow subsequently used the Berlin crises of 1947 and 1948–49 to veto actions by the Western powers—and ultimately to obtain Western acceptance of East Germany as a legitimate state, if a "neutral" united Germany could not be established. The United States (until 1954) publicly supported claims to Germany's 1937 borders, while West Germany itself sustained this demand until 1990–91—borders with Poland and Czechoslovakia were considered provisional. In 1948, concurrent with Marshall aid, the Six Power conference in London decided to integrate all three zones of West Germany occupied by the Allies—in effect, isolating Moscow and establishing a separate West German state. (In addition to demanding that Paris remove Communist ministers from the French Atomic Energy Commission, Marshall aid had been conditioned on French support for an economically "sensible" Germany. Lack of Soviet support for a divided Germany, plus the Soviet crackdown on interwar French allies in Eastern Europe, likewise reinforced France's decision.) Ironically, disputes over Germany hardly touched real German economic capabilities. By the early 1950s, both Washington and Moscow sought to revive German industry as a form of security assistance vis-à-vis the other[14]—at the same time that Bonn hoped to use its economic power potential and strategic leveraging to ultimately achieve unification.

TENSIONS OUTSIDE GERMANY

Soviet pressures to make border revisions in Turkey (related to tsarist claims to Kars and Ardahan), to support Kurdish independence movements, and to make changes in the 1936 Montreux convention that would permit a Soviet military presence in the Dardanelles, were regarded a step toward Soviet expansion into the Aegean and Mediterranean. Initially, senior officials in the army and air force—who were in favor of maintaining the wartime alliance—did argue for concessions: Soviet naval parity should be granted as the United States itself was obtaining overseas bases in Iceland, the Azores, and Pacific islands. The internationalization of the Dardanelle Straits was discussed at Potsdam, but dismissed as Stalin appeared to want to forge a regional Black Sea pact with Turkey.[15] Stalin's demands had a historical precedent: In 1915–17, London promised to grant both the tsarist and provisional Russian governments Constantinople as a reward for staying in the war. Even with the (belated) Soviet entry into World War II, however, the United States maintained the more traditional British policy: to contain Soviet amphibious capabilities by permanent deployment of the U.S. Navy in the Mediterranean in September 1946.

The revolutionary movements in Greece (Macedonia) were primarily supported by Yugoslavia and Bulgaria—and not by Stalin, who opposed Josip Tito's seizure of Trieste in 1946 and Yugoslavia's military presence in Austrian Carinthia. Ironically, in the period 1945–47, Harry Truman, Anthony Eden, and Josef Stalin had a common interest in containing Tito's proposals for an alliance with Bulgaria, Albania, and other Balkan states. (Stalin initially entertained Tito's proposals for an alliance with Bulgaria—but as a means to contain Tito.)[16] A prudent Stalin wanted to limit areas of confrontation with the West based on his "percentages agreement" with Churchill and concurrently limit Tito's independence from Moscow. Tito's actions led Stalin to strengthen his grasp over Central and Eastern Europe (the Czech coup in 1948) and to make sure that Mao, if he gained power, would not look westward to an alliance with the United States. Here, had the Truman Plan been directed against Tito alone (and *not* against the Soviet Union as well) Washington might have been able to work with Stalin in maintaining distinctly defined spheres of influence and security—at the same time that it still supported Greece and Turkey. Washington, however, began a rapprochement with Tito in 1948 (despite his anti-Western actions) as a means to erode the Soviet bloc. Concurrently, Soviet troops stationed in Hungary assured Yugoslav "neutrality."

Soviet withdrawal from Iran in May 1946—under U.S. pressure—put to an end the Anglo-Russian condominium that had been established in 1907, and which was later reestablished in 1942 to supply lend-lease aid to Stalin and to prevent the Shah from sympathizing with Hitler. Here, the British had preferred to sustain controls over southern Iran; U.S. opposition to the essentially Anglo-Soviet condominium raised concerns in both London and Moscow. Although Washington initially urged Teheran not to antagonize Stalin, the Iranian parliament refused to grant Moscow oil concessions—initiating Teheran's efforts to play Moscow, Washington (and London) against each other. Increased U.S. financial and military aid to Iran by 1952–53 then exacerbated U.S.-Soviet rivalry over Iran. Washington was more concerned with replacing British interests and with countering Soviet subversion than with the rise of radical pan-Islamic movements.[17]

Thus, by 1947, the Truman administration (lobbied heavily by London) began formally to take on the former burden of the British Empire, having scared an isolationist Congress enough to commit funds. Europeans, however, needed to show a semblance of self-help by forming their own alliances in the fear that the U.S. Congress might demand a return to isolation—as had been threatened by Franklin Roosevelt. The

1947 Franco-British Dunkirk Treaty then led to the 1948 Treaty of Brussels (which would form the basis for the West European Union), and finally, in 1949, to NATO. Although Western forces had demobilized, Moscow maintained 175 divisions in Eastern Europe, many on an apparent war footing. Soviet actions mimicked tsarist actions of 1815–18 in which the numbers of occupation forces in France were actually increased for police and garrison work, and to defend against anti-monarchist French ideology. But unlike in the year 1818, troops did not return to Russia: Moscow was not included in a new "concert of Europe."

Had the United States opted for the alternative options outlined above, U.S.-Soviet tensions might well have ameliorated; Soviet-East European participation in the Marshall Plan—and steps toward a democratic liberalization of the Eastern bloc—might have been assured. What is more certain, however, is the fact that Stalin *did* compromise with the Washington over a limited relief plan through the United Nations Relief and Rehabilitation Administration (UNRRA), which was earmarked specifically for Ukraine and Byelorussia (1945–47). Ironically, before being canned as pro-Communist, UNRRA permitted U.S. citizens free access to Soviet territory; U.S. policy could accordingly have differentiated among the Slavic states, perhaps leading to a *devolution* of Russian predominance. From this perspective, U.S. demands for sweeping economic concessions under the Marshall Plan missed opportunities to use financial leverage for more limited gains.[18]

BURDEN SHARING AND SOVIET COUNTER-ENCIRCLEMENT IN ASIA

In effect, the Yalta Conference had traded U.S. interests in Asia for those in Eastern Europe; yet it was too late to change that arrangement at Potsdam. The Borton group of the State Department argued that Moscow's interests should be included in the settlement in the Far East; otherwise Moscow might "make things difficult down the road."[19] At the same time, despite minor concessions, the United States opposed anything that would constrain the authority of the supreme commander, General Douglas MacArthur. In September 1945, the United States refused Soviet requests to govern a zone of their own in Japan, or to participate as an equal in the Allied Control Council.

The United States saw West German and Japanese economic development as necessary to help pay for occupation costs (an early form of "burden sharing"), as well as help the general economic recovery in each region; yet Dean Acheson's effort to modify the Supreme Allied

Agreement with respect to Japan was opposed by Moscow.[20] Both West Germany and Japan were offered special trading rights and aid, and the United States tried to use the European Recovery Program as leverage to pressure the Europeans into granting both West Germany and Japan most-favored-nation (MFN) status. Britain and France, however, refused to grant Japan MFN—for fear of domestic opposition.

Concurrently, in the effort to double-contain Tokyo, the United States obtained the Ryukyu and Bonin Islands (later returned), as well as the Marshalls, Carolines, and Marianas (put under UN trusteeship) and established a major naval base at Okinawa. (The latter was later returned by Richard Nixon; the major naval bases, however, were retained by the United States.) The Allies had opposed continued Japanese control over Korea and Taiwan, but the Japanese foreign ministry threatened the possibility of a revanchist movement if Japan did not ultimately obtain the Kurile Islands (Kunashiri, Etorufu, plus Shikotan and the Habomai Islands), as well as Bonin and the Ryukyu Islands. From Tokyo's viewpoint, the Soviets had illegally scrapped the 1941 neutrality pact to attack Japan and take the four Kurile Islands—including the two southernmost islands (Shikotan and the Habomai isles). Tokyo did not regard the latter two as part of the Kurile Island chain. Japan argued that the 1905 Portsmouth Treaty did not refer to the Kurile Islands, and that tsarist Russia had agreed to Japanese control over the Kurile Islands in the 1855 Shinoda Treaty and 1875 St. Petersburg Accords. On the other hand, critics argued that Tokyo had given up the Kurile Islands at the 1951 San Francisco Peace Conference, which led to the U.S.-Japanese military alliance and an abandonment of Japanese acquisitions since 1854.[21] Despite the fact that Moscow did not sign the 1951 San Francisco treaty, Washington tacitly assumed Soviet interests—symbolic of tacit U.S.-Soviet collaboration.

After initially intending to spread Japanese industrial capacity throughout Asia, the United States reversed policy by 1947–48. Tokyo had ridiculed the Morganthau plan and Pauley reports: Japan had lost 45 percent of its industrial capacity; it had to deal with 5 million emigrants; it needed to revitalize exports to buy raw materials; and it feared political instability in the period 1946–47. Much like their West German counterparts, Japanese elites worked from the inside to wring concessions and bend occupation directives in their favor, in part through use of the "Made in America" constitution. By 1949–50, Washington encouraged reemergence of the *zaibatsu* conglomerates, opened the U.S. market to Japanese goods, and continued to accept Japanese protectionist policies (until the mid-1960s)—many of which had been instituted under the occupation. In July 1949, Dean Acheson was particularly concerned that the United States had to "avoid preponderant [Japanese] dependence on Chinese sources" of critical imports which would expose Japan to Chinese blackmail.[22] Imposition of COCOM sanctions on the PRC was intended, in part, to limit Beijing's ability to compete with Japan. While Japanese socialists and communists sought a peace treaty with both China and the Soviet Union, the Japanese foreign ministry— like that of Britain—argued for a rapprochement with the PRC, but Tokyo failed in its efforts to play British versus U.S. interests. Concurrently, the defeat and occupation of Japan, combined with the Japanese disarmament, meant that the United States had not only taken on the responsibility for defense of the Japanese mainland, but also the defense burden of former Japanese spheres of influence and security.

THE KOREAN WAR

Given the apparent impossibility of reconciling Mao Zedong and Chiang Kai-shek, plus suspicions of Stalin's secret support for Mao (such as supplying the Chinese CCP with Japanese weaponry), U.S. national security managers possessed few options, given U.S. unwillingness to intervene in a failing cause. One dubious possibility was General Albert C. Wedemeyer's recommendation for a UN intervention in Manchuria. State Department opposition (the argument that such an action would divide China and give Stalin free reign in the UN occupied area) meant that U.S. efforts to play a "Titoist" Mao against Stalin increasingly gained ground. At Yalta, Stalin promised *not* to support Mao if Roosevelt agreed to Outer Mongolian independence and other concessions from China. Although Stalin may have tried to dissuade Mao from crossing the Yangtze (in the assumption that the United States might have intervened), Stalin ultimately looked to a victorious Mao for an alliance—largely in fear of Japanese resurgence, but also to forestall the possibility that a "Titoist" China might side with the United States. The 1950 Sino-Soviet mutual assistance pact against Japan (and its allies) was forged despite the "unequal treaties" in regard to Manchuria, Mongolia, and Xinjiang province.[23]

U.S. national security managers were accordingly confronted with four dilemmas: (1) to counter or break up the Sino-Soviet alliance; (2) to check *both* Communist (CCP) and Nationalist (KMT) efforts to reunify China; (3) to check *both* North and South Korean efforts to reunify Korea; (4) to gain Congressional finance and political support for a global defense network. Prior to the Korean War, Dean Acheson hoped to head off the Sino-Soviet alliance by enticing Mao closer to the West by *appearing* to promise Taiwan (or else by eliminating Chiang Kai-shek). Thus, in a public address in January 1950, Acheson appeared to exclude both Taiwan and South Korea from U.S. spheres of influence and security—despite the fact that the United States *did* intend to defend both. In effect, Acheson was handicapped by a Congressional mandate to withdraw U.S. forces from South Korea and by a general reluctance to supply funds for a global defense build-up. At the same time, Moscow's withdrawal from North Korea in 1948 made it politically difficult for Washington *not* to retreat, particularly given U.S. budgetary restraints. (Contrary to the general view, U.S. withdrawal represented a move initially supported by General Douglas MacArthur in order to retrench to Japan—but actually stalled by Secretary of State Acheson.)

Moreover, in regard to Korea in particular, U.S. national security managers did not want to negotiate with Stalin through the Four Power accord, particularly at the same time that they hoped to push NSC 68 through Congress. Neither Washington nor Moscow could find an effective way to contain rival Korean claims to unification, all the more so as Seoul itself initiated a number of border clashes in 1949 once U.S. forces left. The North Korean attack—drawn up by Soviet military advisors—was entitled "Preemptive Strike Operational Plan." From this perspective, factions within both the Sino-Soviet and American alliances provided significant reasons to provoke conflict.

On the one hand, Kim Il Sung sought to draw Mao—and a more reluctant Stalin—into support of reunification. Here, Pyongyang feared that Moscow would make a deal with Washington excluding Pyongyang. (Kim Il Sung tended to trust Mao more than Stalin due to the mutual assistance given during the Chinese revolution.) Only by promising that the United States would not intervene did Kim II Sung gain a reluctant Stalin's support: North Korea hoped to achieve a rapid victory in a month's time—before the United States could mobilize forces from Japan. On the other hand, South Korea likewise feared a U.S.-Soviet double containment, or else total abandonment by the United States. Seoul became more aggressive once the United States withdrew its forces: It sought to draw Washington into closer support by engaging in border incursions against Pyongyang throughout 1949–50.

In addition, KMT leader Chiang Kai-shek may have hoped that conflict over Korea would boost U.S. support for his own regime and foil a threatened coup d'état, if not draw PRC troops away from an impending attack on Taiwan. (The war began at a time when U.S. intelligence predicted a CCP offensive against Taiwan, and when the U.S. national security managers anticipated a coup plot against Chiang.) Here, Acheson's initial policy was *not* to abandon Taiwan to the PRC, but to replace Chiang's government with a U.S.-sponsored UN government. The replacement of Chiang was intended to contain KMT demands for unification and help reach a compromise with Mao, but without giving up a neutralized Taiwan. If Chiang would not step down willingly (which he would not), then a coup—or direct U.S. intervention—were considered options.[24]

Stalin used North Korea much as he used Berlin: The 1948 blockade of electrical power by the North on the South coincided with the blockade of surface access routes to Berlin in 1948. Although Stalin certainly did not want to escalate the conflict, he may have hoped to provoke a confrontation between Beijing and Washington that would force Beijing into dependence upon Moscow, forestall Mao's rapprochement with the United States, if not break up the U.S.-European-Japanese alliance. (Washington had decided to underwrite the costs of French involvement in Indochina in May 1950.) Most crucially, Stalin sought to retain leadership over the world Communist movement vis-à-vis his relatively independent Chinese rival.

Since he was more concerned with Taiwan, Mao may have initially hoped that tensions in Korea would draw U.S. attention away from his planned campaign against Taiwan. China was consequently forced to enter the war not merely to counter the United States and Japan, but also to weaken Soviet influence over North Korea—therefore sustaining a regional equipoise. (Mao intended to revise long-standing treaties including Japanese acquisition of Taiwan in 1895; the 1842 Treaty of Hong Kong with Britain, followed by the 1844 Treaty of Wanghia with the United States. Ultimately, Mao also sought to undo the "unequal treaties" signed with tsarist Russia.)

In effect, U.S. policy—designed to play upon "Titoist" tendencies in China—encouraged Mao's claims; U.S. policy failed to forge a neutral Taiwan, and did not, at least initially, break up the Sino-Soviet alliance. Beijing expanded into Hainan Island in May 1950 (to check France in Vietnam) and seized Tibet from India at the onset of the Korean War (to preclude U.S. support for Tibetan independence). The latter action in effect destroyed the buffer between India, the Soviet Union, and the PRC, initially set by the 1907 Anglo-Russian agreement. The Chinese—with Soviet support—also absorbed East Turkistan (established in 1944) to check pan-Turk, pan-Islamic movements in Xinjiang province—seen as supported by Washington.

The Chinese seizure of Hainan revealed the need to defend Taiwan. Here, the United States feared that the Soviet Union could use its alliance with Mao to deploy air and submarine forces on that strategically positioned buffer state. Once the war began, not only did

U.S. jets strike Chinese airbases, but the U.S. airforce also attacked the Soviet airbase Sukhaya Ryechka at Vladivostok on 8 October 1950. Washington at first denied the attack, then "apologized." Paul Nitze opposed making the Soviet role in the war public so as not to inflame American public opinion into provoking World War III. Stalin likewise kept the Soviet role top secret.[25]

The Korean War not only enhanced South Korean and Taiwanese growth through U.S. assistance (and special access to U.S. markets), but also the influence of Japan; at the same time, the United States was angered at Tokyo's refusal to send troops to Korea, and ostensible reluctance to establish closer relations with Taiwan (even though secret links were established). A mandatory mutual assistance pact with South Korea (1953), a bilateral pact with Taiwan (1954), which stated that Taipei could not attack the mainland without consulting the United States, and the 1961 defense pact with Japan—all represented U.S. efforts to assure the double containment. Concurrently, it was the Korean War that not so inadvertently galvanized Congressional support for a global extension of U.S. commitments as advocated by NSC 68.

HEIGHT OF THE U.S.-SOVIET DOUBLE CONTAINMENT: PHASE III, 1953–67

The NATO alliance did not initially include West Germany, but the proposed European Defense Community (EDC) sought to form an all-European army. As the 1951–52 proposal included the integration of West German troops, Bonn hoped to use its military contribution as a means of ultimately gaining "parity" with Western allies. French efforts to kill the all-European EDC ultimately backfired: Despite French parliamentary opposition, Paris ultimately accepted West German military integration into the U.S.-led NATO by the 1954 Paris Treaty, which transformed the Brussels pact into the West European Union (WEU). (In fact, West German participation in NATO helped lighten costs of the military burden for France.) Then, in spite of Eisenhower's announcement of the doctrine of "massive retaliation" in January 1954 designed to reassure U.S. allies, Paris stated its intention to build its own nuclear force—in part because of the U.S. failure to support strongly French interests in Vietnam. (Discussions inside France about developing the atomic bomb as a means to impel U.S. acceptance of Paris as an "equal" in the Anglo-American club began as early as 1944–45.)

Although the concept of an all-European force was accordingly ruled out, the WEU still formed the roots of the not entirely ineffectual

"European pillar" within the Atlantic alliance. The formation of the European Coal and Steel Community in 1951 had helped reconcile French and German political-economic disputes over the Ruhr; it provided France with a way to contain German industrial and war capabilities and then led to the 1957 formation of the European Economic Community (EEC) and the 1960 Common Agricultural Policy. Resolution of disputes over the control of the Saar in the period 1954–57 was also key to gaining French support for West German integration into NATO and the WEU.

EAST AND WEST GERMAN MANIPULATIONS

In March 1952, in part as a response to the EDC proposal, Stalin hinted that a united yet neutral Germany was feasible—an option supported by secret police chief Lavrenti Beria yet opposed by East German leader Walter Ulbricht—as well as by Khrushchev and Foreign Minister Vyacheslav Molotov. Beria's proposal for a neutral yet unified Germany, was coupled with appeals to nationalism in the Western Ukraine, Byelorussia, and the Baltic states—appeals that threatened the legitimacy of the Russian-dominated Communist elite.[26]

Stalin's death in March 1953 promised a period of general liberalization. Khrushchev renounced claims to Turkey, reestablished ties with Israel and Yugoslavia, and, most importantly, ended the Korean War. Khrushchev sought to liberalize the Soviet empire, but at the same time, to discourage nationalist movements through a mix of cooptation and repression (arresting Beria, for example)—despite recognition of the Tito thesis that there were many paths to Socialism.

Khrushchev transferred Russian joint-stock companies (seized after World War II) to East Germany and other East European states in an effort to decentralize economic decision-making. In a return to the New Economic Policy, he permitted limited cultural and national autonomy; halted forced collectivization; and replaced Stalinists with "national Communists"—as a means of forging a "new patriotism" opposed to "bourgeois cosmopolitanism." Khrushchev accordingly handed over the Crimea to Ukraine in 1954 to coopt national Communists who (discreetly) opposed Stalinist rule.[27] These steps enhanced the powers of the "titular" republics created by Lenin vis-à-vis the central government, and thus helped to establish the preconditions for multiple sovereignty that ultimately brought down the Communist Party in 1991.

Following the Korean War, U.S. containment policy as advocated by NSC 68 was then extended by the Eisenhower-Dulles "New Look" in the period 1953–61. Yet except for the implementation of propaganda through Radio Free Europe (1950), Radio Liberty (1953), in addition to Voice of America (1942), efforts to destabilize the Soviet bloc were largely abandoned. Although candidate Eisenhower initially campaigned for rollback, the year 1955 thus represented the height of the double containment. Ironically, the integration of West Germany into NATO was accepted by Moscow as a means of containing its foreign and military policy; Moscow sought to contain East Germany and Eastern Europe's foreign policy through the formation of the Warsaw Pact.

Following Stalin's death, Winston Churchill had called for an immediate Four Power summit—an option delayed until 1955 by the Eisenhower administration, which argued that U.S. concessions could only be granted following sweeping Soviet concessions. Though some progress was made, the 1954–59 Conferences of Foreign Ministers in Berlin were unable to reach a fundamental compromise over the German question. On the Western side, the 1954 Paris Treaties supported German unity but reluctantly: West Germany would have to be tied to NATO, the WEU, and the EEC; it could *not* return to the borders of 1937. Chancellor Adenauer's general strategy (against that of the Social Democratic Party's Kurt Schumacher who argued that a capitalist West Germany would not sufficiently attract East German popular support) was to side strongly with the West until that point in which German unification could be bargained from a position of significant Western superiority. Soviet domestic economic weakness, its lack of an agricultural base to feed its population, plus conflict with China, would not permit Moscow to "simultaneously build up its empire" and "keep pace with the United States in the arms race."[28]

In addition to giving up Austria as a nonnuclear neutral state (Vienna was not permitted to form an economic union with Bonn), Moscow gave back the Porkkala naval base to Finland and Port Arthur to China. Despite these ostensibly positive concessions, the 1955 Austrian peace treaty was regarded as a way in which Moscow sought to reduce its occupation costs, cut economic losses, and split NATO defense lines between West Germany and Italy. Following NSC 68's fears of "neutrality," John Foster Dulles also feared that the Austrian treaty would ultimately lead to the "neutralization" of West Germany.

The delayed 1955 Geneva Summit gave further legitimacy to the control of Berlin by the Four Powers; Khrushchev established relations with Bonn in 1955 but no progress was made on the key issues of German/European security. At the 1955 Conferences of Foreign Ministers, Soviet Foreign Minister Vyacheslav Molotov (backed by East German leader Walter Ulbricht) argued for a treaty that would give more equal representation to East Germany as a part of a confederal state. U.S.

Secretary of State Christian Herter, on the other hand, called for an all-German national assembly and free elections. Adenauer called for the neutralization of the GDR alone (raising questions whether Germany had to be totally "democratic" to reunify).

The Berlin crises of 1957–61 were thus primarily instigated as a means to gain legitimacy for East Germany as an equal to West Germany but they also represented a statement against Bonn's incorporation into NATO as well as proposals to grant Bonn nuclear weapons. The Soviets were also seen as wanting to exclude the Bundeswehr and German economic capability from the Western alliances; it was feared that a denuclearized West Germany would undermine NATO's forward strategy against Soviet conventional force superiority. (NATO's doctrine of forward defense was intended to allay German fears of becoming victims of a conventional war.) On the other hand, if it did step out of NATO constraints, Bonn could initiate its own nuclear program.[29] Proposals for U.S.-Soviet disengagement were thus rejected, even though Khrushchev conceded a possible role of the United States in Europe and of West Germany in NATO. Soviet leader Nikolai Bulganin, who engaged in copious correspondence with the West, proposed both conventional and nuclear force reductions—as did the second (November 1958) version of the Rapacki Plan[30]—reductions most reminiscent of those enacted by President Gorbachev in 1986–88. But these potential compromises (Soviet demands were overplayed by Khrushchev's November–March 1958–59 Berlin ultimatums), were not so much upset by the U-2 crisis as by East German leader Walter Ulbricht.

In this regard, Khrushchev preferred to compromise with Washington than to forge a separate deal with Ulbricht. In fear that tighter Soviet links with West Germany would undermine his power, Ulbricht insisted that unification could only take place through intra-German negotiation. Ulbricht accordingly used fears of a West German takeover and East German economic instability, plus threats to take West Berlin by force, to obtain more significant economic and diplomatic assistance from Moscow. Ulbricht reminded Moscow of East Germany's important military contribution to the Warsaw Pact. He also played his own "China card" to jar Moscow into greater support.[31]

Khrushchev, however, had hoped that John Kennedy would revive the Four Power process belatedly adopted by Eisenhower to deal with Berlin—thus treating Moscow as an equal. Kennedy, however, was too concerned with crises in Laos, Congo, and Cuba to fully address Germany—Khrushchev's primary concern. Moreover, Adenauer counseled against any deal involving the recognition of the GDR, the Oder-Neise line, or the neutralization of Central Europe.[32] Ironically, the Berlin crises resulted in steps to delegate greater powers and rights to East Germany, and thus made Berlin less dependent upon Moscow, and more capable, in the long term, of striking a separate deal with Bonn.

By late 1959–60, the United States proposed the Multilateral Force concept (MLF)—which would have given Britain, France, and West Germany a finger on the nuclear trigger. The effort was intended to head off French plans to develop an independent nuclear program and to weaken Soviet support for a nuclear China. Concurrently, Bonn sought to play off Paris against Washington in an effort to gain greater equality within the NATO alliance and thus supported the MLF. West Germany stated that it would forego the acquisition of its own nuclear weapons— but only if the United States agreed to a nuclear sharing arrangement. Despite these threats, the Johnson administration finally canned the MLF—straining German-American relations. Bonn then refused to renounce absolutely the right to acquire nuclear weapons *unless* Germany's security and eventual reunification were firmly guaranteed by the United States.[33] Moscow opposed the MLF proposal and stated it would not sign the NPT if Bonn possessed nuclear weapons.

THE SUEZ, BERLIN, AND CUBAN MISSILE CRISES

Parallel, but uncoordinated, U.S.-Soviet pressures against Britain, France, and Israel during the Suez crisis, and apparent U.S. compliance in the Soviet intervention in Hungary, appeared to indicate a complacent division of the world. In 1956 the Soviets threatened to use the atomic bomb against both France and Britain during the Suez crisis, and repeated these threats during the Berlin crises of 1957–58. Washington threatened not to support the British sterling, if London sustained its intervention in Egypt. After the CIA overthrow of Iranian president Mohammed Mosadeq in 1953, Eisenhower ironically opposed European actions in Egypt in fear of threats to nationalize U.S. oil firms, which had begun to replace British and French firms since 1945.[34] As Washington formed the Baghdad Pact and then the Central Treaty Organization (CENTO), Moscow supported Gamal Abdel Nassar's pan-Arabism.

The U.S. refusal to support the Euro-Israeli action to regain the Suez accelerated France's nuclear program and ultimately led Israel (then provided nuclear technology by France) to justify its nuclear program. Similarly, as Britain began to retrench from its overseas empire, it accelerated its nuclear program, as stated in the 1957 White Paper. London had already been upset by the 1946 MacMahon Act, which halted Anglo-American nuclear cooperation. Eisenhower's 1953 Atoms for Peace Program and the 1954 Atomic Energy Act then sought to compete with British, European, and Soviet nuclear reactor exports; U.S. firms were permitted to offer nuclear fuel and plants in foreign markets.[35] By 1958, however, following Sputnik and the 1957 establishment of Franco-German nuclear cooperation through the European Atomic Community (EURATOM), Britain and the United States once again agreed to share nuclear technology. (The U.S. Congress refused to revise the MacMahon Act to include France; President Nixon subsequently aided France's atomic weapons program secretly.)

The Soviet build-up of nuclear and naval forces corresponded with the Suez crisis, so that by the early 1960s Moscow was ready to press in interests in Cuba. By pressuring Berlin, Egypt, and then Cuba, Moscow also hoped—through a knight's gambit—to block deployment of nuclear weapons in West Germany, to legitimize Castro's rule in Cuba (and hence offset Chinese criticisms of lack of Soviet support for world communism), and to counter-encircle Washington in its own backyard. Khrushchev deployed some 43,000 troops (combined with 270,000 Cubans); he equipped IRBM missiles with nuclear warheads; and he gave local commanders the rights of command and control over tactical nuclear weapons! Khrushchev then proved willing to pull atomic weapons out of Cuba in exchange for an elimination of U.S. IRBMs that had been temporarily deployed in Turkey (raising Ankara's suspicions of U.S. reliability). Khrushchev thus sought to legitimize Soviet claims to global parity—if not threaten superiority over the United States.[36]

Ironically, Kennedy and Khrushchev's reciprocal understanding of their respective domestic plights led to a condition of mutual empathy that set the stage for détente. On the level of foreign policy, simultaneous U.S.-Soviet support for India against China during the Cuban missile crisis helped forge a closer U.S.-Soviet relationship, resulting in the Partial Test Ban treaty and the "hot line" agreement (agreements regarded as a means of checking French and Chinese nuclear capabilities). At the same time, however, the Soviet military vowed to reach strategic parity through a major nuclear build-up designed to counter—if not surpass—U.S., Anglo-French, and Chinese atomic weaponry. As the Soviets had cut off nuclear aid to Beijing in 1960, Moscow sought to impress the PRC with its nuclear arsenal in an effort to deter the latter from developing its own nuclear program.

After the Cuban missile crisis (which may have also been indirectly intended to check the transfer of U.S. nuclear weapons to Britain), the United States once again had to build up the confidence of its allies. Following the Skybolt crisis, and in part to be in a position to support India against China, Britain had resolved to develop a more independent nuclear force. The December 1962 Nassau Agreement thus meant that Washington would supply London with the Polaris missile. Although the British nuclear force would be pledged to NATO, it could be withdrawn temporarily in case of a "national emergency." British retrenchment east of Aden (as a result of imperial overextension relative to financial capabilities), however, tended to exacerbate U.S. security concerns in Asia and further isolated the U.S. position in Vietnam.

Concurrently, Charles de Gaulle denounced Kennedy's handling of the Cuban missile crisis and argued that U.S. unilateral actions and lack of NATO-member participation in such a dangerous crisis meant that the United States could not be trusted to defend Allied interests. De Gaulle accordingly demanded major NATO reforms (in 1959 he had called for a tripartite directorate); pushed ahead with the 1963 Franco-German treaty of cooperation to strengthen European unity; and rejected the MLF proposal. De Gaulle's *force de frappe* was intended to establish "parity" with the Anglo-American and Soviet nuclear clubs, assert French political-military leadership over West Germany, and impel the United States to support French interests. At first, de Gaulle proposed the "all-horizons" doctrine—aimed at all possible adversaries. After Soviet repression of Czechoslovakia, however, de Gaulle shifted to the Fourquet Plan—a flexible-response option which would establish a triggering link with the U.S. nuclear deterrent intended to draw Washington into support of French interests.

On the one hand, de Gaulle sought a rapprochement with both the Soviet Union and the PRC, and envisioned a new Europe from the Atlantic to the Urals. He argued that Sino-Soviet rivalry would ultimately result in a rapprochement between Russia and Europe—together with an internal liberalization of the Soviet Union. On the other, by recognizing the Oder-Neise line in 1959, he raised German fears of a permanent division—since de Gaulle opposed actual reunification or close German confederation.

In 1963, de Gaulle also blocked Britain's entry into the EEC and sought to assert French/European interests against the United States in monetary and trade issues, multinational investments, technology, nuclear weapons, and nuclear energy. De Gaulle regarded Britain as an U.S. "Trojan horse" and criticized the British failure to forge a common front against U.S. foreign and economic policy—at the same time that he tried (unsuccessfully) to engage Britain in EEC nuclear programs. De Gaulle was subsequently angered by the 1962 Nassau agreement that largely tied British defense to U.S. Polaris submarines. (France was also promised Polaris missiles, but had no suitable subs for delivery. De

Gaulle opposed U.S. entanglements—even though Paris could have obtained a "supreme national interest" clause like that of London.)

De Gaulle also proposed drawing West Germany into a closer nuclear relationship—but discussions appeared to go nowhere, in part because the United States argued that French withdrawal from NATO would undermine the "forward defense" of West Germany.[37] On the one hand, the U.S. refusal to seek a compromise with Moscow over the German question represented a rebuff to the prospects of a French-led Europe. On the other hand, de Gaulle's diplomacy set the foundations for a more polycentric world—a diplomacy subsequently extended by Richard Nixon but that, in U.S. hands, was designed to double-contain European steps toward political-military independence.

DOUBLE-CONTAINING JAPAN

Attempting to relax tensions on both flanks, Moscow also looked to Tokyo for a possible rapprochement in 1955 and offered to return the two southernmost Kurile Islands to Japan. By August 1955 Japan expanded its claims from two to four islands; in effect, Tokyo used its alliance with Washington to pursue its claims against Moscow. Tokyo's threat to make a deal with Moscow then led John Foster Dulles to counter-threaten in 1956 to revise the U.S. position that Okinawa was inherently Japanese territory if Tokyo did recognize the northern two territories as belonging to Moscow. Following NSC 68, Dulles feared that Moscow-Tokyo links would result in Japanese neutrality. With the subsequent signing of the 1960 U.S.-Japanese defense pact, Moscow reneged on its initial offer. (As has been argued, Tokyo had no real intent to make a separate agreement with Moscow.[38] Concurrently, Washington showed no interest in forming a U.S.-Soviet-Japanese security accord.)

In the early 1950s, Japan saw itself involved in an "unequal relationship." Tokyo sought an equal security treaty (seeking rights to grant Washington permission to use Japanese bases); it sought political and economic ties to the PRC and rights of self-determination in regard to its military build-up. Tokyo hoped to use its strategic position following the Korean War and its industrial potential as a lever to gain U.S. support for its position. Like Bonn, Tokyo sought "equal partnership" and "power sharing." Washington, however, sought to incorporate Japan into its global strategy—to rearm Japan, tighten Tokyo-Taipei ties, and establish automatic American basing rights in Japan. At least in the short term, the United States appeared to win on all points in its effort to double-contain Japan.

DAMMING CHINA

In 1954, Khrushchev attempted to allay Chinese anger after meager Soviet support during the Korean War by forging trade, railroad agreements, mining, and industrial projects. Concurrently, Khrushchev hoped to "contain" China by support for India. Thus, in the 1955 Bandung Conference, Moscow began to regard India as an economic partner and potential ally, and as a more influential land bridge to the Afro-Asian world than the more threatening PRC. Support for India gave Moscow a strategic bulwark to counterbalance Chinese influence in South Asia and the Indian Ocean. These steps began to alienate China: Sino-Indian relations were tense once Beijing seized Tibet in 1950. The Soviet opening to New Delhi drew Chinese troops toward the Indian border and enhanced Chinese support for Pakistan and Iran. It was in 1955 that China opted to develop nuclear weapons.

In 1957, following Sputnik (but also in response to closer U.S.-Soviet relations), Mao had proclaimed that an "east wind prevails." Consequently, the PRC intensified its unsuccessful campaign against Taiwan by bombarding Quemoy and Matsu—actions taken to force Moscow into support for China's claims. Moscow, which concurrently pressured U.S. interests in Berlin, did not want the conflict to escalate. As Moscow could match U.S. nuclear deployments in Europe, it was primarily the fear of China's long-run intentions that resulted in Khrushchev's abrupt decision to drop his previous support for the PRC's nuclear program in 1959–60, to plea for a nuclear free zone in Asia (to calm tensions between New Delhi and Beijing), and to ask for nuclear disarmament talks with the United States. (Partial test ban limitation talks began in the period 1958–63.) Though giving lip service to the PRC's claims to Taiwan, Moscow pressured Beijing and hoped to benefit more from U.S.-Soviet cooperation than from that with China.[39]

Accordingly, it is not surprising that Anatoli Dobrynin told a rather astounded Henry Kissinger that during the years 1959–63 "great opportunities had been lost in Soviet-American affairs."[40] Khrushchev had hoped to pressure the United States from a position of perceived strength, but was willing to compromise. Moreover, even during the Berlin and the Cuban missile crises, the United States and the Soviet Union tacitly cooperated in support of India against China during the Sino-Indian border conflict of 20 October 1962. The 1962 Sino-Indian border conflict also led to the Indian decision to develop its own nuclear capability (aided by a Canadian research reactor and U.S., and later, Soviet heavy water). Pakistani nuclear efforts were soon to follow. (U.S. efforts to enlist Pakistan—and Afghanistan—in the Baghdad Pact had already upset India and raised Soviet eyebrows.)

At the same time that Paris denounced U.S. unilateral actions in resolving the Cuban missile crisis, Beijing used that crisis to try to undermine Soviet influence in the developing world. Beijing denounced the "forced" deployment of nuclear weapons in Cuba as well as their sudden removal. Moreover, both Beijing and Paris regarded the Partial Test Ban, NPT, and ABM treaties as superpower tactics designed to double-contain third powers. During the Chinese nuclear tests in 1964–67, Beijing propagandized that its atomic bomb gave encouragement to the Vietnamese, Laotian, Palestinian, and other revolutions to continue their struggle. (Beijing recognized the PLO in 1964 before Moscow became its primary supporter in 1968.) Not so accidentally, as Sino-Soviet rivalry heated up for control of revolutionary movements, pan-Arab goals gave way to pan-Islamic ambitions following the 1967 Arab-Israeli War: Defeated Arab movements looked to wider supports.

Mao had admired de Gaulle's efforts to establish a nuclear deterrent independent of the two superpowers and sought to link China with a Europe "from the Atlantic to the Urals." At that time, Mao criticized Soviet repression in Eastern Europe and Poland in particular; he supported Yugoslav and Albanian independence, appealed to West German and Japanese irredentist claims against the Soviet Union, and claimed not only the Trans-Amur territories, but also the port of Vladivostok and Sakhalin Island. Mao opposed Moscow's tilt to India, and looked to Pakistan and later Iran, concurrently exacerbating Indo-Soviet fears of Sino-Islamic counter-encirclement. Mao also sought to wean Mongolia and North Korea away from Soviet influence, and both Moscow and Beijing set up rival Communist Parties. (Mao opposed the effects of Khrushchev's liberalization upon Chinese society—much as the Chinese elite would later oppose both Soviet *glasnost* and American democratic liberalism in 1989.) Accordingly it was in the mid-1960s that the Soviet Union decided to build up its IRBM systems in order to safely transfer troops from Eastern Europe to the Sino-Soviet border. In 1964, Washington even considered joint military action with Moscow against China's nuclear capabilities.[41]

Moreover, Mao looked to Sukarno of Indonesia in 1962 to counter-encircle the United States, in addition to supporting Ho Chi Minh (having recognized Ho before Moscow did). Mao opposed a U.S.-Soviet détente, which he feared would lead to an anti-Chinese "double containment." Mao thus called for a *bouleversement des alliances* and called for a "third force" that would incorporate China, Western Europe, independent states in Eastern Europe, and Japan—if the latter would renounce its alliance with the United States.

4

An Increasingly Perforated Iron Curtain

A SOVIET ALLIANCE BID: PHASE IV, 1968–77

President Richard Nixon's efforts to establish a more polycentric global system represented the major step toward the disruption of the five-dimensional double containment as established since the mid-1950s. At the same time, Soviet efforts to move beyond détente and *impel* the United States toward an entente or alliance in the period 1970–74—in part to forestall steps toward a possible Sino-American alliance—were rebuffed. Leonid Brezhnev's final 1974 alliance bid—which other states could join—was subsequently dismissed by Nixon as a "condominium in its most blatant sense."[1]

In effect, unable to forge an alliance with the United States, the Brezhnev leadership began to veer toward a more assertive strategy of global counter-encirclement in the effort to draw West Germany, Japan, and China closer to Soviet interests. Concurrently, as the Soviet Union approached strategic nuclear parity with the United States, and as the U.S. economy appeared to atrophy, allied trust in the American deterrent began to wane, reinforcing steps toward European strategic and economic unification. Ironically, while Moscow believed that it was playing Bonn against Washington, and Washington believed it was playing Beijing against Moscow, in fact both Bonn and Beijing were separately playing the United States and the Soviet Union against each other. At the same time, Tokyo also boosted steps to develop a foreign and economic policy more independent of Washington.

DETENTE: THE TILT TOWARD CHINA

By 1966–67, the United States ostensibly began to move toward a more "even-handed" approach toward the two Communist powers, but one that would ultimately "tilt" closer to China. Prior to becoming president, Richard Nixon had advocated a rapprochement with China in an effort to moderate Soviet conduct in general and to bring about an end to the Vietnam War by establishing a new Asian equipoise. (Nixon had advocated establishing ties with Beijing as early as 1960.)

Not so accidentally, following the 1968 global recession, the 1969 Nixon Doctrine announced that the United States no longer possessed the economic resources to take on all defense commitments. A Soviet offensive against Western Europe was considered the most likely contingency upon which to base U.S. war planning; war with China was regarded as less likely.[2] Ties with China would help to reduce Soviet pressure on Western Europe by forcing the Soviet Union to prepare for a two-front war. Concurrently, Sino-Soviet border clashes (which threatened the possibility of a major conventional war between two nuclear powers) helped move the Chinese leadership toward a rapprochement with the United States in spite of the Vietnam War, although Beijing was not beyond feigning a rapprochement with Moscow so as to better improve its bargaining position (see below).

By 1971, following the bombing of Cambodia and Henry Kissinger's "secret" trip to China (kept secret from the State Department), Nixon decided to forge the 1972 rapprochement. In addition to providing a countervailing force against the Soviet presence in Indochina as well as the expected "domino" effects once U.S. troops were to be withdrawn from Vietnam (1973–75), Nixon and Kissinger argued that the new Sino-American rapprochement would pressure Soviet compliance on the SALT I treaty. By 1972, Nixon's Shanghai Communiqué stated that the United States recognized only one China, and that the United States would begin to withdraw military and diplomatic supports from Taiwan—including the removal of Taiwan from the UN Security Council. These steps, linked with the U.S. retraction from Vietnam and the Asian theater in general, represented a policy of "appeasement" which would form the basis of U.S. policy toward the PRC. (Former UN Ambassador George Bush later stated that the Nixon-Kissinger strategy undermined his efforts to prevent Taiwan from being alienated from the UN altogether.)

As Nixon's primary concern was to deal with the Soviet Union over the issues of Vietnam and disarmament, Nixon missed an early opportunity to establish relations with Beijing in late 1968/early 1969, when Chou En-lai's initiative to establish contact was overlooked. Had Nixon moved earlier on the China question, he might have been able to take a stronger bargaining position by threatening to support Moscow against Beijing during the Sino-Soviet border clashes in 1969. An earlier rapprochement might have also permitted Nixon to make less concessions on the issue of Taiwan.[3] But here Nixon was afraid to lose Chinese support on the crucial issue of ending the war in Vietnam in such a way as to counter Soviet advances. The option of reaching a settlement with Moscow's cooperation (and forging a neutral Vietnam) as a means to counterbalance *both* the Soviet Union and the PRC was ruled out.

CZECHOSLOVAKIA

Soviet fears of burgeoning West German political-economic and socio-cultural/ideological influence could be seen in the 1968 crackdown on Czechoslovakia. Prior to the ascendancy of the Brandt government, West German Chancellor Kurt Kiesinger sought to isolate East Germany by recognizing other East European states, but not East Germany. Supplying major financial credits was seen as a means to wean these states away from their ties to Moscow, in part through "debt leveraging" (which ironically exacerbated Western financial liabilities in Eastern Europe). As West German actions were regarded by Moscow as a means to break up the Warsaw Pact, Moscow opted for intervention, though first seeking to assure itself that the United States would not intervene.

Strategically, the "loss" of Czechoslovakia would have isolated Soviet forces in Hungary from those in East Germany and Poland; economically, it would have broken up Council of Mutual Economic Assistance's (CMEA) program for joint stock railways, shared oil and gas pipelines, and electricity grids, including nuclear power. In addition, Moscow feared the loss of Czechoslovakia as a supplier of advanced military technology and uranium. The Soviet crackdown was also intended to prevent "bourgeois" ideas of democracy and national independence from spreading into Eastern Europe, as well as in the Baltics, Byelorussia, and Ukraine.[4] In 1965, Ukrainian intellectuals had openly demanded independence from Soviet/Russian domination.

Chancellor Kiesinger's policies, at least initially, had the effect of tightening the support of Warsaw Pact countries for East Germany, rather than isolating the regime as Bonn originally hoped. Yet the invasion of Czechoslovakia slowed, but did not end, Bonn's strategy of *Ostpolitik*. President Johnson had told Chancellor Kiesinger that the United States would "no longer fight a war of unification" and that "if you want to live in peace in Europe, you have to look for an alternative."[5] The crackdown on Czechoslovakia revealed how sensitive Moscow was to the effects of liberalization upon any regime because of the interconnectedness of the empire. It also helps to explain why in 1989, once Eastern Europe fell, the Baltic states, Belarus, and Ukraine were not far behind.

SOVIET GLOBAL STRATEGY

Though some opportunities presented themselves for a breakthrough before events in Czechoslovakia, American backing for West German "revisionism" (plus moves to support the PRC in 1967–68) threatened the Soviet Union with "encirclement." Moscow attempted to meet this threat (1) by drawing West Germany toward the Soviet Union; (2) by encircling and pressuring China through Vietnam; (3) by efforts to destabilize Iran; (4) by expanding Soviet global outreach through support of pro-Soviet movements during the heyday of high oil prices; (5) by reaching central nuclear-strategic parity with the United States and then by *threatening* nuclear superiority against actual and potential Western military-technological capabilities.

As the United States moved toward closer relations with China, the Soviet Union also sought closer ties with the United States in the period 1969–74, in part to preclude the United States from playing the "China card." Yet as it became clear that Moscow and Beijing would not be able to mend their differences, and as the Sino-U.S. rapprochement deepened and Moscow's bid for an alliance with the United States went unheeded, Moscow drastically toughened its tactics of strategic leveraging by 1975 in an effort to break its perceptions of encirclement.

Ironically, as a means to pressure the United States into an alliance, the Soviets threatened to wean West Europe/West Germany away from NATO, if not to break up the Franco-German alliance along with it. This latter goal was to be achieved by ameliorating East and West German tensions in order to secure the Soviet Union's Western front once Moscow was certain that it had lost the possibility of an alliance with China.[6] From this perspective, the Soviet response to the advent of West German *Ostpolitik* had its roots in increasing Sino-Soviet tensions and the attempt by the Nixon administration to play upon those tensions. (It was no accident that hard-liner Walter Ulbricht was replaced by a more "flexible" Erich Honecker in May 1971.)

This newer form of Soviet strategic leveraging—an amelioration of East-West German relations through the reassociation of the two

German states—meant that West Germany often appeared reluctant to take a pro-Atlanticist stand on certain issues that were contrary to both Soviet and West German interests. Moscow's calls for a Conference on Security and Cooperation in Europe (CSCE) were likewise interpreted as a means to freeze the territorial status quo and gain Western economic assistance.

Not so ironically, Washington had scarcely formed a strategy on how to deal with the new West German *Ostpolitik*. Kissinger's actions were largely reactive; he was suspicious of Willy Brandt and Egon Bahr as they dared to move on their own. Bonn did assure the United States that it would maintain its security relationship with NATO as it cautiously moved toward the East, but it was not clear that the more independent thrust of German foreign policy was in the national American or global interests. Robert E. Osgood, director of the NSC policy planning group, found merit in Brandt's approach; Kissinger, however, feared Brandt's policies could head toward a "new form of classic German nationalism."[7] Kissinger also feared that Bonn was veering toward a separate agreement with Moscow (a "Rapallo pact" in his view)—hence breaking out of the double containment.

The August 1970 treaty between West Germany (FRG) and the Soviet Union resulted in the mutual renunciation of the use of force and guarantees of inviolable borders. The December 1970 treaty between West Germany and Poland provisionally recognized the Oder-Neise line. The 1971 Four Power agreement over the status of Berlin represented the breakthrough that helped to establish the "intra-German" détente, which would ultimately lead to unification in 1989. The 1972 Basic Treaty between the two German states agreed to accept the "reality" of East Germany (GDR), but stopped short of recognizing the GDR as a second sovereign state of Germany in international law, despite the fact that UN recognition of the two German states in 1973 appeared to solidify the division of Germany. Most importantly, the Basic Treaty recognized the right of peaceful change in support of future steps toward reunification, and "allowed Bonn a flexible inner-German policy through its very ambiguity."[8] As Bonn also recognized the rights of the wartime powers, neither the United States, the Soviet Union, France, nor Britain was to be alienated.

Not surprisingly, Beijing, in its effort to prop up hard-line Soviet and East European opinion, responded negatively to the August 1970 treaty and denounced Moscow for not insisting that the FRG formally recognize the GDR. Beijing also stated that the FRG did not renounce the goal of reunifying Germany, and thus Moscow had permitted monopoly capitalism to further permeate and subvert East

Germany.[9] In short, Beijing attacked Moscow's efforts to forge a separate peace with the West that might exclude China.

NIXON SHOCKS AND JAPAN

The 1971 anouncement of a U.S. rapprochement with China ostensibly shocked Tokyo, which had purportedly not been consulted despite assurances three weeks prior to the announcement that no new Sino-U.S. relationship would be forged. Prior to the Sino-U.S. rapprochement, the United States had sought to further reconcile Japan by giving Japan administrative rights over Okinawa, while permitting the United States to keep its military facilities. The 1969 Nixon-Sato communiqué sought to assure Japan as to the U.S. defense commitment in regard to the Kuriles, the Korean peninsula, and Taiwan. (Japan had rebuffed a Chinese alliance offer by Chou En-lai in the mid-1960s.)

In the late 1960s, China propagandized that the "Okinawa" agreement would lead to an "Okinawanization" of all of Japan by turning Japan into a base for U.S. aggression. Moreover, the Nixon-Sato communiqué had been regarded as supporting a "two China policy." Ironically, however, despite Sino-U.S. disputes, Beijing hoped that the United States would continue to sustain its double containment over Japan. (Nixon dangled the threat of a nuclear Japan over China's head at the same time that he offered concessions on Taiwan.) Beijing also believed that an opening to the United States and Japan could help mitigate the prospects of Soviet-American collusion against Chinese interests, at the same time that Beijing threatened a rapprochement with Moscow to raise its bargaining leverage vis-à-vis Washington.

Moscow was pleased with the Nixon-Sato communiqué, as it expected it to help forestall the development of an independent military and/or nuclear force by Japan, as well as to contain China's regional military temptations. On the other hand, China saw the Soviet Union as attempting to make use of the U.S.-Japanese military alliance to isolate China and sabotage Korea's reunification. Beijing probably hoped to discourage Japan's acceptance of Brezhnev's Asian security system (proposed in 1969) so as to drive North Korea out of Moscow's embrace. Having failed to keep Ho Chi Minh out of the Soviet grasp, Beijing wanted to pull Pyongyang closer.

Thus despite China's publicly expressed outrage, the Nixon "shock" permitted a change in the Sino-Japanese relationship. China sought assurances from Japan that the PRC was the sole government representing the Chinese people, that Taiwan was an inalienable part of the PRC, and that the Japan-Taiwan peace treaty of 1952 was illegal. Japan responded that it "fully understands and respects" the Chinese position that Taiwan is an "inalienable part" of its territory. China, despite lack of full recognition of its claims to Taiwan by the Japanese, reacted positively to the U.S. rapprochement and the new Sino-Japanese relationship, seeing the threat of a pan-Asian alliance as a means to check the influence of the Soviet Union, as well as manipulate U.S. interests. Beijing hoped that tacit Japanese recognition of Chinese aims might permit an expansion of Chinese regional influence.

By September 1972, China and Japan established diplomatic relations; yet the Chinese still considered the two powers in a legal state of war. Likewise, a technical state of war existed between Japan and the Soviet Union, which had not formally signed a peace treaty following World War II. Concurrently, both North and South Korea began to look toward reassociation, at the same time that the United States and Japan looked toward a rapprochement with the Soviet Union and China. Nixon removed two U.S. combat divisions from South Korea at the same time that he decided to visit Beijing in 1972. (South Korea, already fearing U.S. troop reductions under Nixon's "Guam doctrine," had secretly threatened a nuclear program in 1970. To forestall such a step, the Nixon administration reaffirmed its nuclear guarantees to Seoul. A suspicious North Korea may have started its nuclear program in the late 1970s.[10])

As a response to increasing Sino-Soviet tensions, Moscow not only sought to ameliorate tensions with West Germany, but also with Japan, during Gromyko's visit to Tokyo in January 1972. Gromyko offered to return two of the southernmost Kurile Islands and to provide access to the Siberian resources and markets. He also promised verbal support for Japan against the PRC, and political cooperation where possible on East Asian issues, "preferably with Japan as an independent power, *but even with Japan as an American ally if Japan so desired*" [emphasis mine]. In return, Gromyko asked for a pledge that Japan would not develop a relationship with China that was detrimental to Soviet 'interests.'"[11] By 1974 the Soviet attitude on the Kurile Islands hardened, in part as U.S. support for China had altered the situation.

Despite the fact that "aggressive" Soviet actions in Asia were in part directed toward China, and could possibly have been channeled in a way to meet U.S. interests through a U.S.-Japanese-Soviet entente, the U.S-Japanese alliance remained aloof to Soviet offers. Nixon thus passed up an opportunity to forge a compromise with Moscow over Germany/Europe and Japan in his effort to obtain a rapprochement with the PRC. Nixon rejected Brezhnev's last bid for a U.S.-Soviet "condominium" against the PRC, thus thwarting Soviet efforts for a rapprochement with the United States. Although claiming that Moscow had no intention of attacking China, Brezhnev warned that if China ever arranged a military agreement with the United States, "that would confuse the issue."[12]

THE VIETNAM WAR

The fact that the United States had remained bogged down in Vietnam had permitted the Soviet Union to build up its strategic nuclear force to rough parity and begin to press for "superiority" in heavy land-based nuclear systems (see Chapter 7). U.S. involvement in Vietnam itself weakened the U.S. ability to reassure its allies in Europe that the United States would, in fact, defend Europe. U.S. allies believed that they were indirectly financing the Vietnam War and that the United States was using borrowed money to buy up European assets with inflated dollars. (The United States, however, had indirectly financed the French role in Indochina in 1950–54—in part to buy French support for German rearmament. Refusal to seek a political settlement after Dien Bien Phu, and the subsequent refusal to cut U.S. losses, forced Ho Chi Minh, initially supported by Mao, into the Soviet camp as the United States expanded the war.)

Having opted for a military, rather than political, solution, U.S. inability to prosecute the war in Vietnam was also due to the Korean War "syndrome": U.S. reluctance to cross the seventeenth parallel in Vietnam was due to the belief that China would intervene as it had done in Korea. On the one hand, the United States could not strike certain geographic thresholds for fear of bringing in the PRC. On the other hand, Nixon's rapprochement with China did permit Washington to step up the bombing campaign in Cambodia and North Vietnam. (Of note, Hanoi actually held Soviet sailors hostage in an effort to limit U.S. bombing and protect key defense sites—thus attempting to draw Moscow into closer support against Washington.)

But here it was dubious that even a limited American military intervention in the north (ostensibly taking advantage of China's weakness during the Cultural Revolution) would have helped to convince a highly suspicious Chinese leadership of American "good" intent. U.S. intervention would have strengthened the pro-Soviet viewpoint in China, as Mao at least feigned a possible rapprochement with Moscow in 1970. The very threat of even a so-called limited intervention would have prevented the implementation of President

Nixon's higher-level grand strategy designed to wean the Chinese into the so-called equidistant U.S. policy vis-à-vis the Soviet Union and PRC, as a means to check Soviet global outreach and Japanese political-economic influence.[13]

CHINA AND THE NIXON DOCTRINE

China's motivation for accepting the Nixon initiative was not merely based in fear of Soviet pressure along the Sino-Soviet border and its opposition to the Brezhnev doctrine permitting Soviet intervention in Czechoslovakia in 1968. It also lay in Beijing's effort to break its perceptions of a U.S.-Soviet double containment in the aftermath of the Korean War, and its efforts to press for unification with Taiwan.

From this perspective, after the bitter intra-Party feud between Lin Biao and Chou En-lai, Beijing opted for a strategy that would pit "barbarian against barbarian" while concurrently learning from barbarians. Beijing could use its already strong trading relationship with Japan, plus new trade ties to be forged with the United States and Western Europe, to help modernize its economy. (By 1965, Japan was China's major trading partner, the Soviet Union second, despite Japan's lack of diplomatic relations with the PRC.) Close relations with Japan, in effect, *threatened* a pan-Asian alliance against both Moscow and Washington. Ironically Beijing hoped to use its new relationship with the West and Japan to counter the Soviet Union, while expanding its outreach into the Asian littoral once the U.S. presence began to recede following American withdrawal from Indochina.

Beijing could also feign closer relations with the Soviet Union to ameliorate tensions and, at the same time, frighten the United States into a rapprochement. Moreover, Moscow itself proposed a number of measures to reduce border tensions, including the August 1970 proposal for a nonaggression agreement; the January 1971 proposal of a treaty to prohibit the use of force or threatened use of force, including conventional, nuclear, and missile forces, in settling bilateral disputes; and an expressed willingness to accept the Thalweg principle for determining riverline boundaries, and draft a new treaty regarding river rights.[14] In effect, Moscow hoped to forestall closer Sino-U.S. ties.

The opening of Sino-American ties was also regarded as a means to pressure Soviet behavior vis-à-vis the Indo-Pakistani conflict. Here, the United States began to tilt toward China's ally Pakistan contrary to both State Department and CIA advice. The latter two had both stated that the United States should work through India and the Soviet Union to cool tensions. Nixon's decision to move an aircraft carrier group into the Bay of Bengal to support Pakistan was thus intended to impress Beijing of the symbolic U.S. commitment, and the United States conveyed a willingness to provide assistance to China if the Soviets attacked either Pakistan or the PRC in November 1971. These actions fit into Nixon's new global strategy—even though neither the Soviet Union nor India considered initiating a conflict at that time.

NIXON, THE SHAH, AND CENTRAL ASIA

In addition to playing the China card, Nixon also played the Iranian card. Following the collapse of the dollar, the Shah of Iran was able to use the oil weapon, plus threats to move closer to the Soviet Union, as a means of strategic leveraging to obtain a "blank check" from the Nixon administration to buy U.S. armaments. The Shah's efforts to become a major power in the Persian Gulf and Indian Ocean, and the preeminent bulwark against Soviet and Indian expansion (which Teheran also sought to counter by ties with Pakistan and China), impelled Iraq to sign a fifteen year friendship treaty with Moscow and led Saudi Arabia to increase defense spending as well. In addition, the Shah attempted to establish a pan-Islamic union of non-Arab nations stretching from Turkey to Pakistan (plus an Indian Ocean common market)—an effort to wean Central Asian Soviet republics, such as Tajikistan, away from Moscow's grasp.

The Shah's financial links with "neutral" Afghanistan and India were efforts regarded by Moscow as a lever to draw Kabul and New Delhi away from the Soviet orbit. (The United States and Pakistan also provided aid to influence the Afghan Daoud regime.) Concurrently, Moscow continued to pressure the Afghan Daoud government and likewise support "national liberation" movements, such as the Pushtun irredentism against Pakistan, in addition to seeking to destabilize Iran itself.[15] Moreover, U.S. policy hoped that a strong Iran would discourage pro-Soviet (and pro-French) Iraq from pursuing its irredentist claims against the Arab emirates (i.e., Kuwait), at the same time the United States sought to "contain" Iran's own irredentist claims in the region—which also included Kuwait.

THE QUESTION OF U.S.-SOVIET PARITY

While the United States was largely forced to accept Soviet efforts to establish strategic parity (until the buildup of American central strategic nuclear systems in the late 1970s), Washington did not at all accept Soviet efforts to achieve global political parity. On the one hand, Nixon and Kissinger sought to play upon contradictions in the Communist world to contain and pressure the Soviet empire and its alliances; on the other hand, Nixon and Kissinger also sought to sustain a more cooperative U.S.-Soviet relationship in managing global affairs.

The dilemma with this strategy is that it assumed precisely what the Nixon administration attempted to deny—the legitimacy of the Soviet role in the five-dimensional double containment. This essential contradiction (which continued to plague U.S. policy) led to accusations from the right that Nixon had sold out to the Russians; and from the left, that Nixon was seeking a U.S.-Soviet condominium. Ironically, as Moscow approached central strategic "parity" with the United States, and as Washington and Moscow were seen as moving toward closer collaboration, allied trust in Europe and Japan in the American deterrent began to wane—much as De Gaulle had forewarned.

Even Britain, for example, began to widen its options. Following British political-economic decline and withdrawal from the Middle East (east of Aden), Britain began to move closer to Europe and away from its "special relationship" with the United States by joining the Common Market in January 1973. British steps toward Europe followed Nixon's rapprochement with China, the suspension of the Bretton Woods monetary system, and the U.S. tilt toward Pakistan in the 1971 Indo-Pakistani War. At the same time, however, London remained tied to Washington through its nuclear relationship—but a relationship that provided London a limited and relative independence.

The 1973 U.S.-Soviet agreement on preventing nuclear war appeared to represent a new double containment. In effect, Nixon sought to cooperate with the Soviet Union on arms control issues, yet sustain a policy of multilateral geopolitical containment. Thus he concurrently supported the 1973 "Year of Europe" in an effort to get allies to assume greater responsibility for regional defense and security affairs; the United States was to be concerned with global affairs. The cooptive Nixon-Kissinger approach, which emphasized a linkage between U.S. military protection and European political-economic concessions, angered European allies.[16]

European opinion was furthermore outraged after Nixon ordered an alert of U.S. nuclear forces during the October 1973 Arab-Israeli War without warning NATO members. Nixon's pro-Israeli policy sought to make sure that European states (which were heavily dependent on Arab oil) did not make separate deals with Arab leaders. U.S. actions worked to bolster resolve to create a European political and defense policy more independent of American policy. EC foreign ministers drafted a "declaration of European identity" and sought joint defense projects, including the neutron bomb.

By June–July 1974, Nixon rejected Leonid Brezhnev's final efforts to forge an alliance at Summit III, arguing that the offer smacked of "condominium in the most blatant sense." Thus, without an agreement to guarantee a U.S.-Soviet entente, the Soviets continued to press their global claims as a strategic lever to ultimately impel the United States into an alliance and as a preemptive effort against a potential NATO-PRC-Japanese "encirclement." Concurrently, despite Nixon's refusal to forge an alliance with Moscow, his efforts to sustain détente (and grant the Soviet Union nuclear parity) reinforced European efforts to obtain greater autonomy.

By 1975 the Soviets supported a short-lived pro-Soviet coup d'état in Portugal (which controlled Angola and the Azores). The coup in Portugal helped to decapitate Portuguese control over Angola by 1976; the Soviet Union had supplied Cuban forces in Angola in 1975 with logistical support. Such an action was also directed against burgeoning Chinese interests and Maoist movements in Africa. The coup likewise raised concerns that the United States might lose basing rights in the Azores; German financial assistance, however, helped to bring the pro-Western Portuguese Socialist Party into power.[17] Moscow also tacitly supported Euro-Communist parties in Italy, France, and Spain (despite apparent ideological divergences with Moscow) to frighten NATO interests; East Berlin supported the terrorist faction, the Red Brigades.

Despite the deterioration of détente, the 1975 Helsinki Accords were signed and provided a legal framework for human rights at the same time that they *appeared* to permit the United States and Soviet Union to freeze the territorial status quo. Charged with "appeasement" by conservative critics of détente and Helsinki (as Saigon became Ho Chi Minh City), the Ford and Carter administrations found themselves on the defensive because of the perception that the Helsinki Accords guaranteed permanent "spheres of influence." Japan was likewise concerned that the CSCE accord (Basket I) could have been interpreted as a recognition and final settlement of the Kurile Islands question.

It would not be until the advent of the Gorbachev regime that the Helsinki Accords would be acknowledged and supported by Moscow, however. In effect, rather than appeasing Soviet interests, the Helsinki

Accords continued the new dialogue between the two Germanys and the two Europes, first established by the 1972 Basic Treaty between East and West Germany, and permitted West European states—for the first time—to better coordinate their strategy toward the East. This dialogue helped to set the conditions of the intra-German détente that would ultimately move beyond German re-association and toward unification.

THE INTENSIFICATION OF ENCIRCLEMENT: PHASE V, 1978–84/87

Following the brief occupancy of the White House by President Gerald Ford, President Jimmy Carter came to Washington with a Wilsonian evangelical and ecological vision. Initially, Carter sought a rapprochement with the Soviet Union, unilateral restraints and arms control, and cooperation in the Middle East, as well as recognition of Vietnam. Under the increasing influence of Zbigniew Brzezinski, however, Carter was converted to efforts to seek the break up of the Soviet Union by encouraging Polish and East European independence.[18]

To a large extent, Carter's policies enraged Soviet hard-liners who opposed American meddling in domestic affairs. In part, Carter's ostensibly universal support for human rights tended to adopt an anti-Soviet bias under National Security Adviser Brzezinski's direction; U.S. criticism of the PRC was largely blunted. At the same time, Carter's support for vaguely defined human rights gave hope for *both* pan-nationalist forces (i.e., his attack on President Ford's refusal to meet with pan-Slav proponent Aleksandr Solzhenitsyn) *and* "democratic" forces for change (support for dissident Andrei Sakharov).[19] Hence Carter sent conflicting messages to divergent factions which opposed the Soviet regime.

U.S.-Soviet détente began to break down following President Carter's attempt to significantly lower Vladivostok II guidelines, which had originally been agreed to by President Ford in 1974 (see Chapter 7). It was in late 1977 that the Carter administration adopted a tougher policy toward the Soviet Union—*prior* to the Soviet invasion of Afghanistan. In effect, Carter's efforts to exclude Moscow from the Middle East/Persian Gulf alienated Moscow. In October 1977, Carter had signed the U.S.-Soviet declaration for a joint approach to Middle East conflict, but then—under protest from Tel Aviv—signed the Camp David accords in November 1977, isolating Moscow. After being forced out of Egypt by Sadat, and in the effort to counter both the Shah of Iran and burgeoning Chinese influence in the region, Moscow strengthened efforts to undermine Israel and other U.S. allies by supporting the PLO,

Iraq, Syria, and revolutionary pan-Islamic movements.

As Moscow pressed a more assertive policy, the Carter administration decided to reach out for a closer defense relationship with Beijing. Between 1978 and 1979, National Security Council Adviser Brzezinski, after winning the vicious inter-bureaucratic battle with Secretary of State Cyrus Vance, decided to play the so-called China card by permitting European arms sales to China as a countermeasure to the Soviet role in Ethiopia and the Ogaden, heightening Soviet involvement in Afghanistan, Libya, and South Yemen, Soviet support for anti-Shah revolutionary activities, the use of former U.S. naval facilities in Vietnam, the deployment of SS-20s (1977) and Soviet military threat to Europe, Japan, and China, and to forestall a Soviet crackdown in Poland.[20] In addition, the 1977 Conventional Arms Limitation Talks (CAT) broke down over the U.S. refusal to discuss the Asian region.

By 1978, the United States and China had established formal diplomatic relations and terminated the mutual defense treaty with Taiwan, ignoring the Joint Chiefs of Staff recommendation to insist that the PRC renounce the use of force in the Taiwan Strait.[21] Contrary to Brzezinski, Vance believed that the so-called even-handed approach originally intended by Nixon should continue to be pursued. Vance, for example, sought (unsuccessfully in part because of initial Vietnamese demands for "excessive" war reparations and obstruction by Brzezinski) to recognize Vietnam for purposes of regional balance. Without a balanced strategy, Vance argued that the Soviets would fear a "tacit NATO-PRC encirclement."[22] Moreover, the diplomatic recognition of Hanoi was also blocked by the Vietnamese thrust into Cambodia (1978–79) that was intended to crush the irredentist claims of the Chinese-backed Khmer Rouge to Vietnamese territory. Regarding Vietnamese actions as part of Moscow's counter-encirclement strategy, Beijing opted to "punish" Hanoi in February–March 1979. Moscow accordingly threatened military intervention if Beijing prolonged the attack or struck Hanoi. China's military setback against experienced Vietnamese troops ultimately led Beijing to revamp its military capabilities.

By late December 1978, Brezhnev sent a letter to President Carter implying that no further progress on arms control was possible unless the United States and its allies prevented the sale of arms to China. At the Guadeloupe summit, the Western allies stated their support for the SALT process, but also affirmed that the Western normalization of relations with China should not alter the state of "détente." Likewise, before signing SALT II, President Carter assured the Soviets that the China card would not be played. Thus, in the period 1978–81, the United States and China entered a period of entente against the Soviet Union which generally militarized Soviet behavior: The Soviet elite continued to strengthen the Soviet Union's more vulnerable Asian flank in preparations for a possible two-front war. And concurrently with the U.S. rapprochement, the Chinese established closer links with both the EC and Japan. In October 1979, Chinese Prime Minster Hua Guofeng called for German unification on his trip to Bonn.

Carter flipflops also upset U.S. allies despite his emphasis on trilateralism. His efforts to prevent nuclear proliferation were often interpreted as means to sustain the U.S.-Soviet double containment. The 1978 Nuclear Control Act brought the United States into conflict with France, Germany, Japan, as well as semiperipheral states. Carter's opposition to the fast-breeder reactor at Creys-Malville angered French plutonium economy advocates (but at a time when U.S.-French strategic nuclear cooperation was very tight). Carter's opposition to Japan's breeder reactor at Tokai Mura was seen as blocking Japan's "energy independence" and making Japan increasingly vulnerable to energy imports: Carter's policy was thus called as significant as the Nixon "shocks." (For the decade 1966–76 Japan had been reluctant to sign the NPT, the Japanese Diet only signed the treaty in part as Japan would still be permitted to produce plutonium for potential nuclear weapons development.)

The United States was also able to block Taiwan's efforts to separate plutonium, thus obtain the PRC's approval at a time when the United States was seeking to forge a close entente with Beijing. Bonn, however, was angered by Carter's efforts to block sales of reprocessing-technology equipment to Brazil. In addition, Carter administration efforts to find a technological alternative to the plutonium producing fuel cycle helped to make misuse more difficult, but failed to find an alternative to the use of fissionable materials.[23] (Carter's presidential efforts to counter the relative decline of the U.S. nuclear industry, such as sales of Westinghouse nuclear reactors to Iran, led to accusations of U.S. hyprocrisy.) Until the 1980s, German nuclear proponents had already regarded the Non-Proliferation Treaty (NPT) as part of the double containment—and even denounced NPT as a "second Versailles"! German criticism was very effective in watering down regulatory and inspection rights of the NPT regime. (With no backup from the military-industrial complex to subsidize German nuclear development, the German nuclear industry was more dependent upon exports than the American, Canadian, French, or British nuclear industries.) Both Paris and Bonn refused to adopt full-scope safeguards against nuclear proliferation until the late 1980s.

JAPANESE DOUBTS

As the United States moved to recognize the PRC, it was not accidental that Japan signed a defense treaty with the United States in 1978 as a counterpoise. This pact sought to extend Japan's naval defense perimeter to guard the Straits of Malacca and thus permit the U.S. fleet greater flexibility in the North Pacific and Indian Ocean as well as in the Persian Gulf. This treaty provided for substantial joint planning and permitted the United States to pursue a forward defense strategy so as to put greater pressure on the Soviet navy and bases in the Northern Pacific (Moscow's largest fleet) and the increased Soviet military presence in the Kurile Islands. In addition, for the first time, Japan and Europe set up regular bilateral security consultations in the 1980s, and limited joint defense cooperation, largely involving naval exercises.

From the period of the Nixon rapprochement with the PRC until 1978, Japan had threatened to move closer to China: The threat to sign a Sino-Japanese "treaty of peace and friendship" with a mutually agreeable "anti-hegemony" clause brought Andrei Gromyko running to Tokyo in 1976, where his proposals for a return of two of the four Kurile Islands were once again rebuffed. Japan also began to play the United States against the Soviet Union, but leaned toward Washington in most issues. Having already taken a pro-Arab stance in the 1970s (freezing economic relations with Israel), in 1978 Japan began to develop a more independent policy in regard to Cambodia and Afghanistan, and sought out stronger ties with Australia and the ASEAN states in addition to China. Tokyo also remained a major trading partner with South Africa despite U.S. efforts to enforce sanctions. Tokyo also pursued relations with Iran during the hostage crisis—fearing that Washington could no longer guarantee access to oil.[24]

At roughly the same time, however, China began to make conciliatory overtures to the Soviet Union in the wake of the 1978 U.S.-Japanese defense treaty. The July 1979 Carter decision not to withdraw troops from South Korea (Seoul threatened to "go nuclear") also angered China. The fact that Carter had campaigned on the promise to reduce U.S. troops in Korea seemed to represent a concession to both Beijing and Moscow. Carter's flipflop on the issue also angered Tokyo: Carter did not consult Tokyo in 1977 as to his decision and then suddenly shelved the idea in July 1979. These facts (coupled with previous Nixon shocks) helped raise Japanese skepticism of U.S. goals and leadership, at least prior to the December 1979 Soviet invasion of Afghanistan—which then impelled both Tokyo and Beijing to move closer to Washington.

AFGHANISTAN

The war in Afghanistan stiffened U.S. resolve to forge an anti-Soviet alliance. Moscow had initially opposed sending in ground troops in fear that direct intervention would—as it subsequently did—strengthen the anti-Soviet camp. Concurrently, Washington attempted to use the Afghan war to rein in European allies who appeared to be moving toward more neutral positions. Most crucially, Germany refused to take a tough stance against the Soviet invasion—in the effort to sustain détente for as long as possible.

Before the Soviet thrust into Afghanistan, the Carter administration had flipflopped on providing aid to Pakistan (because of fears that Pakistan was developing its own nuclear capability). The Soviet invasion, however, led the Carter administration to open the gates to massive U.S., Saudi, and Chinese assistance to Pakistan as the state that would, in effect, most coordinate the Afghan resistance. (Japan also provided significant aid to Pakistan under U.S. urging; secret military aid also came from France and Britain.) These actions intensified Indo-Pakistani conflict, and increased rivalry between pan-Shi'ia Iran and Sunni Moslem states to support the Afghan resistance. (India supported the pro-Soviet Afghan government.) At this point, the Carter administration drew the line: the fear of a Soviet thrust into Pakistan or Iran would represent a *casus belli*. While not directly attacking Islamabad, Moscow did support subversion and terrorist attacks: Much as tsarist Russia pressured the Afghan buffer to gain leverage vis-à-vis Britain in the Turkish Straits, the Soviet Union also pressured Pakistan as a lever to support Cuba and the Sandinista revolution in Nicaragua in addition to attempting to block Pakistani assistance to the Afghan resistance.

THE REAGAN YEARS: THE INTENSIFICATION
OF ENCIRCLEMENT: PHASE V CONTINUED, 1984–87

The advent of the administration of Ronald Reagan expanded the effort to intensify encirclement and the defense buildup begun in the late Carter years. In addition to the buildup of central strategic systems, the U.S. defense budget largely emphasized naval forces to counter Soviet geostrategic weaknesses in peripheral regions. The United States likewise sought to incorporate major U.S. allies into "burden-sharing" arrangements as much as possible; concurrently, Reagan policy sought to assure U.S. leadership of the alliance through the double containment. Thus policy would initially begin to change in 1984—then crowned by the 1987 INF agreement (see Chapter 7).

Reagan's first term in office was characterized by advisers who differed on whether Washington should negotiate with Moscow "from a position of strength," or whether it should pressure the regime to the point of collapse.[25] Ironically, despite its anti-Communist rhetoric, the Reagan administration was not at all able to sustain the strong 1979–81 U.S.-Chinese entente, nor was Washington able to stop West Germany from ultimately pursuing its policy of *Ostpolitik*, which the Reagan administration feared would result in an anti-nuclear German neutrality. In addition, as the Reagan administration pressed demands on Japan to become an "unsinkable aircraft carrier," Tokyo began to demand greater "power sharing"—but within the aegis of the U.S.-Japanese alliance. Japan also threatened to move closer to either Russia or China through "yen" and "microchip" diplomacy.

President Reagan's doctrine of "horizontal escalation" represented a form of "quasi-global war" designed to roll back "pro-Soviet" regimes and anti-American regimes or movements in peripheral regions. Largely abandoning the "balance of power" approach, the doctrine of "horizontal escalation" argued that the United States could support "freedom fighters" in Afghanistan, Ethiopia, Nicaragua, Angola, Mozambique, Cambodia, Somalia in 1982 (in addition to supporting South Africa and Zaire among other states) to counter or "roll back" Soviet power projection. Not wanting to become another John F. Kennedy (who had permitted the Castro regime to survive in the U.S. sphere of influence), Ronald Reagan's first priority was to eliminate Soviet and "third world" influence in Central and Latin America, in particular Nicaragua; and to support anti-Communist governments in El Salvador and Guatemala, for example. In addition to threatening Cuba with invasion, Reagan also opposed other Latin governments which sought political and economic policies more independent of Washington (such as that of Michael Manley in Jamaica). The long-term consequences of U.S. actions (the threat of a perpetual destabilization of regional conflicts) appeared to be given little consideration, as military actions were initially preferred over political settlements.

Unlike the Carter administration, which sought a political settlement, the Reagan administration gave the green light to an Israeli invasion of Lebanon intended to wipe out the "pro-Soviet" PLO. In addition, the United States used its naval and air power (and other more clandestine means of strategic leverage) to pressure radical regimes, such as Iran and Syria, including air attacks against Libya. The doctrine of horizontal escalation argued that these largely peripheral conflicts would not escalate to nuclear war because the United States and Soviet Union possessed a rough nuclear parity—but with the United States moving toward superiority.[26] In the Mediterranean, the United States had been dissatisfied with European efforts to counter apparent Soviet advances in relation to Libya and Syria, as these states sought European, Soviet, and PRC support against Israel.

In the case of Afghanistan, the United States through Pakistan, and with the secret cooperation of PRC, sought to undermine the Soviet political-military presence, costing the Soviet Union a U.S. estimated $5 billion a year. In March 1985 the CIA sharply escalated U.S. covert actions in an effort to undermine the Soviet army and to counter Soviet offensives. In addition to providing the Mujahedin with Stinger anti-aircraft missiles (weapons that could be turned against U.S. interests for terrorist attacks), CIA targets included military installations, factories, and storage depots *within* Soviet territory. (At the same time, factions of the Mujahedin threatened to turn Afghanistan into another Lebanon, if Pakistan or the United States tried to seek a diplomatic settlement with Kabul.) By November 1986, unable to convince Washington that a Soviet defeat by pan-Islamic forces would also represent a defeat for U.S. interests in the region, Mikhail Gorbachev opted for withdrawal, but not without extending new overtures to both Beijing and Iran. (In late 1993 Egyptian President Hosni Mubarak stated that Afghan Mujahedin elites, purportedly trained by the CIA, had aided pan-Islamic revolutionary movements in Egypt and Algeria.)

REAGAN AND EUROPE

In terms of Reagan policy toward Europe, President Reagan, at least initially, sought to intensify a strategy of encirclement. In order to deter the two Germanys from seeking a "neutral" or "non-aligned" reunification and in an effort to counter perceived Soviet efforts to break up NATO, the Reagan administration began a renewed military buildup, the biggest since the Kennedy administration.

On the one hand, both Britain and Socialist France supported 1983 INF deployment as a double containment of Germany and the Soviet Union (see Chapter 7). On the other hand, the American invasion of tiny Grenada angered the Conservative Thatcher government, as British interests were involved. U.S. efforts to arbitrate between Britain and Argentina over the Falkland/Malvinas conflict tended to alienate London, which did not feel the United States had supported Britain to the fullest; concurrently, Washington criticized Britain for utilizing forces dedicated to NATO defenses, including nuclear-armed submarines. U.S. efforts to control allied trade with Moscow also angered Europeans (see Chapter 6).

Although President Reagan publicly called on Gorbachev to tear down the Berlin Wall, the United States still feared that a unified Germany would adopt a stance of "neutrality" that would deny NATO access to German military and economic capabilities, even if Germany did not shift to an overtly pro-Soviet stance. It was also feared that Germany could possibly opt to create its own nuclear deterrent. U.S. policy thus actually attempted to stall the prospects of German unification, much as it attempted to forestall closer European and West German ties to the Soviet Union, by linking West Germany tightly within NATO defenses and Western multilateral organizations (and by limiting closer German and European trade/technology with the Soviet Union). The deployment of INF forces was key to sustaining the double containment of Germany; yet even when the INF talks collapsed in 1983, the two Germanys were able to sustain an "intra-German" détente in the midst of superpower confrontation until the 1987 volte-face of the Reagan administration—which ultimately opened the doors to German unification (see Chapter 7).

CHINESE MANIPULATIONS

At first, the Reagan administration had sought to revitalize a strictly anti-Communist containment, but President Reagan's anti-Communist (anti-Soviet and anti-PRC) campaign rhetoric, as well as his opposition to the PRC's claims to Taiwan, led Beijing to question the close entente relationship established with the United States between 1978 and 1981. In particular, Brezhnev's 1981 Peace Offensive sought to ameliorate tensions with China. At this point, U.S.-Soviet competition for sustained influence over China's geostrategic and political-economic allegiance began to heat up.

As argued, China's alleged "fear" of the Soviet Union did not preclude Sino-Soviet flirtation to ameliorate trade and border tensions and to threaten the United States with the prospects of a Sino-Soviet re-alliance. After U.S. diplomatic recognition in 1978, China looked toward an amelioration of tensions with the Soviet Union in 1979. Following the Soviet thrust into Afghanistan, however, China did break off normalization talks with the Soviets, but resumed them following Brezhnev's March 1982 Tashkent address. The latter gave

Soviet diplomatic support for Chinese irredentist claims in regard to Taiwan and raised U.S. fears of closer Sino-Soviet cooperation.

Brezhnev's Tashkent speech was delivered at roughly the same time that the Reagan administration was proceeding with a $60 million sale of military parts to Taiwan. The Reagan stance suddenly shifted from a general opposition to all forms of communism to a primarily anti-Soviet stance, when the PRC threatened to downgrade relations with Washington if the arms sale to Taiwan was permitted. The United States then followed up with the Second Shanghai Communiqué of 17 August 1982, which pledged that U.S. military sales to Taiwan would not exceed the 1979 level in either qualitative or quantitative terms. For Beijing, this meant that after thirty or forty years, U.S. government arms sales to Taiwan were to drop to zero.[27] (On the other hand, the United States argued that private technological transfers to Taiwan fell outside the parameters of the agreement. This remained a point of contention with Beijing.)

Although the period 1979–81 thus represented one of close Sino-U.S. collusion and intense anti-Soviet agitation, the period 1982–87 increasingly represented a Chinese effort to cajole both the United States and Soviet Union into coming to terms with China on specific issues. (Following the Soviet thrust into Afghanistan, Beijing tested its first ICBM in May 1980.) By 1982, as U.S.-Soviet rivalry for China's political and economic allegiance intensified, the Reagan administration thus attempted to draw China into position as a "passive strategic counterweight" against the Soviets, at the same time as Washington began to urge the Japanese to become an "unsinkable aircraft carrier."

This fact tended to push the PRC even closer to the Soviet Union, at the same time that Japan began to demand greater aspects of "power sharing" in exchange for greater "burden sharing." Japan threatened to spend more than its self-imposed limit of 1 percent of GNP on defense spending—raising fears in the Soviet Union (which opposed its demands to return all four Kurile Islands) and throughout Asia. Ironically, China feared that a more independent Japan would assert its own interests if the United States continued to back into isolation and to push Japan toward "burden sharing." To counter this possibility, Beijing increasingly looked to Moscow for support.

In July 1985, for example, immediately following U.S. military and trade discussions, the Chinese met with high-level Soviet officials to discuss trade and the three major stumbling blocks to Sino-Soviet reconciliation. In July–August 1986, the Soviets offered nominal troop reductions in Afghanistan, Mongolia, and along the Sino-Soviet border, and pressured Vietnam to begin troop withdrawals from Cambodia. Concurrently, Moscow's talks with Beijing threatened a Sino-Soviet reconciliation to get the United States to reduce its support for the Afghan Mujahedin as well as to gain better terms in the 1986 strategic arms talks, prior to the November U.S.-Soviet summit. (Prior to the Sino-Soviet rapprochement, Soviet troops in Afghanistan pressured the Wakhan corridor and Chinese nuclear facilities at Lop Nur; between 1968 and 1979, the Soviet buildup accounted for some 80 percent of the total increase in Soviet military spending; there were approximately 100,000 more troops along the Sino-Soviet border than were placed in Eastern Europe.

The 1987–88 removal of Soviet troops from Afghanistan in exchange for an end to U.S. support for the Mujahedin thus not only represented a decision to cut losses, and a move to restore the Soviets' influence in the Moslem world, but also an attempt to establish a far-reaching entente with China. Beijing had, in the past, pushed for a "military solution" to the Afghan war and unconditional removal of Soviet troops; yet a significant irony was that neither the Soviet Union nor the PRC desired a militant "pan-Turkish" or "pan-Islamic" state on its borders as such a state could potentially undermine Soviet controls in Central Asia and Chinese controls over Xinjiang province.

CHINA AND JAPAN

China tried to construct a close "economic symbiosis" with Japanese capital. In 1984, twenty years after Mao had called for a Sino-Japanese alliance with West Europe (if Japan could cease to be America's lackey), Zhao Ziyang called for a more unified Europe coupled with a Sino-European alliance; China would continue to support steps toward European unity. At the same time, Zhao looked for increased Sino-Japanese strategic and economic cooperation.[28] In effect, Beijing attempted to both cajole and pressure Japan into alliance.

Through Japanese "Yen diplomacy," Tokyo spread its interests, largely in accord with U.S. global concerns, but also tried to open some room for maneuver between Moscow, Beijing, and Washington. Tokyo sought to shore up states in Latin America, Turkey, Pakistan, the Philippines (a mini-Marshall Plan), Cambodia, and Yugoslavia. Its financial assistance to Egypt helped to widen the Suez Canal for the passage of U.S. aircraft carriers. Although unwilling to send a mine-sweeping force in 1987 to aid the Gulf crisis during the Iran-Iraq War, Japan promised $10 million to help construct a navigation system and aid regional states.[29]

WASHINGTON AND MOSCOW

On the Soviet side, Soviet policymakers during the Reagan years appeared to be split between those who sought a more U.S.-oriented approach, those who sought better relations with Western Europe and Japan, and those who sought better relations with China. Prior to the 1985 U.S.-Soviet summit, Gorbachev began an (unsuccessful) campaign to enter into direct bilateral negotiations over nuclear matters with both Britain and France (much as the Soviets did in the early 1960s). In addition, Soviet proposals to eliminate all intermediate and short-range nuclear weapons from Europe were initially regarded as a ploy to split Western interests—that is, if not ultimately accompanied by *asymmetrical* reductions in Soviet conventional forces.

In September 1984 Andrei Gromyko had been invited to the White House; new talks began on Star Wars. Steps toward better relations thus preceded Gorbachev's ascension to power—as Secretary of State George Schultz's efforts of "realistic re-engagement" with Moscow had, in part, been blocked by the Soviet shooting down of South Korean airliner 007 in 1983. (Hints of a more cooperative relationship may have actually aided Gorbachev's arrival to power against more hard-line elements.) The 1985 U.S.-Soviet summit agreed to initiate secret talks on regional "hot spots." The quasi-global war began to subside as the United States and Soviet Union attempted to forge political settlements in Nicaragua, Afghanistan, Indochina, Southwest Africa—and South Africa itself—among other disputes. Washington opened discussions with the African National Congress (ANC), and the Palestine Liberation Organization (PLO), and took steps toward possible recognition of Vietnam (all efforts that had failed miserably during the Carter years). Moscow took steps to recognize Israel, South Korea, and reduced support for Castro's Cuba.

Concurrently, the Soviet leadership sought to repress burgeoning independence/democracy movements throughout Eastern Europe. Yet rather that resort to direct military intervention, Moscow supported the ultimately futile efforts of the Polish military leadership of General Woiciech Jaruzelski to repress the Solidarity movement. While given political support by most Western countries, Solidarity only received limited financial support from the CIA, in part because of fears that destabilization of Poland would lead to default on Polish loans. (In fact, Jaruzelski purposely paid back loans to private banks, but withheld payments for loans by Western governments.) Ultimately, it would in part be the legalization of Solidarity in April 1989 followed by the restoration of democracy in Poland that would help to undermine Soviet controls throughout Eastern Europe.

By 1987, both the United States and the Soviet Union tended to support Iraq against Iran, and both acted separately to protect Kuwait (which was supporting Iraq) against Iranian missile threats. It was in part because of the efforts of the tiny oasis state of Kuwait (prior to the Iraqi invasion of Kuwait in August 1990) to play Soviet against American interests that helped lead to tacit U.S.-Soviet defense cooperation, and which also helped to enhance West European Union (WEU) naval cooperation during the Gulf War. Brezhnev's proposals in 1980 for an international treaty on the Persian Gulf had previously been rejected by the United States on the grounds that such a treaty would legitimate the Soviet naval presence in the region. Both superpowers then declared formal "neutrality" in regard to the Iran-Iraq War (1980–88); but by 1987 both the United States and the Soviet Union took separate, but parallel efforts, to clear mines from the Persian Gulf following Kuwait's call for assistance. Had Kuwait's demands for joint U.S.-Soviet cooperation been heeded, could Iraq's later invasion in 1990 have been averted? (Interestingly, the United States forged a defense pact with Kuwait and Saudi Arabia after the Gulf War; the new Russia then forged a defense pact with Kuwait in November 1993.)

5

Not So Inadvertent Roll Back

FROM MINIMAL U.S. INTERVENTION TO OPERATION DESERT STORM: PHASE VI, 1988–91

Having set the stage for a closer U.S.-Soviet relationship in 1984 following conversations with Andrei Gromyko prior to Gorbachev's ascension to power, the Reagan administration moved toward what appeared to be a closer U.S.-Soviet cooperation leading toward détente. Ironically, however, this stage really turned out to be the stunned aftershock of what was, in effect, a technical knock-out. Gorbachev's statement, as relayed by French President François Mitterrand (1989)— "As soon as German unification is announced, a two-line communiqué will announce that a Soviet marshal has taken my place"—was taken to be a mere scare tactic to gain concessions from the West.

U.S. efforts to gain military-technological and political-economic superiority had begun to pay off as the Soviet system became politically, economically, and ideologically bankrupt. Gorbachev's efforts to revitalize the Soviet empire failed miserably. His belated efforts to devolve Soviet controls over Eastern Europe led to the collapse of the Warsaw Pact; Soviet controls over its global and domestic empire likewise began to implode. Time ran out for any effort to manage the devolution of the Soviet empire in such a way that might have been able to avert potentially destabilizing consequences.

Although President Reagan himself showed great enthusiasm for the new, albeit belated, U.S.-Soviet relationship, the Bush administration (despite the fact that Bush was Reagan's vice-president) remained skeptical and began a long reassessment of Reagan policy—only meeting with Gorbachev in Malta in December 1989. (This fact appears to parallel Eisenhower's reluctance to move toward a closer U.S.-Soviet relationship following Stalin's death.) President Bush promised to implement a new foreign policy designed to go "beyond containment" and integrate Moscow into the community of nations (based on National Security Directive 23); but Bush's actions continued to be reactive rather than innovative. Using a condescending "tough love" metaphor, Secretary of State James Baker, in effect, argued that the United States had to play the role of a strict parent who must wait for a child to learn from his own mistakes before granting forgiveness. In his 1990 State of the Union address, however, President Bush no longer pledged to go beyond containment, as the situation within the Soviet bloc and the world was fraught with "great uncertainty."

In February 1991, Secretary of Defense Richard Cheney argued that civil unrest in the Soviet Union was now a greater threat than military expansion. Fear of Soviet "instability" or "uncertainty" replaced the Cold War fear of a Soviet attack on Western Europe. (Perceived Soviet efforts to split NATO were now based on Soviet weakness, not strength!) In effect, prior to the failed August 1991 coup attempt in the Soviet Union, Washington began to fear the consequences of Soviet political-economic instability—an instability caused, in part, by American unwillingness to compromise with Moscow at earlier stages of the Cold War.

After his initial hesitation to follow through on President Reagan's 1987 diplomatic breakthrough, the Bush administration continued to pressure Moscow through nuclear weapons modernization (see Chapter 7). While pursuing the START I talks, the Bush administration also demanded higher levels of Japanese "burden sharing" and supported German reunification under the aegis of NATO. (Secretary of State Baker subsequently renamed U.S. demands for "burden sharing" as "responsibility sharing.") In addition, issues such as Soviet support for Cuba, the failure of the Gorbachev regime to implement market-oriented reforms, coupled with U.S. hesitation to provide substantial financial assistance, continued to plague U.S.-Soviet relations. The publication of "To the Stalin Mausoleum" by "Z"—a pessimistic indictment of Gorbachev's reforms and Gorbiemania—was rumored to represent the Bush administration's equivalent of George Kennan's 1947 "X" article.[1]

Unlike the Nixon era which resulted in closer U.S.-Chinese relations, U.S. relations with Beijing became acrimonious following the 1987 sale of Silkworm missiles to Iran and the March 1988 sale of IRBMs to Saudi Arabia—prior to the crackdown on "pro-democracy" demonstrators in 1989. Nixon's so-called China card had, in effect, become a wild card. In addition, U.S. relations with a newly unified Germany and Japan began to deteriorate. A unified Germany continued to advance foreign and economic policies more independent of the United States and its EC compatriots. Japan feared that the retraction of the U.S. security umbrella in the Pacific region might invite Soviet or PRC expansion, if not result in instability on the Korean peninsula; the United States and Japan had yet to resolve serious trade/monetary disputes. Japan opposed the "European" orientation of U.S. policy and sought to maintain Chinese stability and give more attention to tensions in Asia, where the Cold War had not entirely ended.

Moreover, it was not entirely accidental that as the Soviet role in the fifth dimension of the double containment continued to unravel, the United States moved from minimal intervention to Operation Desert Storm. During the Cold War, direct or indirect U.S. intervention had been circumscribed by Soviet and/or Chinese efforts to check U.S. actions and allies by providing sufficient supports to those revolutionary groups or states challenging U.S. or allied interests. Concurrently both the United States and the Soviet Union generally tried to prescribe the actions of their respective allies. The collapse of the Soviet will to "co-guarantee" global security, however, also meant the collapse of Moscow's ability to rein in its allies.

Until the U.S.-led UN-coalition attack on Iraq in 1991, the "Vietnam syndrome" was still evident in the minimalist character of U.S. interventions. President Reagan had been able to galvanize domestic support by minimalist intervention in Grenada and Libya (despite the marine barracks fiasco in Lebanon). The Reagan administration's so-called managed revolution in the Philippines and Haiti obtained popular support as well. President Bush's move into Panama was, at least initially, supported as minimalist intervention. The U.S.-led UN intervention in Kuwait (which paralleled British intervention in 1961 against Iraq, secretly backed by the United States) however, opened up new debates.

The invasion of Kuwait by Iraq (neither Iraq's 1980 attack on Iran nor its 1990 invasion of Kuwait was counseled by Moscow) took place in circumstances of Soviet impotence. U.S. policy was likewise caught off guard: Washington's efforts to quell Baghdad's revisionist demands through illegal financial and technological assistance prior to the invasion of Kuwait (and simultaneously play Baghdad against Teheran, resulting in both "Iraqgate" and "Irangate"), failed miserably. (From the Iraqi perspective, the invasion was provoked by Kuwaiti refusal—under U.S. pressure—to permit the price of oil to rise high enough so Iraq could pay off debts incurred during the Iran-Iraq conflict—a war in which Iraq saw itself as containing the forces of pan-Islam in the interests of the West. By arming both sides, however, Washington, Moscow, and the other core and semiperipheral arms exporting powers hoped to use the Iran-Iraq War as a means to weaken both states. Only a few countries remained loyal to one side.)

Washington subsequently refused to appease Iraq after its invasion of Kuwait: Baghdad's actions were judged as violating "vital" U.S. global security and economic interests. On the other hand, the United States appeased Syrian claims to northern Lebanon in order to entice Damascus to join allied forces against Iraq (and, it was hoped, to settle its dispute with Tel Aviv over the Golan Heights). At the same time—Israel was restrained from acting unilaterally to prevent the allied Arab coalition from breaking up. Negotiations towards a peace settlement for the entire region—backed by the United States, EC, and a Soviet Union/Russia increasingly obsessed by domestic crises—went forward, but only following Iraqi defeat. (Middle East peace talks were not to be seen as a capitulation to Saddam Hussein.)

President Bush was initially reluctant to intervene: British Prime Minister Margaret Thatcher's experience in the Falklands War may have influenced his decision. U.S. interventionists argued that Washington had to take a more unilateral role in stemming the rise of powerful weapons states. U.S. interventionists were worried that a powerful Iraq could ultimately assist Soviet interests as a regional ally (despite actual Soviet assistance in describing Iraq's military capabilities). Iraq's attempt to control roughly 20 percent of the world's oil supply, and eliminate the Kuwaiti power to influence world oil prices, threatened regional predominance over Saudi Arabia and Israel.

Non-interventionists worried that conflict in the Gulf might draw the United States into a deeper imperial quagmire; they opposed intervention in favor of long-term sanctions and selective military intervention. In addition, many feared that American intervention might help fuel pan-Islamic movements throughout the Middle East and North Africa—particularly Algeria and Egypt. Interventionists, however, argued the United States should have "gone to Baghdad" or at least moved into southern Iraq; the Bush administration instead opted for the limited goal of liberating Kuwait only. (General Colin Powell defined the conflict as a "limited-objective" and "limited-means" war[2]—despite substantial damage to Iraqi civilian infrastructure with perceived dual-use capabilities. U.S. efforts to eliminate Iraqi nuclear capabilities were really a consequence and not a cause of the war. Interestingly, the Pentagon was hesitant to attack known Iraqi biological warfare facilities for fear of spreading contamination.)

In addition to the U.S. refusal to play "imperialist," the fact that Saddam Hussein remained in power after the war was in part due to the fact that U.S. regional allies (Turkey and Saudi Arabia) feared that Kurdish and pan-Islamic Shi'ia movements might gain strength. It was argued that the Shi'ia, which represent 55 percent of the Iraqi population, could strengthen the position of Shi'ia Iran; support for an independent Kurdistan could polarize Turkish society. And it was not clear whether a pro-Western leadership would necessarily come to power in Iraq. (Both Iraq and Bahrein possess a majority Shi'ite population, but a Sunni leadership.)

The U.S.-led UN intervention in Kuwait was intended to send a warning signal to states that might attempt to challenge the former bipolar global order; following the 1991–92 break-up of Yugoslavia, however, it is not at all clear that all states (and pan-national movements) received the same message.

GERMANY: A PERFORATED IRON CURTAIN CRUMBLES

Deliberating at first, the Bush administration was slow to accept the West German call for German "reassociation" moving toward "reunification." Initially, the preferred U.S. strategy had been to work toward German reassociation within NATO-dominated Conventional Force-in-Europe (CFE) talks involving twenty-six nations. Yet as the pace of reunification went forward, the United States, under pressure from the West German government, sought a more simplified framework for negotiations involving the two Germanys and the four powers with legal rights over the Germanys (the United States, the Soviet Union, Britain, and France)—the two-plus-four arrangement. This formula first initiated discussions between the two Germanys to arrange a national framework for German unification. The Four Powers responsible for the occupation of Germany then set the terms for Germany's international security—but in a framework largely established by Bonn alone. Decisions would then be "ratified" in an all-European CSCE framework.

The two-plus-four arrangement represented an attempt to find a compromise between the two apparently irreconcilable extremes of the U.S. preference for a united Germany within NATO and the stated Soviet preference for a neutral Germany, in which East Germany would not lose its "socialist" character. In essence, the plan for German reunification proposed by German Foreign Minister Hans-Dietrich Genscher sought to bind West Germany to the NATO alliance and yet permit a contingent of Soviet troops to remain within East Germany for a "transition" period (until 1994) during which Germany would take steps towards unification. In large part because of Chancellor Helmut Kohl's promises of a "reinsurance treaty" between Germany and the former Soviet Union, the two Germanys then opted for a federal system under West German control (see below).

Much as Konrad Adenauer predicted, Western superiority did force German unification largely on Bonn's terms. Communist proposals for a loose confederation and proposals by the East German New Forum movement for a "special way" between capitalism and communism were defeated in large part because of Chancellor Kohl's Ten Points and promises to significantly raise the East German standard of living. Initially, Chancellor Kohl's Ten Points program supported a confederal approach, but Kohl's hopes to become the "unification chancellor," Gorbachev's willingness to cut a deal (combined with German fears that this might represent the last chance) led to more rapid steps. Although Moscow requested assurances that a unified Germany would not become a political-military threat, Moscow had no strategic leverage with which to block German unification (in part because of significant East German indebtedness to West Germany). In addition, Margaret Thatcher's steps to halt or at least slow down the unification process, and forge a confederal Germany, failed. In her view, French President François Mitterrand (having initially taken tentative steps towards a rapprochement with East German leader Erich Honecker and Mikhail Gorbachev that enraged Bonn) believed it was too late to halt Bonn's drive for unification. France then opted to contain a unified Germany within a pan-European federal structure—opposed by Thatcher.[3]

Moscow would have preferred to discuss security arrangements first in a four-plus-zero framework, and then consider the domestic issues resulting from German reunification second. Moscow feared that a more militarily and economically powerful state could ultimately evolve through German unity than if East Germany joined as part of a loose German confederation in which Moscow would retain some influence. Moscow also feared that the Christian Democratic Union (CDU) and Christian Socialist Union (CSU) might ultimately demand the incorporation of the former GDR into NATO defenses as German Defense Minister Gerhard Stoltenberg had advocated. Moscow's hard-liners (such as Yegor Ligachev) argued that NATO might opt to deploy a "forward defense" if German military capabilities were not strictly limited. As East Germany represented the "keystone" of the Soviet empire, Soviet hard-liners not only feared the collapse of the Warsaw Pact, but also the breakup of a European Russia, and pressed for a crackdown on East Germany. (Former Soviet Foreign Minister Eduard Shevardnadze later stated that such a crackdown might well have led to World War III.)

Some Central European states, however, sought to convince Gorbachev that a "neutral" reunified Germany would not indefinitely accept largely self-imposed restraints on conventional and nuclear armaments if not part of a larger U.S.-Soviet or all-European security system. Czech President Vaclav Havel and other Central European leaders pointed out that a reassociated Germany tied temporarily to NATO and then ultimately tied to an all-European security system, would be in Moscow's best interests. As Warsaw still feared Bonn's revisionist claims, it supported a continued double containment of Germany in NATO, plus a NATO-Warsaw Pact entente. In addition, NATO promised to move toward a "nonoffensive defense" if the Soviets would make *asymmetrical* military cuts in Eastern Europe. (By October 1991, the Visegrad "three" [Czechoslovakia, Hungary, and Poland] sought membership in NATO—for protection against an instable Soviet Union and the indirect consequences of war in Yugoslavia.)

The final settlement resulted in the German renunciation of the development of nuclear, chemical, and biological weaponry (on its territory) and stated that the NPT would continue to apply to a united Germany. German forces were limited in size to 370,000 men. After withdrawal of Soviet forces in 1994, German units assigned to alliances (NATO and the WEU) could be stationed in the eastern region of Germany, but they could not deploy "nuclear weapons carriers." Foreign forces and nuclear weapons could not be deployed in the east. (But NATO could still move into the region if Article 6 went into effect.) In addition, Germany signed a separate "peace" or "reinsurance" treaty with the Soviet Union—the Treaty of Good Neighborliness, Partnership, and Cooperation—which stated "if one of the two states should become the target of aggression, then the other side will give the aggressor no military aid or support."[4] Since Bonn argued that NATO is a "defensive" alliance, then NATO would not attack the Soviet Union.

In order to contain Germany within a multilateral framework, the Bush administration also encouraged the formation of a "European pillar" within NATO designed to grant Europeans a greater sense of "power sharing." Thus, by April 1990 the United States began to back Franco-German plans to pursue European political, economic, and strategic integration by 1993 (the "European pillar"), as a means to prevent Germany from sliding into "neutrality" or military independence; in December 1991 the United States offered the former Warsaw Pact states greater consultation with NATO through the North

Atlantic Cooperation Council—but only after heavy German lobbying.

As the United States began to revamp NATO policy, in November 1990, Soviet hard-liners, such as the Soyuz faction of the Supreme Soviet, began to assert their power in the Kremlin (prior to the August 1991 coup) in an effort to block Gorbachev's New Union Treaty, to stall German unification, as well as to sustain Soviet nuclear and military interests in the aftermath of the collapse of the Warsaw Pact. Moreover, the Soviets appeared to stall on troop removals from East Germany and Poland, in part to gain more German finance to pay the costs of the troop withdrawal (few jobs or homes available for troops returning to the Soviet Union), as well as in a vain effort to gain greater bargaining leverage on the START I agreement. These hard-line efforts appeared to weaken by April–May (after the signing of the two-plus-four-treaty), and at the time of the Yeltsin-Gorbachev compromise (when Boris Yeltsin was playing the national-republic card against Mikhail Gorbachev's new federalism).

The efforts of Soviet hard-liners to block Gorbachev's reforms convinced the German leadership that Germany must push its interests more assertively. As German Foreign Minister Hans Dietrich Genscher put it: This "still unaccustomed resurgence of German self-assurance began on 15 March 1991. . . . Something changed . . . when Tererkhov handed over the documents" (the signed and ratified copy of the two-plus-four treaty confirming Germany's sovereignty). "Until then, we exercised great restraint," Genscher stated, "those who later launched the August coup in Moscow were against ratification and had tried to prevent it."[5] Thus, after March 1991, Germany began to favor Baltic independence and sovereignty for Ukraine. Bonn (influenced in part by the state of Bavaria) pushed for the recognition of Croatia, Slovenia (and then Bosnia) against pan-Serb expansionism after the failed August 1991 coup attempt in the Soviet Union. (Contrary to Genscher, it can be argued that the entire push for reunification was not at all an exercise in "great restraint.")

While Germany was active in Europe, Bonn was not as active in supporting U.S. interests in the Persian Gulf. Following the Iraqi invasion of Kuwait, Washington was angered by both French and German reluctance to intervene; Bonn did pay up to $11.4 billion of the costs of the war, plus assistance to states affected by the war; yet it had allocated some $50 billion to unification. Whereas Paris had significant investments and arms interests in Iraq, and feared that the war might sour Franco-Arab relations (and help fuel pan-Islamic movements in North Africa), Bonn argued that the U.S.-imposed Constitution prevented it from engaging forces in out-of-area, non-NATO missions.

JAPAN: MORE DOUBTS

Unlike Reagan, President Bush did not publicly urge Japan to forge itself into "an unsinkable aircraft carrier." Japan nevertheless possessed the then third-largest defense outlays in the world. Japan continued to expand its naval and military capabilities, slightly above the 1 percent GNP limit, and was urged by the U.S. Congress to increase defense spending (to as much as 2–3 percent of GNP!), to coordinate strategic planning with NATO, to participate in SDI research, and to upgrade its naval outreach to be able to cover the Persian Gulf. With the deterioration of Sino-American relations in the 1980s, Japan became the linchpin of U.S. geostrategy in the region—despite the rise of U.S.-Japanese political-economic tensions. In accord with the call for "responsibility sharing," Secretary of Defense Richard Cheney pressed for a 10 percent cut in American troops in Japan, and demanded a 50 percent increase in military contributions from Japan, in February 1990. He also asked a reluctant South Korea to increase its share of the defense burden.[6]

Japan's major security concerns included the Soviet occupation of the Kurile Islands and Soviet naval bases in the Sea of Okhotsk, its fear of the potential withdrawal of U.S. security guarantees, particularly if coupled with the additional "insult" of burgeoning U.S. and European economic protectionism. In addition, Tokyo engaged in a thus far "silent" naval rivalry with China: Japan feared China's ambitions and military capabilities in regard to its March 1988 seizure of the Spratly Islands and 1974 seizure of the Paracel Islands and claims to Taiwan (90 percent of Japanese oil passes by the Spratly Islands). China's apparent desire for "peaceful" Korean reunification (largely on North Korea's terms) likewise worried Japan. The issues of World War II war reparations also continued to divide the two.

In the short run, following the Tiananmen Square massacre in June 1989, Japan sought to mitigate the Chinese sense of isolation by seeking to minimize sanctions. Japan hoped that its offers of trade and investment would deflect Chinese claims to hegemony over the region. On the other hand, Japan refused to transfer high technology that might assist China's competitive capabilities in the economic sphere, or its military capabilities in the security sphere, such as its decision to block the sale of flying refueling pumps to China through COCOM. Japan also announced an increase in defense spending in the week of Tiananmen Square (and in the midst of its own political scandals).

Even though Moscow significantly reduced the number and scope of its naval exercises in the Northern Pacific to signal Japan its "good" intentions, Japan still feared Soviet intent. Thus, although Moscow reduced the size of its overseas forces, it ironically began to concentrate forces closer to Japan; Moscow also continued its naval and submarine force modernization. The April 1991 Soviet-Japanese summit failed to bring any significant compromise between the two powers, despite the fact that the December 1988 Soviet-Japanese Communiqué implicitly recognized for the first time a more "balanced" negotiating approach to Japanese claims to the Kurile Islands. Japanese conservatives were concerned that the Soviet diplomatic offensive was intended to "pigeonhole" the territorial question in order to gain high technology, and that Soviet military reductions had been supplanted by qualitative advancements and armament modernization. President Gorbachev's pleas for $30 billion in Japanese investment fell largely on deaf ears, as Japanese businessmen refused to invest in politically and economically instable conditions. On the Russian side, Soviet military leaders refused to compromise over the Kurile Island dispute, arguing that the Soviet Union would lose its great power status if it gave up its control over the two northernmost Kurile Islands. Giving up the islands could also strengthen the claims of the PRC to Soviet territory. Newly elected Russian President Boris Yeltsin compared the Gorbachev's proposed deal with Tsar Alexandr II's sell out of Alaska.

As Japan watched the Soviet hold over Eastern Europe crumble, it hoped that Moscow would ultimately cave in to its demands. Moscow feared that Tokyo might also be seeking greater political-economic influence over Siberia and the Sakhalin Island before it agreed to ameliorate relations with Moscow. In addition, Japan's refusal in April 1991 to accept Gorbachev's offer of a U.S.-Japanese-Soviet alliance and a compromise over the Kurile Islands was not merely a result of a lack of U.S. support for a joint U.S.-Soviet-Japanese defense treaty, but also because of Japan's concern with the ultimate intent of the PRC, which has opposed greater Japanese political-economic influence and collusion with Russia in northeast Asia.

In addition to Soviet military pressure and burgeoning Chinese maritime capabilities, Japan feared that instability in the Philippines would ultimately lead to the U.S. withdrawal from Clark Air Base or Subic Naval Base, thus leaving a strategic no-man's-land in the South Pacific which either Japan or potentially China could fill—if a declining Soviet Union could not.[7] After the Iraqi invasion of Kuwait, some Japanese officials were more worried about maintaining a secure supply of oil than pressing Iraq to leave Kuwait. Following the 1973 crisis, Japan had reoriented its domestic economy to conserve energy. Who actually controlled oil was seen as an issue for the United States, but not Japan.[8]

Thus, during the Persian Gulf War, Japan was criticized for not sending a military presence to defend its assumed interest in securing sea lines of communication (SLOC); but it did pay the costs of "burden sharing." Japanese doves pointed to the U.S.-imposed constitution, which permits only a "defensive" military capability as an aspect of the double containment. (The Japanese constitution does permit "defensive" nuclear weaponry, but so far Japan has upheld the "three nonnuclear principles.") On the other side, Japanese hawks sought more direct intervention. Tokyo found a compromise by permitting Japanese mine-sweepers to move as far as the Persian Gulf so as to protect Japanese shipping. In addition, the need to reach a peace settlement in Cambodia raised the question whether Tokyo should alter its U.S.-imposed constitution mandating only the deployment of "defensive" military capabilities and involve Japanese troops in UN peace-keeping measures.

U.S. actions and calls for "burden sharing" may have accordingly accelerated Japanese efforts to produce an indigenous defense capability. In postponing the joint development of the FSX fighter jet, for example, the U.S. Congress feared it would give away critical high technology and lose superiority in aircraft manufacturing to Japan; Congress also thought Japan should buy the jet "off the shelf" so as to reduce the U.S. trade imbalance.[9] In addition, Japanese foreign policy critics, such as Shintaro Ishihara, threatened to oppose the United States and to play the microchip card so as change U.S. policy, particularly in relation to the Soviet Union. This group wanted to revamp the Japanese self-defense force and make it more loosely linked to the United States, in part by developing Japan's own reconnaissance satellites and fighter jets.[10] In reaction to the FSX controversy, the Japanese Defense Agency thus started several large-scale development programs, including efforts to replace U.S. missiles, jet engines, and helicopters with Japanese models. (The issue of "techno-nationalism" likewise plagued proposed technology sharing of SDI defenses.)

Whereas Congress sought to apply sanctions (Super 301 legislation was regarded as a "crowbar" to open Japanese, South Korean, and Indian markets) and counter "unfair" trading practices resulting in major U.S. trade imbalances, the Pentagon sought to maintain a strong military-technological cooperation with both South Korea and Japan and to prevent South Korea and Japan from becoming serious rivals. As long as Japanese prohibitions of military exports (except to the United States) remain in place, the United States and Japan can develop a comprehensive strategy; but if Japan expands its production of defense-related materials beyond domestic capacity to absorb them, then "military exports may become a structural imperative."[11] As 90 percent of Japan's weapons are produced domestically, Japan's strategy of *Kukusanta*—technological autonomy—sought to reduce Japanese dependency on the United States, despite higher costs involved.[12] Inability of Washington to cooperate with Tokyo in the military-technological field thus would, in effect, end the double containment of Japan.

CHINA: THE WILD CARD

The fact that the tacit NATO-Japanese-PRC encirclement of the Soviet Union began to break up by 1982 represented a fortunate circumstance in that it worked to abate global tensions. Ironically, the Reagan administration's initially strong anti-Soviet, anti-PRC policy reduced the pressure of "encirclement" upon the Soviet Union as the PRC moved toward a position more independent of the two "superpowers" following Brezhnev's 1981 Peace Offensive—an outcome which was not the original intent of Reaganites, who hoped to forge a strong anti-Communist alliance.

Not so ironically, however, as U.S.-Soviet relations finally improved in 1987, U.S.-Chinese relations soured because of fear of a renewed U.S.-Soviet condominium, Tokyo's military buildup and role in SDI, continued direct and indirect U.S. military support to Taiwan, difficulties faced by U.S. businessmen in China, sanctions placed on certain high-tech products between October 1987 and March 1988 as a protest on Chinese Silkworm missile sales to Iran (1987) and Eastwind IRBMs to Saudi Arabia (1988). Congressional demands to repeal China's MFN status, criticisms of China's human rights abuses, plus denunciation of the Chinese invasion of Tibet in 1950 and the Dalai Lama's visit to Washington, also heightened tensions. (Chinese IBRM sales were in part a consequence of Congressional refusal to sell F16s to Saudi Arabia.)

By May–June 1989, the rise of the "democracy" movement was seen by Beijing as encouraged by Voice of America. Beijing saw U.S. propaganda as an effort to disrupt Gorbachev's May visit and the Sino-Soviet rapprochement. Even prior to the crackdown in Tiananmen Square, Sino-U.S. relations had reached the lowest point since normalization. Then, following Tiananmen Square, the United States suspended military sales and contact of high-level officials. Additionally, the United States sought to postpone new loans to China by international lending institutions; but concurrently the United States began a secret rapprochement. Only superficially reminiscent of the "secret" trip of Henry Kissinger to Beijing, National Security Adviser Brent Scowcroft appeared in Beijing at least twice following the Tiananmen Square repression. The rapprochement with China was depicted as a means to bring Beijing out of its "angry isolation," strengthen "moderates" in the Chinese leadership, and find areas of mutual agreement in regards to regional conflicts in South Asia, Indochina, and the Korean peninsula. Without strong U.S. ties, it was feared China would seek out European, Japanese—if not Soviet— technology and investment to the exclusion of the U.S. interests.

By reaching out to Beijing, Bush also hoped to reinforce the trend toward a reduction of Soviet military pressure on NATO by keeping the pressure on the Soviets through the PRC. When the Nixon administration reached out to China in the period 1969–71, it had hoped to take advantage of Sino-Soviet border clashes; in 1989 the Bush administration hoped to preclude the possibility of tighter Sino-Soviet cooperation. (By December 1989, Moscow sent its own Valentin Falin mission to Beijing.[13]) Although many analysts argued that there were no longer any strategic cards for the major powers to play against one another, the Chinese elite did not accept either Soviet or American versions of "new thinking."

The Sino-Soviet rapprochement worked to reduce the Chinese fear of encirclement by reducing the Soviet military presence along the Sino-Soviet border. Gorbachev withdrew Soviet forces from Afghanistan (though Moscow continued to supply military equipment and IRBMs to the Afghan government) and began to pull Soviet forces from the Asian region, including naval units from Vietnam's Cam Ranh Bay. By May–July 1991, the Soviet Union and PRC had settled border disputes over islands in the Amur and Ussuri Rivers (such as Damanskii Island) that had set off the Sino-Soviet border clashes in 1969. These factors, to a certain extent, permitted the Chinese to pursue a more maritime-oriented strategy of defense, as concerns with continental defenses against the Soviet Union no longer appeared as necessary.

Prior to Tiananmen Square (and the late 1987 economic retrenchment), Zhao Ziyang sought to build China's economic base rather than invest heavily in the military. This led Chinese hard-liners to fear the "danger zone"—the period during economic and military modernization in which China might be vulnerable to attack. At roughly the same time as the 1987 INF U.S.-Soviet accord which indicated steps toward closer U.S.-Soviet ties, Yang Shangkun, then second in command of the PLA, stated that China would become a world power of the first rank within sixty years, but to do so, it needed to avoid the Japan model of becoming just a prosperous country that is not militarily powerful.[14] This statement, in effect, represented an attack on Zhao Ziyang's program of economic liberalization and marked a move away from the emphasis on "economism" toward a greater emphasis on "geostrategy" on the part of the Chinese elite. In the period 1987–89, China began not only to fear new steps toward U.S.-Soviet condominium, but it also began to fear U.S. support for Tibetan and Taiwanese independence, as well as the forces of democratic dissent.

In an additional sign of a more assertive Chinese policy, coming in the same month as the announcement of the sale of IRBMs to Saudi Arabia, China seized some of the Spratly Islands in March 1988. Although these islands were controlled by Hanoi (not given support by Moscow), this action raised the concerns of the Philippines, Indonesia, Malaysia, in addition to Taiwan, Japan, as well as the United States and Soviet Union. These strategically placed *points d'appui* that guard access to oil in the South China Sea, as well as the sea lines of communication (SLOC), can be used "as bases for sea lane defense, interdiction, surveillance, and possibly for the launching of land attacks."[15] Some of these same islands were used by the Japanese for attacks during World War II. Beijing was also regarded as eyeing the oil-rich James Shoal in possible rivalry with Japan.

From this point of view, China had attempted to manipulate both the United States and Soviet Union into accepting its claims to Taiwan following the 1981–82 Brezhnev Peace Offensive, which gave Soviet diplomatic backing to China's claims to Taiwan. Mainland China hoped that the offer of greater trade, investment opportunities, and cultural exchange could ultimately lure Taiwan into accepting the "two systems, one country" formula, which could grant the PRC strategic naval and SLBM access to the South China Sea and the Pacific. Beijing regarded U.S. government promises to withdraw support from Taipei as disingenuous: private investment (and the development of indigenous Taiwanese military capabilities) continued to increase.

Beijing continued to challenge U.S., Japanese, and Taiwanese interests, despite the attempted Sino-U.S. and Sino-Japanese rapprochement. By December 1989, as China continued its crackdown on supporters of the democracy movement, the PRC issued at least seven warnings against the public advocacy of Taiwanese independence by the opposition Democratic Progressive Party in the first nationwide elections held since the lifting of martial law in 1987. In addition, the rise of China as a major arms supplier to the Middle East (Iran, Iraq, Egypt, Syria, and Saudi Arabia) threatened to upset the U.S.-Soviet double containment of the Middle Eastern tinderbox. The sale of

Silkworm missiles to Iran in 1987 and the Eastwind IRBM to Saudi Arabia in 1988 served to isolate Taiwan (by cutting diplomatic ties between Saudi Arabia and Taiwan); the sales also served to pressure Japan's SLOC by providing PRC military supports to countries which provided Japan's oil (see Chapter 6).[16]

China's March 1989 declaration of martial law in Tibet likewise raised the suspicions of India. After the Bush administration's July 1990 decision to open discussions with Cambodia and Vietnam, China vowed to double its support for the Khmer Rouge, if the United States supported the pro-Vietnamese Cambodian government of Hun Sen. In effect, China's "sweet and sour" strategy continued to threaten the Asian littoral in order to gain concessions from the United States and Japan.

In essence, the Bush administration opposed the continuing "isolation" of China, and sought a nostalgic return to a "business as usual" with the PRC. Initially, the Bush administration attempted to "buy" China's allegiance (through the sale of more than $600 million in defense materiel, among other incentives) in the hope that it could avert a closer Sino-Soviet entente, forestall Chinese supports for North Korea, and simultaneously compete with both European and Soviet arms sales to the PRC—efforts of appeasement that proved "disappointing" in President Bush's own words.

As China opened to the forces of democratic liberalism, regional differences became exacerbated because of the emphasis on free-enterprise zones in the south. The new freedoms had abetted black-market profiteering, both at the level of factory managers and on the street. Moves toward "bourgeois-liberalization" such as the 1980 "Democracy Wall" movement were at first repressed. The year 1984 saw the Chinese "anti-spiritual pollution" campaign. Large-scale pro-democracy student demonstrations (with some worker and urban support) took place in major cities throughout China in late 1986–87, and millions participated in the May–June events in 1989, though the majority peasant population did not participate. On the other hand, signs of xenophobic hatred for the Western, and particularly Japanese, presence were seen in student demonstrations in 1985 and again, against African students, in December 1988.

Between 1987 and 1989, China increasingly began to retrench its policy of economic reforms in an effort to foster centralization, control provincial governments, and slow down an overheated economy. In part, the turn toward Moscow (and sponsorship of a Sino-Soviet summit in May 1989) was not merely designed to modernize Soviet made weaponry and retool factories built by the Soviet Union in the 1950s, but also designed to appeal to anti-Western, anti-capitalist hard-liners. On the other hand, as was the case for Khrushchev's reforms during the Cultural Revolution, Gorbachev-style reforms of *glasnost* and *perestroika* also presented a dilemma for the Chinese leadership. As the Warsaw Pact collapsed, the Chinese leadership placed the PLA on alert, and sought to strengthen China's internal-security apparatus. Fears of a Polish-like Solidarity movement and breakup of the Warsaw Pact were ultimately used to justify a crackdown on Tibet and the Chinese democracy movement—a movement which initially intended to establish a student union independent of Communist Party controls.

By selectively purging pro-democracy supporters within the party itself (and particularly free market followers of Milton Friedman), and by intimidating those who supported reform outside the control of the party, and most importantly, by bringing the PLA back into the political decision-making process, Deng Xiaoping hoped the Communist Party could survive any succession crisis following his death. Some reforms would occur under the guidance of the party, and enough measures of liberalization would return to appease rival European, Japanese, and American "capitalists," who were, in effect, willing to sell the rope to hang themselves in the Leninist view. The CCP hoped to maintain itself in power by a dual-track policy of cooptation and selective repression, coupled with appeals to xenophobia and "defense education."[17]

Willingness to repress its own population (despite opposition at high levels), development of a rapid deployment force, PLA training with tactical nuclear weapons, raised the prospects of an increasingly assertive policy. Following the Persian Gulf War, China announced an increase in military spending of nearly 12 percent, despite its record budget deficit of $2.8 billion. The increase in government defense spending was justified as needed to modernize weapons and equipment, as well as to meet security concerns of a "complex and volatile international situation."[18] (In fear of setting a precedent—as Iraqi claims to Kuwait could be seen as parallel to PRC claims to Taiwan—China abstained on UN Resolution 678 to use "all necessary means" against Iraq.) Then, during the August 1991 putsch attempt in Soviet Union, Chinese forces went on alert; following the failed coup, CCP leaders moved to reaffirm the party's control over the military.

THE SOVIET UNION: NEW THINKING, NEW CRISES

With his accession to power in 1985, Mikhail Gorbachev launched a "revolution" in Soviet foreign policy. After denouncing the Brezhnev era policies, Gorbachev returned to strategies pursued by Khrushchev in the period 1955–56 (and to a certain extent pursued by Kosygin and Brezhnev in period 1970–74). Gorbachev intensified the efforts launched by Brezhnev in 1981–82 to reach a rapprochement with China; he then sought reconciliation with the United States, Germany, Japan, as well as states such as Iran.

In essence Gorbachev's strategy represented a diplomatic offensive designed to end the Soviet Union's "encirclement" and prevent the breakup of the country. It definitely failed to prevent the latter, and may have also failed to prevent the former as well. The liberation of Eastern Europe was also intended to forge a far-reaching entente with both the United States and Germany/Europe. If Moscow failed to reach an entente with Washington, however, then Gorbachev would attempt to forge a closer relationship with Germany. In many ways, Gorbachev's strategy paralleled Lenin's strategy at Brest Litovsk to limit Soviet liabilities. Whatever the ultimate result, Soviet retrenchment would force the West to pay the consequences.

Soviet calls for "nonthreatening defense" and "sufficient deterrence," Gorbachev's apparent aversion to the use of force, and his appeals for constitutionally mandated change, the policies of *perestroika* and *glasnost*, promises to permit a multi-party system, and the acceptance of the principle of asymmetrical arms reductions all represented a radical shift in both domestic and foreign policy at least ostensibly designed to forge an entente, moving beyond détente, with the United States. Gorbachev's policies (dubbed the "Sinatra Doctrine"), resulting in the liberation of East Germany and East European states from Communist Party monopoly by letting East European states "do it [their] way," had replaced the Brezhnev Doctrine with the wilting of Soviet spheres of influence.

Gorbachev's preferred strategy was to forge a concerted effort with the United States to form a new "European home," find a compromise in response to Japanese claims to the Kurile Islands, and manage a resurgent, yet unstable, China, in addition to coordinating strategy in the still unstable Central Asia and Middle East (as well as peripheral regions). This strategy was expected to bear the fruits of cooperation in both the developed and developing worlds without risk of conflict with the United States. It was accordingly expected that Soviet "unilateral" offers were to be followed by reciprocal gestures on the part of Washington in order to seal a more constructive long-term relationship. U.S. support for West German and Japanese compromise with the Soviet Union was to help legitimize Soviet security interests through a more concerted global relationship.

Yet Gorbachev's efforts to establish better relations with Europe and Japan tended to be interpreted by the Bush administration as a means to wean these states away from U.S. hegemony; some U.S. strategists argued that the real intent of Soviet strategy was to break up American alliances. Although Soviet reform efforts were applauded, Henry Kissinger, for example, feared that, should Gorbachev's reforms prove to be successful, then Moscow could emerge as an even stronger rival. Concurrently, Kissinger more correctly noted that the failure of Soviet reforms could result in dangerous instability.

In regard to China, it is not entirely accidental that Gorbachev's foreign policies (which inadvertently liberated Eastern Europe from Communist Party controls), followed closely upon the heels of the Sino-Soviet rapprochement in May 1989. In effect, by seeking a rapprochement with China, Gorbachev sought to protect the Soviet eastern flank, before he exposed Moscow's western flank to U.S. and German/European influence. Gorbachev thus extended Brezhnev's efforts to forge a rapprochement with the PRC by negotiating with China over the "three obstacles" to improved Sino-Soviet relations (see the previous chapter). And Soviet steps to establish a far-reaching entente with Iran in June 1989 represented an effort to reduce Iranian support for pan-Islamic movements within the Soviet Union itself and help contain demands for a unified independent Azerbaijan.

Gorbachev's rapprochement with Beijing was a major factor in compelling the Bush administration to reaffirm strong Sino-U.S. relations hastily following the bloody June 1989 Tiananmen Square massacre and in the aftermath of the May 1989 Sino-Soviet summit and the December 1989 Valentin Falin mission to Beijing, followed by Chinese Premier Li Peng's trip to Moscow in April 1990. Gorbachev thus hoped to maintain a Sino-Soviet détente in order to resolve issues that led to the Sino-Soviet border clashes of 1969 and to counterbalance U.S. (and European) strategic cooperation with the PRC, and as a means to pressure Japan. In the short term, then, both Moscow and Beijing could use the *threat* of a closer alliance as a means to bargain with and manipulate Washington and Tokyo. Additionally, Moscow looked to an economically rising Beijing to help support its overseas burden, if not bolster its own economy by bartering arms for consumer goods.

Prior to the May 1989 Sino-Soviet normalization, Gorbachev's Krasnoyarsk speech in September 1988 promised a Soviet withdrawal from its naval bases in Vietnam in exchange for a U.S. withdrawal from its Philippine bases. Such a "deal" really represented a continuation of Soviet efforts to woo China. The arrangement was to relieve Chinese fears of naval encirclement in the South Pacific, in addition to encouraging anti-U.S. dissent (and hostility in the Philippine Senate toward the presence of U.S. bases) in an increasingly instable Philippines. As the roots of the Sino-Soviet reconciliation lay in Soviet diplomatic support for Chinese claims to Taiwan, the real intent of Gorbachev's strategy was to deflect China's strategic and economic capabilities away from the Soviet Union and toward the Pacific.

Concurrently, however, as Gorbachev moved to establish better relations with China, he also had to reassure India, which suffered a breakdown in the system of supply and credit in the last year of Gorbachev's rule; Gorbachev thus visited India in 1986 and 1988. He promised to supply India with a nuclear power station and advanced MiG-29 fighter jets. Soviet sales to India were intended to "counterbalance" Chinese and Pakistani pressures: Chinese arms sales (anti-aircraft weaponry) to Nepal, for example, caused a strong Indian reaction and a virtual shutdown of Indian and Nepalese trade in 1989. Chinese influence in Burma, and to some extent Sri Lanka, also raised Indian concern. Concurrently, as India attempted to play the United States and the Soviet Union against each other, India increasingly looked to the United States for high technology and arms.

In many ways, steps toward a Sino-Soviet détente permitted the Soviet Union to take a more relaxed attitude toward U.S. denunciation of the "evil empire"—at the same time as Moscow continued its defense policy buildup until 1987. From this perspective, it was the steps toward Sino-Soviet reconciliation, and not necessarily the Reagan hard-line policy, that permitted the Soviet Union to readjust its policy vis-à-vis the United States. Gorbachev's gambit thus threatened a Soviet version of the China card against U.S. Pacific interests. At the same time, Gorbachev's gambit appeared to promise the possibility of U.S.-Soviet cooperation over a "democratized" Eastern Europe—that is, if the United States did not refuse Gorbachev's offer of alliance.

As Gorbachev and Soviet reformers sought to cultivate states such as Israel, Brazil, Argentina, Morocco, Turkey, and South Korea, Soviet hard-liners had hoped to sustain relations with the more radical states, such as Cuba, North Korea, Nicaragua, Iraq, Syria, Libya, and Vietnam, despite the strain most of these states put on Soviet finances. (Here, Gorbachev's 1990 decision to recognize Seoul led Pyongyang to accelerate its drive for a nuclear capability.) The loss of Soviet footholds abroad, however, exacerbated the fears of isolation of neo-

Brezhnev hard-liners who staged the failed August 1991 coup. (Was the show trial and execution—ostensibly for drug trafficking—of Cuban General and war hero Arnaldo Ochoa Sanchez in 1989 at the time of revolutions in Eastern Europe, for example, related to Castro's fears of a coup supported by Gorbachev and the KGB? Or was the CIA taking advantage of the situation?)

With the resignation of Eduard Shevardnaze in December 1990, hard-liners, such as the Soyuz faction of the Supreme Soviet, gained the ascendancy in an effort to block Gorbachev's New Union Treaty and stem secessionist demands within the Soviet Union itself. And yet, despite the tensions over influence in Eastern Europe, Moscow continued at least tacitly to cooperate with the United States in many areas, particularly in regard to Iraq. Moscow, for example, gave its approval in the UN for largely U.S.-led efforts to remove Iraqi troops from Kuwait, at the same time that Soviet Black Beret special forces moved into Vilnius to crack down on demands for secession. (Here, there appeared to be a parallel between U.S.-Soviet cooperation over Iraq and the Soviet crackdown in Vilnius, and the 1968 U.S. bombing of Hanoi and the Soviet crackdown in Czechoslovakia, as well as the earlier U.S.-Soviet pressure on Britain, France, and Israel during the Suez crisis, and the Soviet crackdown on Hungary. In addition, when U.S. forces moved into Panama in 1990, Secretary of State James Baker stated his support for Moscow to intervene in Romania—if Moscow deemed such action necessary!)

Gorbachev's efforts to reform the Soviet empire failed: His reforms of *glasnost* and *perestroika* resulted in the formation of a system of "multiple sovereignty" in the Soviet Union—the deconcentration of central power and the rise of local and republican powers. Prior to the August 1991 coup, the question of the Party's efficacy, issues such as the Chernobyl disaster, plus the Soviet defeat in Afghanistan (plus the local/regional Communist Party leaders seeking to coopt that dissent) led the general population to question the very legitimacy of the Communist Party itself.[19]

As the power of the central ministries was cut back (creating a reaction among the *nomenklatura*), it was the rise of multiple sovereignty with its conflicting and divided claims of authority, combined with the absolute decline of Communist Party legitimacy, which helped to split loyalties within the central leadership, the republics, and the localities (particularly Moscow and Leningrad). The effort to create pseudo-democratic bodies—the Congress of People's Deputies, a restructured Supreme Court, and a new presidency—appeared to parallel failed 1906–17 tsarist reforms "from above." But real power moved from the Kremlin to Lenin's "titular" republics, which began to assert powers previously denied—thus undermining the ability of hard-liners to use force and to seize power. At the root of the domestic conflict was the question of what system of government was to replace the ideologically and materially bankrupt Communist Party. (Over one hundred political parties had been created.)

In addition, the fact that the intergenerational mobility of workers in the middle and professional classes continued to decline[20] led to the questioning of Communist Party authority among the elite, and not merely among groups such as striking miners, and the average consumer upset by higher prices and shortages. Gorbachev's efforts failed to coopt dissent into supporting party efforts; his high moral tone seemed designed to attract supporters of Andrei Sakharov, for example, but these elites failed to be coopted even after Sakharov's release from Siberian exile. To the right, followers of Alexandr Solzhenitsyn's calls for pan-Slavic unity helped undermine Soviet legitimacy as well.

Despite efforts to end the war in Afghanistan, Gorbachev's dealings with Soviet nationalities failed, as he was caught between efforts of national party and state bureaucracies to stop his reforms, and the rise of popular movements which sought more radical change. His attempts to eliminate top nationalist leaders (replacing a Kazakh party chief, for example, with a Russian) in a series of purges in the Transcaucasus and Central Asia in 1985–88 alienated opinion. (Many of these protests had been given CIA support since 1985, as CIA Director William Casey then augmented propaganda efforts to denounce Soviet repression in Uzbekistan and elsewhere.)

By 1989, nationalist forces, who opposed the "federalism" of Gorbachev's New Union Treaty, began to organize; in February of that year, Gorbachev publicly expressed the fear that his reforms would fail if opposed by a mass movement in Ukraine. In September 1989, the Central Committee Plenum on Nationalities rejected options involving either republican independence or confederation. By June 1990, Boris Yeltsin became president of Russia as the Russian parliament declared itself a sovereign republic (as did Kazakhstan in October), leading Gorbachev to attempt to form the New Union Treaty with nine of the Soviet Republics. Gorbachev's New Union Treaty, however, did not provide a mechanism for the republics themselves to work out their disputes; such issues would have been left to the central "federal" government. This was a major fact resulting in Yeltsin's rejection of the New Union Treaty after the August 1991 coup, which was staged at a time so as to block the signing of the Treaty on the 20 August 1991. In many ways, opportunistic former Communist Party leadership through-out the former Soviet empire became "more nationalist than nationalist" in order to coopt such movements led by republican boyars—Boris Yeltsin in Russia, Leonid Kravchuk in Ukraine, and Nursultan Nazarbayev were former Communist leaders (the latter a protégé of Brezhnev).

Domestically, the coup leaders were thus unable to usurp the political influence of Boris Yeltsin. It was fundamentally the formation of multiple sovereignty within the Soviet Union that helped to split the hard-line leadership and resulted in a refusal of members of the KGB and the army to obey the putschist orders. Unlike the Chinese leadership (who were finally able to unify the military to support the Tiananmen Square repression in June 1989), the Soviet leaders were indecisive and unable to use force against their own people.

Rather than permitting Gorbachev's Leninist mix of cooptation and repression to "save" the Union, by August 1991 Soviet hard-liners accomplished by themselves what they themselves most dreaded. Ironically, much as Trotsky used the forces of "dual sovereignty" to bring down the tsarist empire, the rise of multiple sovereignty resulted in the dissolution of the Soviet empire, the central Kremlin leadership, and demise of the Communist Party itself.

6

U.S. Economic Atrophy, Soviet Collapse, and Global Geoeconomic Rivalry

FIVE PHENOMENA NOT CONDUCIVE TO GLOBAL STABILITY

NSC 68 stated that "foreign economic policy is . . . an instrument which can powerfully influence the world environment in ways favorable to the security and welfare of this country. It is also an instrument which, if unwisely formulated and employed, can do actual harm to our national interests . . . it is an instrument peculiarly appropriate to the Cold War." Despite these warnings (which indicated that American national security managers did *not* overlook the importance of economic factors—or so-called low policy—in the formulation of global strategy), the dynamics of American strategic leveraging have resulted in five phenomena not conducive to global stability.

First, the indirect effects of Cold War rivalry (coupled with centralized Soviet inefficiencies) have left the former Soviet empire virtually bankrupt. Prospects of hyperinflation—which has already threatened the stability of Ukraine—have thus been raised. The 1992–93 G-7 plans—what Secretary of State Warren Christopher called a "strategic investment"—have been most reminiscent of the Dawes plan (see Chapter 2) designed in contemporary circumstances to forestall the rise of Russian revanche and to "buy" the peace between Germany and Russia. (The quantity of aid—roughly $43 billion promised but not yet provided—does not yet amount to a new Marshall Plan, which would roughly be the equivalent of $80 billion in 1992 dollars.) Here, U.S. policy has impelled Moscow to accept potentially destabilizing market-oriented reforms; concurrently, Moscow has expected that the reform process will ultimately lead to a closer U.S.-Russian entente and that

Washington will accordingly accept the legitimacy of Russian spheres of influence. As Russian Foreign Minister Andrei Kozyrev put it: "Spheres of influence will manifest themselves in the form of commercial wars. . . When Russia will become a true ally of the Western democracies, it will equally participate in these economic wars.[1]

Second, U.S. emphasis on "burden sharing" has led to the relative rise of Germany and Japan, which have *threatened* to forge new regional economic "blocs" to lessen their market dependence upon the United States, at the same time that they place themselves in position to obtain geoeconomically advantageous real estate. Whereas Germany was more willing to float the U.S. economy throughout the 1960s and 1970s in order to help share the costs of the NATO military burden, Bonn became less willing to do so once the U.S.-Soviet détente broke down in the late 1970s. Then, following the collapse of the Soviet Union, Bonn argued that it could not float the U.S., the EC, the former Soviet Union, the military foray against Iraq, as well as the vastly underestimated costs of German unification. It is also not clear that Japan will continue to float the U.S. economy as it did in the 1980s, as Tokyo attempts to cope with its "Japanese style recession," political scandals, and as it strives to become less dependent upon U.S. defenses. U.S. pressures to open up Tokyo's markets through the Structural Impediments Initiative and "managed" or "results-oriented" trade against Japanese demands that the United States begin to resolve its government deficit must soon be resolved, if tensions are not to disrupt the U.S.-Japanese alliance.

Third, while Germany/Europe and Japan have appeared to be the more immediate threat to U.S. economic interests, the PRC may represent a longer-term concern, as Chinese growth—albeit its highly uneven character—could surpass that of Japan by 2010 assuming a minimum of social resistance. China and the United States have been at loggerheads over trade imbalances, intellectual property rights, and human rights among other issues. The debate over whether to revoke China's MFN status has—in part—been stimulated by U.S. domestic interests, which seek to block Chinese imports, potentially alienating Chinese entrepeneurs (and multinational corporations investing in China), if not further militarizing the Chinese Communist Party elite.

Fourth, the relative atrophy of U.S. economic capabilities, following the 1971 "Nixon shock" and decision to drop out of the Bretton Woods system of monetary management, has meant the end of dollar "diplomacy." Subsequent U.S. foreign-economic policies risked not only destabilizing the Soviet Union, but have also limited financial options available for dealing with crises. Although steps to forge NAFTA may buoy U.S. capabilities in the long term, relative American economic atrophy has weakened the U.S. ability to sustain the allegiance of U.S. allies at the very time that many allies have been augmenting their demands for increased aid and assistance, as well for access to U.S. markets, as conditions for granting U.S. basing rights, for example. Calls for Marshall-type plans for Grenada, Panama, Eastern Europe, the Middle East following the Persian Gulf War in 1991 (including Palestine after the 1993 Israel-PLO peace agreement), as well as for the new Russia and the CIS, have generally been felled by more somber realities.

And last, hopes for a more interdependent global economic system may be foiled by increasing trends toward regional economic groupings. The last minute conclusion of the Uruguay round of the GATT talks in December 1993 can help mitigate the dangers of trade diversion and protectionism, but this fact by itself will not necessarily forestall fierce geostrategic and political-economic tensions on the next economic upswing, as new patterns of trade and investment begin to bypass previously developed or protected sectors (exacerbating regional and domestic tensions), as the former Soviet bloc and PRC attempt to adjust to global market realities, and as new regional "blocs" seek to sustain or obtain prime geostrategic positions and real estate so as to best compete for new markets, access to resources, and trading opportunities.

BURDEN SHARING AND THE ECONOMIC CONTAINMENT OF THE SOVIET UNION

By 1966, the United States saw that its policy of economic embargo on Eastern Europe was largely counterproductive. It was recognized that the Western boycott of Eastern Europe merely reinforced Stalin's diversion of Eastern European trade away from the West. At first, and largely in deference to West Germany, increased trade and aid for East bloc countries sought to isolate East Germany and encourage "polycentrism"—at the same time, however, West Germany quietly supported intra-German trade as a means to sustain an intra-German détente and block East Germany from entering into close arrangements with third states. By the 1970s, West German *Ostpolitik* opened relations with East Germany, and used more overt economic aspects of strategic leveraging to pry East Germany and Eastern Europe away from the Soviet grasp through trade liberalization, joint ventures with East European firms, and German credits and technology transfers. These efforts, involving debt leveraging, ironically extended East European financial liabilities to the West.

In addition to supporting the rapid growth of West Germany and

Japan as economic bulwarks against Communist influence, by 1969–71 the United States also began to extend trade benefits and sales of military technology to the PRC. This was done in the hope that the PRC might force the Soviet Union to prepare for a two-front threat, provide new markets for U.S. trade and investment, and counterbalance European and Japanese influence in Beijing. Great Britain and France had originally opposed the U.S. embargo on trade with the PRC (as did American multinational corporations in the 1950s). In 1957, West European states had abolished the policy of the "China differential" (in which COCOM restricted some 200 commodity groups more than those available on the revised list for Soviet bloc states in 1954). It was only a matter of time for the United States to adopt a similar policy.

The long-term geostrategic and political-economic implications of the relative loss of U.S. hegemony were first realized by the Nixon administration, following the "gold war" with Charles de Gaulle—initiating European efforts to establish a monetary system more independent of the United States. In 1969, following the 1968 recession, the Nixon administration decided that the United States could not afford to sustain the predominant share of the world's defense burden. Nixon's export surcharge on the European and Japanese allies was, in effect, a form of "burden sharing" designed to impel U.S. allies to help pay for the escalating costs of the Vietnam War and the U.S. defense burden, its balance of payments crisis, as well as U.S. social welfare transfer payments. Confronted with a major recession, President Nixon attempted to boost U.S. competitiveness by devaluing the dollar, initiating new international trade negotiations, and opening trade with Communist countries so as to counter West European and Japanese competition for Soviet bloc and Chinese markets.

The general recession in the United States consequently led to a greater interest among both business and conservative labor groups for trade with the East. The 1971 Peterson Report called for a new trade policy with the East; it sought to reverse policies of economic warfare and to grant MFN status for the Soviet Union and export financing for firms doing business with Communist countries. As in 1944–46, U.S. firms were interested in the Soviet Union as a source of raw materials, particularly following the OPEC embargo and threats of future OPEC-type organizations (in bauxite, for example).

Nixon's commercial agreements with the Soviet Union attempted to remove shipping obstacles to trade; increase commerce between the two countries (particularly grain); and settle Soviet lend-lease debt, which paved the way for Soviet access to private credits. By declaring that U.S.-Soviet trade was in the national interest, Nixon permitted the Export-Import Bank to extend loans to Moscow. Ostensibly, Nixon sought a "balanced approach" to Soviet and PRC trade; but his global strategy tilted decisively toward the PRC and against the Soviet Union only in part because of opposition by Congress.

In addition to attempting to control the costs of the arms race by the SALT process, the Nixon-Kissinger strategy of linkage was intended to sustain continued leverage over Soviet conduct through long-term infrastructure projects. In 1973, Nixon had submitted the Trade Reform Bill which enhanced presidential powers to conclude trade agreements, including MFN status, to state trading companies. Nixon, however, had missed the chance to obtain MFN for the Soviets in 1969 (when he opposed liberalization of the Export Control Act); and yet, by 1974, Congress blocked his efforts. The failure to obtain MFN status for Soviet bloc countries has been described as "tragic" for détente.[2] But the extent of the tragedy has only been really understood following the collapse of those economies. Despite the fact that MFN status would have had little effect on the price of Soviet raw materials entering the United States, Moscow regarded MFN as a means to gain important political status. MFN status would have given Moscow greater incentive to improve commercial manufactures for export over the long term.

The 1973 Trade Act finally became law in January 1975, but in watered-down form. This is true as the 1974 Jackson-Vanik amendment to the Trade Act made MFN status for the Soviet Union contingent upon its emigration policy. The Stevenson amendment to the Trade Act also placed a $300 million limit on loans from the Export-Import Bank to firms doing business in the Soviet Union. Richard Nixon subsequently argued that these amendments worked to limit U.S. strategic leverage during the Soviet thrust into Afghanistan, for example.

Toward the end of the Cultural Revolution, the United States began to relax restrictions on trade with China. Soviet trade with China had fallen off nearly 45 times from 1959 to November 1970. (Since 1960, Beijing had complained that they were forced to pay high interest, that the sale of their strategic minerals went to produce Soviet weapons, that Soviet aid merely paid for Soviet military equipment for Chinese use, and that they were forced to pay unequal exchange rates.[3]) Nixon's policy attempted to stimulate U.S. trade with the Soviet Union and the PRC (Pepsi went to Moscow; Coca-Cola to the PRC); he also continued to press for protectionism against American allies. The Sino-U.S. rapprochement risked the alienation of Japan as the reduction of COCOM restrictions began to enhance China's competitive advantage vis-à-vis Japan, and as the Nixon "shock" had been accompanied by a 10 percent surcharge on Japanese exports to the United States.

By 1978, and once again to Chinese favor, Beijing signed a major trade agreement with Tokyo. The Soviets condemned the "anti-hegemony clause," but were unable to obtain a similar pact with the Japanese, who feared that such a pact with the Soviets would prevent them from regaining the northern territories. Concurrently, the 1978 U.S.-Japanese Defense Pact was regarded by Tokyo as a means to guarantee Japanese access to U.S. markets.[4]

In the mid-1970s, both Beijing and Moscow sought better relations with the EC. In 1978, a five-year nonpreferential trade agreement was signed by the EC and China, but negotiations between the Soviet-backed CMEA and the EC stalled. In 1979, at the UN Conference on Trade and Development (UNCTAD) IV Conference, the Soviet Union began to explore ways to enter the world market despite its previous support for the New International Economic Order in the late 1960s/70s. The Chinese won again vis-à-vis the Soviets when they obtained MFN status from the United States in July 1979 (a humiliation for Moscow); Beijing became eligible for Export-Import Bank financing. Both made inquiries about entering GATT as "observers." As pointed out, Moscow refused to accept U.S. conditions dealing with emigration law set by the Jackson-Vanik amendment. Beijing's emigration and human rights policy was not ignored, but instead was quickly dismissed. Chinese leader Deng Xiaoping told President Carter, "If you want me to release ten million Chinese to come to the United States, I'd be glad to do so."[5] (Deng Xiaoping subsequently raised the ante in the 1980s and threatened Secretary of State George Shultz with twenty million emigrants!)

By 1979, Sino-U.S. trade had grown, but fluctuated. After the establishment of diplomatic relations, Foreign Trade Minister Li Qiang agreed to permit U.S. firms to enter into joint ventures with Chinese trading corporations, but also suggested a reluctance to repeat the fate of dependent nineteenth-century China. In September 1979, the Export Administration Act had been originally intended to minimize controls and facilitate licensings of exports to the Soviet Union; in January 1980, however, following the Soviet thrust into Afghanistan, President Carter imposed a grain embargo (opposed by U.S. agri-industry) and suspended licensing of all high-tech (placed on a case-by-case review); of note, he wanted to "establish a difference in COCOM between the Soviet Union and China."[6]

By 1981, following the inauguration of President Reagan, the Sino-U.S. entente weakened because of Reagan's publicly stated support for Taiwan. This permitted Moscow to rekindle trade negotiations with Beijing despite the yet unresolved "three obstacles" to Sino-Soviet rapprochement. At the same time, President Reagan lifted the grain embargo that Carter had imposed, basing his argument on the grounds that grain sales forced the Soviet Union to lose hard currency (the same argument that Dean Rusk had used in 1964 to justify U.S. grain deals with the Soviets), even though domestic lobbying was the more likely factor involved. (Moscow, citing U.S. unreliability and demanding "sanctity of contract" legislation, initially refused to increase grain purchases from the United States—seeking grain from Canada, Argentina, and Australia.) The threat of Soviet intervention in Poland then delayed the signing of a long-term grain agreement in 1981.

The Reagan administration also took a broad interpretation of strategic-economic goods that should be denied the Soviet Union and, in 1981, implemented a top-secret directive dealing with East-West economic warfare. The 1982 Pentagon "defense guidance document (DGP) sought to put as much pressure as possible on a Soviet economy already heavily burdened with military spending."[7] The 1983 SDI initiative was also, in part, intended to strain Soviet resources.

From 1980 to 1982, the United States engaged in major trade disputes over the Western European pipeline and high-tech sales to the Soviet Union (which paralleled U.S.-European strategic-economic disputes in 1962–63). The Europeans argued that they were merely diversifying energy supplies, and not becoming dependent on Moscow. Reagan's actions also resulted in Moscow's favoring some Japanese over American firms. Even staunch conservative Margaret Thatcher opposed U.S. actions, as they affected British firms. In general, U.S. actions served to intensify European efforts to seek political-economic unity through the Single European Act (signed in 1985, promulgated in 1987).

Sanctions against the Soviet Union increased the importance of the China market; yet U.S. investment had not been as forthcoming as the Chinese hoped—in part because of China's own bureaucratic "red tape." The real winners in the new Sino-U.S. relationship with China were really Japan and the EC. In the years 1985–88, the EC became China's second-largest trading partner after Japan (which was increasingly criticized for its trade surplus with China), if Hong Kong, which is to be absorbed into China in 1997, is excluded. In terms of direct investment, the EC, however, fell behind the United States and Japan, again if Hong Kong is excluded; at the same time, China complained that the Japanese were unwilling to sell it high technology. Thus, most importantly in terms of China's modernization program, the EC as a whole became the largest technology exporter to China.[8]

Whereas China looked primarily to Europe for high-technology transfer, the United States and Soviet Union continued to battle for Chinese allegiance through investment and/or trade. As some 80 percent of Chinese military equipment was based upon Soviet designs from the 1950s, and as many factories were also based on Soviet blueprints, renewed Sino-Soviet ties were important for upgrading the Chinese military and retooling industry. In April 1984, the director of China's Scientific and Technological Commission stated that Moscow had promised to sell nuclear reactors to China "unconditionally." In July 1985, Moscow signed a multi-billion dollar trade pact with China, and another major Sino-Soviet deal followed in 1986, which included aircraft and helicopters to China in exchange for consumer goods and food. In competition, in 1985, the United States made a multi-million dollar reactor deal with China, ignoring substantial evidence of China's complicity in Pakistan's nuclear program.

As Sino-Soviet ties warmed, Sino-U.S. ties began to sour by 1987 before the 1989 Tiananmen Square crackdown. Concurrently, U.S.-Soviet ties began to warm in 1985 as stronger trade and financial credits and less restrictive COCOM regulations preceded the Reagan administration's efforts to revive a U.S.-Soviet détente in 1987–88. A 1987 report by the National Academy of Sciences argued that U.S. export controls penalized U.S. exporters more than they hurt the Soviet Union. (At the same time, the report was concerned with the sale of "process control technology" which could enhance Soviet manufacturing capabilities.[9]) By May 1991, COCOM reduced the number of categories of technology permitted to be exported to the Soviet bloc (see below).

During the May–June 1990 U.S.-Soviet summit, the Bush administration agreed to urge Congress to drop the Jackson-Vanik and Stevenson amendments. Yet the Bush administration's decision to sign a new U.S.-Soviet trade amendment, and temporarily waive the Jackson-Vanik agreement in December 1990 (which did permit the Soviet Union to obtain $1 billion in U.S. agricultural credits), was conditioned on the decision of the Soviet parliament to codify emigration law. (The Bush administration's promises may have been designed to win Soviet acceptance of U.S. policy vis-à-vis Iraq.) By May 1991, the Soviet legislature did lift curbs on travel and emigration, but the issue of MFN status had not been resolved as of the April 1993 Clinton-Yeltsin summit. Ironically, as Russia finally made it easier to emigrate, the United States (and Western countries except Israel) made it harder to immigrate—in opposition to a potentially destabilizing influx of refugees from both the east and the south. (Here, Russian fears of the "brain drain" need to be matched by reciprocal Western technical assistance so as to offset the "loss" of "human capital.")

Whereas "democratic" Russia still had difficulty gaining MFN status, China and Ukraine did not. President Bush promised Ukraine

MFN status in May 1992, despite clear resolve by Kiev to commit itself to economic reforms. In 1991 and 1992, President Bush unconditionally renewed MFN status for China with a promise to look into specific violations of Chinese trading practices; Japanese and German firms also pressed for greater trade and investment in the PRC to overcome restrictions placed after Tiananmen Square. (Net foreign investment in the PRC—except in the hotel business—actually increased following Tiananmen Square.) Prior to the end of Bush's term, China appeared to make significant trade concessions involving intellectual property rights and other issues, in part because of Bush's threat not to accept the PRC in GATT. Candidate Bill Clinton threatened to cut off China's MFN status; President Clinton—by late 1993—sought a policy of "constructive engagement"—much like the Bush administration before him (see Chapter 8). At the same time, Congress threatened retaliatory action if China did not open its markets by December 1993—and continued to hold open the threat of cutting off China's MFN status.

THE ISSUE OF COCOM AND DUAL-USE TECHNOLOGY

In June 1992, Washington announced the expansion of COCOM to include CIS and East European states so as to bring the export of computers, machine tools, telecommunications equipment, and measuring instruments, under control. Pushed by Germany since 1990, the purpose was to widen the number of states involved in COCOM management so as to minimize the spread of chemical, nuclear, biological weaponry, and missile technology. At the same time, however, the fact that East European states were also the object of COCOM restrictions might make compliance difficult to implement. In addition, countries like South Korea, Taiwan, Singapore, India, Brazil, and Argentina may demand to become members of COCOM's consultative mechanism. In June–July 1993 President Clinton promised to abolish most COCOM restrictions on Russia. A substitute for COCOM, which could include Russia and the PRC, has been considered—moving the regime from an East-West to a North-South focus. Russian membership in a reformed COCOM is largely dependent upon its ability to control its own dual-use exports.[10]

In addition to core states such as Japan and Germany (the latter has taken the lead in attempting to relax restrictions on the sale of dual-use telecommunications and space equipment to Moscow), many semiperipheral states have also begun a high-tech export offensive. Of twenty technologies listed by the Defense Department in its 1990 "Critical Technologies Plan," at least fifteen are "dual use." Japan is a leader in many of these, but nations such as South Korea have been catching up: In the 1980s, the United States denied as much as 50 percent of South Korea's applications to export U.S. origin technology to third countries.[11] (This fact raised questions as to the long-term implications of potential Korean unification.) Beijing has also entered the high-tech and nuclear market, selling nuclear materiel to North Korea, Pakistan, Iran, South Africa, Algeria, Brazil, and Argentina.

U.S., British, German, French, Swiss firms aided Iraq's nuclear program. Initially, Iran's Islamic regime halted the Shah's expensive nuclear program, but it later restarted it—seeking assistance from Brazil and China; Teheran may possess a nuclear capability by the year 2000. In addition to Russia and China, Germany has been a major contributor of dual-use technology to Iran. Israel, South Africa, and Taiwan have sought nuclear cooperation agreements among themselves, as did Brazil, Argentina, and Iran before the fall of the Shah. NATO ally Turkey purportedly helped Pakistan acquire equipment to enrich uranium.[12]

The breakup of the Soviet Union resulted in an even greater competitive relationship among former Soviet republics and the West in terms of arms, nuclear, and dual-use technology sales. Ironically, Moscow—more so than the European allies—generally supported U.S. efforts to control proliferation—after initially aiding Beijing's's nuclear program. (India may be an exception—India's bomb was made possible by a Canadian research reactor—but both Washington and Moscow sold it questionable amounts of heavy water.) In the 1980s, Moscow threatened not to support the U.S. nonproliferation stance because of U.S.-Soviet rivalry for the China market and the apparent U.S. inability to halt the acquisition of nuclear capabilities (and delivery systems) by Israel, South Africa, and Pakistan, among other states.

In February 1992 Boris Yeltsin issued a Presidential Decree banning trade in a range of strategic goods; by September Russia promised to put export tariffs on dual-use and strategic high-tech. (Nuclear and high-tech export control systems are almost nonexistent in non-Russian republics.) An additional fear is that former Soviet nuclear scientists may sell their services on the open market. The Russians themselves are more worried that their scientists will first look to rival former Soviet republics for positions and then look abroad. Russians counter that U.S. nuclear scientists (as their jobs are reduced from 30,000 to 14,000 by the year 2000) may also put their skills on the open market. In March 1992, "scores of warheads" were reported missing from former Soviet weapons inventories: Mafia groups in Kazakhstan may have provided Teheran with tactical nuclear weapons. By 1994 Bonn reported some 350 cases of the illegal export of plutonium from the former Soviet

Union; Moscow itself reported 900 attempts to gain illegal entry to nuclear installations and 700 cases of nuclear smuggling.

Many of the new exporters (including the PRC, Ukraine, Kazakhstan, and Belarus, in addition to Russia, India, and Argentina) have entered the dual-use high-tech market and have been reluctant to apply full-scope safeguards in regard to nuclear technology. Russia consequently began export offensives in arms, nuclear technology, and other strategically oriented dual-use high tech, such as aerospace equipment—in part because of its rivalry with Ukraine among other states. (The January 1994 U.S.-Russian-Ukrainian agreement stipulates that Ukraine must ship all nuclear warheads to Russia for reprocessing. The enriched uranium will then be sold by a U.S. firm, with profits divided between the three—minus Kiev's debts to Moscow.)

In general the need to expand a company's industrial base through exports has been assisted by the reluctance of governments to place impediments in the way of overseas sales. In addition to Japanese and European violations of COCOM restrictions, the United States itself has been accused of initiating 80 percent of all COCOM violations.[13]

SOVIET COLLAPSE—AND THE NEO-DAWES PLAN?

In February 1992, President Boris Yeltsin warned that a new Russian dictatorship could take power if the West did not assist Russian reform efforts. These warnings did not, however, provide an incentive for investment. After stalling in March 1992, by April 1992 the Bush administration finally agreed to support a G-7 and IMF $24 billion package—a $6 billion fund to stabilize the ruble and $18 billion in aid over the next three years to pay for Russia's balance-of-payments deficit. Congress then sat on the measure—roughly $14 billion in assistance actually arrived. By April 1993, the Clinton administration sought a more massive plan, $1.6 billion in U.S. aid as a "strategic investment" to sustain a pro-Western leadership in power and to encourage the other G-7 nations, particularly Germany and Japan, to promise roughly $43 billion (including assistance not provided in 1992) before the April 25 national referendum took place in Russia. (G-7 aid continues to be contingent, however, on Russian reforms.)

Initially, the United States itself had given the G-7 plans only reluctant support. This was in part because of the unpopularity of foreign aid; financial limitations of the United States itself; the Bush administration not wanting to be seen as taking the first step to aiding a former adversary; disputes involving the repayment of at least $80 billion in former Soviet debt; fears of continued CIS instability as well as the difficulties facing republics to "open" themselves sufficiently to make U.S. investment feasible by implementing stable property, tax, and investment laws; the Jackson-Vanik amendments; plus efforts to pressure Russian troops to withdraw from Cuba and the Baltic states. In addition, the breakup of the Soviet Union reduced the attractiveness of a large integrated market. Critics argued that the West already put as much as $44 billion into the former Soviet Union with few results.

To a large extent Soviet collapse stemmed from the Brezhnev era. The Soviet Far Eastern build-up cost Moscow twice perhaps three times, the cost of its build-up in Eastern Europe.[14] Soviet forces committed to China alone accounted for 25 percent of Soviet defense spending in the 1970s and 1980s; Soviet forces in Afghanistan and guarding Central Asian republics probably added another 10 percent; defenses against a revolt of East Europeans and against the integration of Japanese "self-defense" forces into the American Pacific command probably accounted for an additional 10 percent of the budget.[15]

Concurrently, in its arms rivalry with the United States, the accelerated Soviet military build-up after 1965 meant that defense procurement grew at a rate higher than GNP and that the economy no longer generated the capital stock necessary to enhance the quality of Soviet production, and to raise the level of Soviet technological capabilities, except in the area of military hardware.[16] In the 1960s, Moscow was also confronted with a major agricultural crisis (affecting Russian relations with Ukraine); the fact the Soviet Union became a net importer of grain meant a significant loss of hard currency. While reformers sought to forge an entente with the West as a means to reduce defense expenditure and enhance agricultural and consumer production, the "metal eaters" pushed for heavy industry and a tougher stance toward the West. The oil boom of the 1970s, however, gave the grossly mismanaged Soviet economy an artificial lease on life. It can also be argued that the Western effort to break OPEC cartel pricing also represented an attempt to lower Soviet hard currency earnings.

By the late 1980s and early 1990s (after the collapse of the world oil market during the Iran-Iraq war and search for new reserves), Soviet production in key commodities such as oil and gold production collapsed precipitously. CIA studies of the Soviet economy, however, continued to exaggerate its strengths. In its 1989 report, the CIA estimated that Soviet output was nearly 50 percent of U.S. production and that its military spending was about 16 percent of its GNP. Gross Soviet output was really closer to one-fourth of that of the United States, and military spending was closer to 20–25 percent of its GNP.

Consequently, in order to overcome its tremendous economic difficulties (and sustain its global outreach as much as possible), Moscow began to look both east and west for supports, in addition to limiting liabilities in Eastern Europe, Vietnam, Cuba, and other overseas interests. In early 1991, Moscow looked to South Korea and Taiwan for aid and trade, after being snubbed by Japan. In the 1990s, continuing trends of Sino-Soviet détente, China offered trade and credits to the Soviet Union so as to ensure the latter's stability—indicative of the new "equipoise" that has developed as the PRC's power capabilities have risen relative to those of Russia.

The Gorbachev regime was not entirely responsible for efforts of the Brezhnev era to cover over the system's defects, but such factors as the decline of revenue from the anti-alcohol campaign; fall in the price of oil; expenditure on a rising subsidy bill; cost of the Chernobyl disaster; pressures to spend more on health and housing; high military spending; and the refusal by central ministries to make decisive budget cuts, all contributed to the Soviet collapse.[17] In addition, there was also a deeper structural inability to compete and to adopt new management techniques of the micro-computer and high-tech revolutions.

The botched August 1991 coup additionally accelerated the collapse of the Soviet economy by disrupting internal supply lines by cutbacks from former CMEA allies. A rapidly shrinking tax base and growing welfare payments widened Russia's burgeoning budgetary deficit. Former Soviet republics did not contribute fully, and oil exports fell to half of 1990 levels; gold and precious stones reserves were sold heavily in 1990 to pay off debt (if not stolen or hidden in large quantities to stage a future comeback—though not necessarily under the guise of Communist ideology). CIS economies contracted 18 percent in 1991; a 15–20 percent contraction was expected in 1992 according to the OECD Semi-annual report—deemed a "supply-side depression."[18] Concurrently, by the end of 1992 Ukraine entered hyperinflation. The Ukrainian GDP fell 14 percent in 1992, and about 20 percent in 1993. With the rise in oil prices to close to world levels, heavy subsidies for Ukrainian industries, and efforts to buy off striking miners and disgruntled sailors, inflation in 1992 reached 2500 percent. Kiev's decision to adopt "coupons" helped disrupt the ruble zone, resulting in August 1992 in a two-tier CIS, which was in danger of an overall trade collapse. (Some 80 percent of Ukrainian trade is with Russia.)

In September 1991 (when the new Russia obtained informal membership in the IMF), the G-7 group began work to help the CIS avoid default—then estimated at $77 billion. Sixty billion dollars were owed to the West (mainly Germany, with roughly 5 percent owed to the

United States); $17 billion was owed to Eastern Europe, China, and India. By December 1991, former Soviet foreign debt had risen to $81 billion; Soviet debts to the West thus quadrupled from 1985 to 1989 and could reach about $100 billion by 2000. Russians estimate the debt owed to the former Soviet Union at about $146 billion, but it is unclear how and if (and in rubles or dollars) this debt is to be paid back![19] (At the same time, in 1990–93, some $85 billion in investment was promised in the energy sector alone, ultimately raising prospects of growth.)

Questions arose as to whether the plan represented an effort to thoroughly assist Russian modernization and development. The 1991–92 G-7 plan also did not include an estimated extra $20 billion desired by other CIS states. The G-7 plan furthermore fell considerably short of the estimated $76–$167 billion a year which would be needed to thoroughly modernize and stabilize Russia for the long term. (The West would need to provide yearly $18–$30 billion in direct aid; $15–$50 billion in rebuilding infrastructure, particularly transport; $25–$45 billion to the energy industry to stabilize output, especially oil; $5–$15 billion on modernization of power stations; $5–$10 billion on agriculture and distribution; $5–$10 billion on training and welfare payments to the unemployed; $3–$7 billion on supplying consumer goods.[20])

Russian economic adviser Jeffrey Sachs argued that lack of decisiveness by the G-7 in January 1992 to provide Russia with a $6 billion ruble stabilization fund provoked the slide into higher inflation and budgetary deficits—and helped explain the late 1992 turn to Brezhnev era conservatism. At the time the Bush administration could not coordinate government aid to Russia; it was split as to whether priority should be given to technical assistance, credits, or ruble convertibility. President Bush also put security concerns up front (without reflecting upon the linkage between security and political-economic stability). It was argued that aid should be not be granted before the START talks were finalized. Critics, on the other hand, argued that Russia's own inability to decide on firm monetary and fiscal policies (plus indecision as to whether Ukraine, Belarus, and the Baltic states would remain in the ruble zone) prevented implementation of more substantial Western aid.

In April 1992, Boris Yeltsin refused to accept the first draft of the IMF assistance plan. By June 1992, G-7 and IMF guidelines became less strict—the IMF was to provide an early line of financing ($1 billion) for vital imports; in the second phase, Russia and the IMF were to forge a broad economic reform package to clear the way for more IMF lending; the third stage was to permit Russia to begin using a currency stabilization fund. But the last step could not be taken until other republics decided what currency they would be using, and until an adequate central banking system was established.[21] (By August 1993, Moscow suddenly decided to eliminate pre–1993 rubles so as to force former Soviet republics to choose the ruble as the key currency and to strengthen central bank control.)

By promising to change its property laws and open up its economy, Moscow looked to Western investment—consequently raising fears of becoming "dependent" upon Western firms. Concurrently, however, the lack of a stable ruble and codified legislation, the reluctance to privatize state property and create a market system, plus constantly changing laws, involving investment and taxation, have weakened the prospects of foreign investment aiding Russian development, as has the initial loss of a vast, potentially unified market. Russian populists, hard-liners, and the *nomenklatura* attempted to block the reform efforts by postponing the rise in energy prices, lowering taxes, raising social security and military benefits, and obtaining 200 billion rubles in credits for Russian industry. The effort of Yegor Gaidar's government (under IMF pressure) to suppress government credits to otherwise bankrupt heavy industries failed in May–June 1992, as the power of the industrial lobby grew. The Union of Industrialists represented, for example, an effective lobby group to represent interests of state enterprises. Local government leaders also opposed privatization; large enterprise managers sought to establish highly subsidized industries formed into oligopolistic syndicates that are supported, but not controlled, by the state. Other enterprise managers sought noncompetitive buy-outs that will give them control at bargain basement prices. Additional sociopolitical disputes revolve around the extent of manager and employee ownership and control: foreign and domestic ownership by interests outside the individual firm helps to offset control by the former *nomenklatura*.[22] (Roughly twenty–three percent of all Russian firms had been privatized by December 1992.)

The G-7 plan was also criticized as selling out Russian interests and creating a dependence upon Western multinational firms, of not providing a significant opening to global markets, and of not providing outright grants and low-interest loans. In addition, the plan was regarded as "debt creating" because there has been a net outflow of financial resources from Eastern Europe and the former Soviet Union. In 1992 between $10–$15 billion left Russia—roughly fifteen percent of its GDP.[23] There has thus been a tension between the free-market vision of IMF bureaucrats, and planned political-economic approaches (involving both geopolitical and sociopolitical interests) of Russian bureaucrats (who continued to support inefficient state enterprises with government subsidies). Here the postponement of raising energy prices in the summer of 1992 was in part because of the necessity to calm tensions with Ukraine and other republics dependent upon subsidized Russian energy—in addition to dealing with rivalries for state funds among Russia's still powerful state ministries. By May–June 1993, however, Moscow stated its intention to raise oil prices to near the world level—instigating a political-economic crisis in Ukraine. There has also been intra-West tension between the European Bank of Reconstruction and Development (seen as providing excessive credits and supporting the public sector) and the IMF (seen as restricting growth).

The failure of Gorbachev's 500–day reforms under Stanislaw Shatalin to make key structural reforms of a highly centralized military-industrial complex should have initially lowered Western expectations as to how rapidly (and realistically) Moscow could install a market-oriented economy and a convertible currency—*prior* to the fall of the Gaidar regime in December 1992. Much as the East German experience has indicated, it will take many years to convert state properties and resources to market values. Legal issues involving property rights and privatization, changing laws regarding foreign investments (fears of the West buying up Russian enterprises with worthless rubles) and fears of black marketeering and the Russian Mafia represent domestic factors that blocked the rapid development of a liberal "free" market economy and a fully convertible ruble.

By April 1993, the United States, Russia, and the EC engaged in talks to expand Russian trade; Russia saw East European states gaining an advantage. (In terms of net direct investment, German firms had invested as much as thirty times more in Hungary than in Russia in 1992; and U.S. firms in the first quarter of 1992 had put about three and one-half times more into Poland than Russia.) At the same time, Moscow complained of an EC decision to block sales of cheaper Russian uranium. The Clinton administration proposed $1.6 billion in assistance to Russia as a means to prod the other G-7 countries to grant funding. The latter came up with roughly $21.4 billion in additional assistance to that pledged for 1992 for a total of roughly $43 billion. The 1993 package did include the $6 billion needed for ruble stabilization. But G-7 aid was also to some extent self-serving in that $10 billion went for loans and guarantees for exports to Russian enterprises, for example. The majority ($700 million) of U.S. aid went to credits for U.S. agricultural purchases, though the rest went to encourage small Russian enterprises ($50 million); training for banking and accounting ($95 million); medical supplies ($25 million); plus a mere $215 million to dismantle nuclear weapons. Much of the aid was made conditional upon Russian reforms.

Only after Yeltsin's dissolution of the Russian parliament in October 1993—an action taken in part because of that parliament's voting of excessive credits that could have bankrupted the state—did Bonn promise $5 billion in debt rescheduling—but still tied to Russian market-oriented reforms. (In December 1992, Bonn had promised to reschedule $15 billion out of $80 billion of former Soviet debt after the Kohl-Yeltsin "sauna diplomacy" in the same week in December 1992 that a Brezhnev-era apparatchik, Viktor Chernomyrdin, came to power.) The EU then promised a more liberal trade accord by the end of 1993 and to establish a free-trade area with Russia by 1998. The United States promised to speed up its $2.5 billion aid package. Russia also tightened conditions for membership in the ruble zone: The IMF and World Bank then concluded that the collapse of the ruble zone could save Russia more than $15 billion in subsidies, but concurrently, such an action would exacerbate economic crises in Uzbekistan, Kazakhstan, Armenia, Georgia, and Azerbaijan—as well as Ukraine.[24] Following the rise of revanchist parties in the second Russian parliament (December 1993), Washington pressured the IMF to deemphasize "shock therapy" and to boost funding for a "safety net" for the poor, elderly, and jobless (pressure resisted by the IMF which wanted Moscow to get inflation under control and cut subsidies). Russian Prime Minister Chernomyrdin declared the era of "shock reforms" over. By January 1994, the Paris Group of major creditor countries debated the need for debt forgiveness on Russia's inability to service its $54 billion (out of $85–$90 billion) external debt. Concurrently it was reported that as much as $1–$2 billion a month in capital flight had occurred since the December 1993 parliamentary elections (out of an overall total of $30 billion in 1993).

A RELATIVE ATROPHY

With the rise of core and semiperipheral states, combined with the former Soviet military challenge, the paramount position of the United States atrophied since the period 1968–71. There has been a general "leveling off" and "equalization" of differences between the core and semiperipheral states. At the same time, however, much as the EU has hoped to revitalize Europe through greater political-economic integration, the United States has moved to build NAFTA (which could possibly include states such as Chile). Tokyo forged an Asian Free Trade Zone in 1992. Concurrently it was hoped that a GATT agreement could forestall moves toward trade-diverting and protectionist blocs.

After 1960, the United States sought German assistance to help stem the outflow of gold: An increase in German "burden sharing" was seen in the effort to balance foreign exchange costs with the costs of keeping U.S. troops in Germany. In 1965, the traditional U.S. trade surplus with Japan turned into a trade deficit; by 1971 the United States faced a long-term and burgeoning merchandise trade deficit. As has been well examined, President Nixon ended the Bretton Woods system, suspended the convertibility of the dollar into gold, and imposed an export surcharge "to force the Europeans and Japanese to revalue their currencies against the dollar."[25] The December 1971 Smithsonian agreement thus resulted in a relative decline in U.S. world leadership and hence a compensating need for "economic summitry" among the non-Communist powers. The United States reluctantly accepted the need to adopt a more concerted policy to keep the U.S. and global economy afloat—but only at the G-5 meeting of 1985![26]

In October 1978, President Carter had announced a new restrictive monetary policy designed to protect the dollar—for the first time the United States altered its domestic economic policy in response to international monetary concerns. Yet, just as in 1971, the West German refusal to subsidize the U.S. deficit led the Federal Reserve in October 1979 (in a significant departure from previous policy) toward a policy of managing the size of the U.S. money supply, rather than managing interest rates alone. President Carter could not force Germany to inflate, symbolic of a substantial loss of American strategic leverage. Bonn saw the United States as forcing Germany to accept ill-advised economic policies and readjustment to U.S. budget deficits. From the German point of view, Bonn propped up the United States as well as the EC. (Bonn, for example, financed a major portion of EC nuclear research, as well as U.S. defense costs in Europe.[27]) As German-U.S. tensions went unabated, Bonn not only sought to strengthen the EC, and forge a closer Franco-German partnership, but also to open closer relations with East Germany.

By 1981, the Reagan administration attempted a unilateral "cowboy" policy—a combination of tight monetary policy and high domestic spending (particularly defense spending). Tax cuts and "supply side" economic policy were intended to generate greater capital formation in an effort to meet international competition. Reagan policy, however, did not result in higher private and corporate savings, in part because of leveraged buy-outs that resulted in record corporate mergers (and bankruptcies). By deficit spending, and maintaining a tight money supply resulting in high interest rates, the Reagan administration was able to finance its massive military build-up (and those social welfare programs it could not eliminate or cut) with money borrowed from abroad, primarily from Japan, Germany, and oil-producing states such as

Saudi Arabia. In effect, President Reagan's monetary policy (stemming from the Federal Reserve's 1979 decision to tighten monetary policy) worked as an economic form of "strategic leverage" to assert U.S. influence over its allies (and economic rivals) and attempt to revitalize the U.S. economy by capital inflows from abroad, but at the expense of skyrocketing U.S. debt and initially rising export prices.

By the 1985 Plaza agreement, however, Washington finally realized that the key to global stability meant that G-7 countries needed to coordinate economic "planning." By April 1986, the United States became a net debtor nation for the first time since 1913; yet debt before World War I had largely been placed in national production.[28] Thus during the two terms of the Reagan "peace through strength" policy (including pork barrel military projects), gross public debt actually tripled from $1 trillion to about $3 trillion in 1988, and rose to $4 trillion by August 1992. (The latter debt did not include government obligations of $6 trillion for crop guarantees, farmer and student loans, and government insurance programs. By 1993, the defense dollar represented roughly one-half of all discretionary federal spending— including interest on the national debt and military entitlements.[29])

In terms of foreign "assistance," it was Japan that had provided a substantial fraction of the $100–$120 billion a year that subsidized the U.S. deficit and that was invested heavily in all types of U.S. assets. Japanese finance was essential to stimulate U.S. consumption and assist the Reagan era military build-up. The tilt to Japan can be seen in the fact that in 1979, West Germany had refused to support the U.S. dollar and the Carter administration military/defense build-up, which upset détente and German *Ostpolitik*; Bonn's actions simultaneously raised U.S. Congressional calls for German "burden sharing" at the same time the executive branch feared that Bonn might opt out of the double containment. Thus, by the mid-1980s, Japan had largely replaced West Germany as the prime foreign financial backer of American hegemony— in part as a means to pay for the defense build-up against Moscow. (In the 1980s, Japan bought about 30–40 percent of U.S. Treasury bonds; in effect, the 1985 Plaza agreement made it the world's leading creditor.)

The federal budget deficit, the trade deficit, burgeoning corporate and private indebtedness (a record low of about 2 percent of GNP), and an increasing gap between rich and poor, are all factors that could throw the U.S. and global economy into disequilibrium. Other issues involve a $200 billion bail-out of two thousand bankrupt Savings and Loans companies; the need to fix plutonium reprocessing plants, nuclear reactors, waste dump sites, and to restructure transportation infrastructure. Moreover, some 40 percent of U.S. exports and trillions of dollars of bank loans depend upon developing country solvency.[30]

In addition, the United States may lose its leadership in military innovation because of its declining ability to compete in the dual-use high-tech field, and its decline in the manufacturing sector vis-à-vis its service sector. Innovations are increasingly arising from consumer research and production and then moving toward the military-industrial complex.[31] There is now a "spin-on" effect that is permitting military/consumer dual-use technology to become increasingly available to other states. The root cause of the U.S. relative decline in high-technology, then, is an inability to innovate for the global market which is, in turn, making the U.S. military more dependent on foreign suppliers for key components (as seen in efforts to obtain spare parts during the 1991 Persian Gulf War).

Although the NAFTA and GATT agreements may ultimately help boost U.S. productivity, the dilemma is that the U.S. call for increased "burden sharing" as a means to cut defense costs has also risked alienating key allies, which have demanded that "burden sharing" be accompanied by "power sharing"—meaning the power of concerted decisions. Critics of U.S. defense policy have argued that major savings could occur by reducing overseas deployment. (Costs of U.S. deployment in Europe represent roughly $150 billion in annual expenditure, some 50–55 percent of the defense budget. Costs of Pacific defenses including Hawaii and California have been estimated between $36–$50 billion annually.) In 1992, President Bush proposed lopping $50 billion off the Pentagon budget over five years, in part by unilateral cuts, plus reducing costs of research, development, and production. Further cuts in manpower in Europe can be expected in the mid-1990s under President Clinton, who initially hoped to cut $88 billion from defense by 1997. (In the 1980s, the United States spent roughly 6.5 percent of its GDP on defense; the UK spent 4.7 percent, France 4 percent, Italy 2.4 percent, and Japan 1 percent. Likewise, in 1987, the U.S. merchandise trade deficit was $170.3 billion—roughly 22 percent of the trade deficit was to NATO allies; and 41 percent of the aggregate deficit was to U.S. allies in the Asian Pacific region. Total merchandise trade deficit could reach up to $3.5 trillion or 32 percent of GNP by 1999.[32])

The issue is not merely a question of "guns against butter" in terms of the distribution of domestic resources, however. Rather, relative U.S. atrophy (and the relative decline in technological innovation) weakens the U.S. ability to sustain its "military viability" and overseas political-economic outreach. Inability to sustain open markets and military-technological superiority may make it more difficult to cultivate allies, or else the United States may have to make greater sacrifices (in terms of technology sharing and market access) to sustain those allies. If not eventually boosted by the NAFTA and GATT accords, U.S. options to utilize all aspects of strategic leveraging may remain limited. Accordingly, what is at stake is the U.S. ability to sustain its present alliances—and forge new ones.

TOWARD NEW REGIONAL BLOCS?

In part in response to relative American atrophy, and new markets created by the collapse of the Soviet Union, the world has appeared to be moving toward regional economic groupings or "blocs"— whose formation, however, continues to be tempered by political and economic disagreements, special interest groups, and labor opposition. Threats to form regional blocs to some extent represent bargaining chips to pry open other markets—but such threats could result in trade diversion and closed markets, if no compromise is reached.

Although a European resurgence had been expected following EU economic integration in 1993, the high cost of German unification (along with continued intra-EU political-economic disputes) began to stymie EU recovery and steps toward integration. West German surplus had been expected to rise (from $45 billion to $85 billion by 1992), but the costs of German unification were overestimated. The first all-German government raised taxes by $31 billion. Out of a $255 billion budget, $50 billion went to unification costs. Costs of privatization and accumulated East German debt reached $260 billion to be repaid starting in 1995, not including costs to reform vital rail links between east and west. The 1991 German government deficit was estimated to be about 5 percent of West Germany's GNP (relatively greater than the U.S. budget deficit), and it was expected to double in four or five years.

The focus on the rapid development of the former East Germany created what former German Finance Minister Jürgen Möllemann called a "vicious circle"—failure to spark self-sustaining growth in eastern Germany, undermining a unified German recovery (and indirectly fomenting labor strikes, neo-Nazi protests, and terrorist attacks on refugees and foreigners). In part because of lack of clearly defined property laws and problems of investing in the east, Germany found itself confronted with 2.6 million unemployed out of an 8 million former East German workforce in April 1991. (EC unemployment as a whole hovered at about 11–12 percent in 1992–93.)

In addition, the German Bundesbank complained that Germany can no longer bear the brunt of assistance to the Soviet Union. The

Germans have been the main creditors to the former Soviet Union and East European countries: By 1991 Germany supported 40 percent of all financial transfers of the twenty-four OECD countries to Eastern Europe and accounted for an estimated $29 billion or 34 percent of the $65 billion Western debt to the Soviet Union alone, of which 75–80 percent is covered by an increasingly indebted German government guarantee. Bonn is thus the most exposed Western financial power should the Russian economy collapse. By 1992, Germany was expected to invest to 180 billion DM into Eastern Europe and the CIS, up from 140 billion DM in 1991—but with no self-sustaining recovery in the CIS yet in sight.[33]

Steps by Germany to raise interest rates following the December 1991 Maastricht summit indicate that Europe must follow the German lead. France, Italy, and especially Britain have also been under pressure from growing trade deficits with Germany. Concurrent with the narrow passage of the Maastricht treaty in the French referendum in 1992, Britain and Italy fell out of the European Exchange Rate Mechanism (ERM)—in part because of German actions. The inability of all states to sustain membership in the ERM raised questions as to the possibility of European unity, and led to some speculation about a secret Franco-German deal over a "two-speed" Europe.

The key question is whether Europeans will discriminate against both non-European goods and foreign firms that have invested in Europe. Both the United States and Japan still fear the possibility of a "fortress Europe," resulting in external tariffs and content legislation. This is particularly true in areas of strategic economics if the EC, for example, does carry out proposals to regulate military imports from third countries—mainly from the United States. (After the Thomson-CSF purchase of the Missile Division of LTV, the U.S. Congress also threatened similar legislation in the so-called "Thomson Amendment" attached to the 1992–93 U.S. Defense Authorization Act prohibiting purchase of U.S. defense contractors by foreign government owned firms.) The formation of the Independent European Program Group—an organization of European defense ministers—is to assume the role of negotiating defense collaboration with the United States on behalf of a united Europe.[34] (To counter EC protectionism, the United States in 1990 and Japan in 1991 sought a special accord with the EC.)

Factors such as German unification, and the breakup of the Soviet empire into newly independent states with individual currencies, have thus exacerbated political feuding as to how *deep* and how *wide* Europe should become. The UK sought to keep Europe open to free trade but stall its further deepening and widening. Germany and France, however, began to compete for new markets in Eastern Europe and

Russia. Germany sought the admission of Austria, Finland, Sweden, and Switzerland into the EU—countries which would enhance Germany's political influence relative to France. Except for Switzerland, these states could enter the EU in 1995. Norway might enter later. In 1992, the EC signed association accords with Poland, Hungary, and the former Czechoslovakia; these accords promised EC/EU membership in the long term but did not offer significant trade concessions. (Membership in the European Free Trade Area [EFTA], however, may provide a backdoor for East European countries to enter the EU.) Questions arose over Turkish membership in the EU, however—possibly alienating Ankara.

The passing of NAFTA raised Russian and European concerns that the Clinton administration had made concessions to protectionist interests in the United States in order to pass the agreement; the GATT agreement (brokered by Germany), however, should help mitigate overt protectionism. A "Yukon to Yucatan" trading bloc was thus formed as Canada is to eliminate all tariffs on U.S. goods by 1998, and as the Senate supported the Bush administration's efforts to forge a free trade agreement with Mexico. (1992 election year politics temporarily blocked NAFTA: The Clinton administration sought agreements on labor and ecological standards before pushing NAFTA through Congress.)

Japan threatened to establish a yen bloc in Pacific Rim countries, and established in 1992 an Asian Free Trade Area (AFTA). This action was intended as strategic leverage to open market access in NAFTA and the EC, particularly as the United States began to implement "managed" or "results oriented" trade. Congress threatened to revise "Super 301" legislation. The 1990 U.S.-Japanese Structural Impediments Initiative (SII) was ostensibly designed to augment Japanese imports of American products; but Tokyo generally opposed efforts to liberalize agricultural trade. One dilemma is that Japan, as imports from Southeast Asia have been increasing and U.S. imports have been declining, may well increase imports but not necessarily buy U.S. products. The United States, on the other hand, may not be able to balance its budget and reduce interest rates—hence resulting in a new round of U.S.-Japanese imprecations.[35] NAFTA accords did involve some promises to American special interest groups that might prejudice Japanese and Asian products. If Japan ultimately does find itself at a disadvantage vis-à-vis NAFTA and EU-EFTA blocs, then Tokyo may seek a formal yen bloc in an East Asian Economic Caucus as proposed by Malaysia.[36] On the other hand, as Clinton's November 1993 summit with the Asian Pacific Economic Caucus (APEC) indicated, Washington could play a potential Asian bloc against that of Europe.

Though considered the primary economic "threat" today to the

United States and the EU in certain key high-tech sectors, Japan's predominance could begin to wane as the PRC, Taiwan, and South Korea continue to compete. (A potentially unified Korea, however, may focus inwardly, at least initially.) By 1992, Japanese growth began to stall; the fall of the Nikkei index shook confidence and resulted in a "Japanese-style recession." By the years 2010-20, Japan could lose to predominance to China in GDP. The PRC (plus Hong Kong) could disputedly become the world's biggest economy, as its growth is outpacing Japan, Taiwan, and South Korea.[37] (In 1991 the combined GDP of China, Hong Kong, and Taiwan represented the seventh-largest economy in the world, not counting overseas investments.)

Despite China's wide-ranging problems (and the prospects that it, like the former Soviet Union, could break up), the contemporary focus on Japanese industrial/financial power should not ignore Chinese potential. The Chinese have been obtaining whole petrochemical plants, computerization, automated assembly lines, high-tech manufacturing plants from the West, Japan, and Russia. Since the United States opened diplomatic relations with China, Tokyo opted for the cheaper oil and mineral resources available in China, losing their interest in Siberian development and giving China some elements of strategic leverage against Japan. China is likely to become a major economic rival for Asian markets, once its technology improves, particularly when linked to the infusion of Western and Japanese finance, and once it begins to integrate Hong Kong (1997) and Macao (1999)—if not ultimately Taiwan—into the PRC. With better global marketing, and more sophisticated computerization, the PRC could become a major economic power through international joint ventures, increased exports of cottons and textiles, the shipping industry, arms sales, and better ties with Hong Kong businesses.

Such a probability, however, assumes a minimum number of economic downswings and relatively ineffective political resistance to the "capitalist road." China's burgeoning population, about 1.2 billion, also forewarns of crisis ahead. China's economic success also depends upon conflict between hard-line party members, "new authoritarians," and the "democracy" movements, as well as the growing imbalance between coastal and inland provinces. In addition, the absorption of Hong Kong (1997) may not result in the benefits hoped by Beijing if Hong Kong business moves out, and if the center of trade relations shifts to other regions in Asia, such as Singapore or Bangkok. Though China ranks second, behind Mexico, among the world's non-OPEC oil producers, its oil production has increasingly gone to meet domestic demand. (Major oil finds in 1987 in the Bohai Sea and at the mouth of the Pearl River appeared to reduce Chinese imports; but by 1994–95, China could become a net importer of oil, resulting in a net loss of foreign exchange.) China's demand for oil in the South China Sea, coupled with a quest for unification with Taiwan, plus efforts of the Communist Party to cling to power, could continue to generate tensions in Asia.

The new Russia has been attempting to keep newly independent republics in a single-ruble "commonwealth." Ideally, Russia would like to forge a Russian-Ukrainian "energy-grain symbiosis." The main concern, however, is that Ukraine did not want to bear the burden of Russia's budget deficit or remain dependent upon its oil and gas. Ukraine thus took steps to create its own currency in June 1992, looked tentatively to Iran and Tajikistan for oil and argued that Russian liberalization strategy was inappropriate for non-oil-producing members of the former Soviet Union. Ukraine also sought to convince the EC that it is the only former Soviet republic capable of joining a wider Europe. By September 1992, Russia blocked financial transactions between Ukraine and Russia—an action regarded as likely to deepen the recession in the former Soviet Union as Russian-Ukrainian trade represented 70 percent of CIS trade. By November 1992–January 1993, under pressure from Western lending agencies, Ukraine and Russia appeared to reach a tentative compromise—but still raising speculation of a "two-tiered" CIS as Ukraine refused a Russian-proposed charter on closer political-economic ties leading to a defense alliance. By mid-1993, as it moved into hyperinflation, Ukraine considered—not without political resistance—integrating its currency more closely with the ruble. (Concurrently, Belarus has also resisted moving into the ruble zone.)

Russia, Ukraine, and Turkey have looked to form a Black Sea free trade area. Poland, the Czech Republic, Hungary, and Slovakia formed a Visegrad group in 1991. Turkey, Iran, and Pakistan discussed the formation of an "Islamic Commonwealth" with Kazakhstan and four other former Soviet Central Asian states in 1992. Turkish actions may be intended to gain U.S. and EU concessions, yet a pan-Islamic bloc could alienate India, as the latter concurrently attempts to adapt to a market economy, and project its interests in potential conflict with China, Pakistan, and Iran.

In conclusion, U.S. political-economic relations with Russia, China, Japan, and the EU do not appear capable of complete resolution in the near future, all the more so as each regional grouping possesses its own intramural conflicts. China's 1993 trade surplus with the United States ran to $22.7 billion, almost four times the trade imbalance of 1989. In 1992 the United States threatened up to $3.9 billion in retaliatory measures; Congress placed a 31 December 1993 deadline on

China to open up its markets. (Part of the trade surplus is due to investment from the U.S., Hong Kong, Japan, Singapore, and South Korea investment.) In 1993 China's overall trade deficit reached $9–$10 billion. Japanese-American relations were also tense as Japan's current account surplus with all countries was estimated to reach about $120 billion in 1992, up from the $87 billion record set in 1987. Some 40 percent of Japanese trade was with the United States. The 1993 U.S. trade gap with Japan reached $59.8 billion. (Tokyo argued that its surplus was significantly less than it appeared as U.S. multinational corporate investment represented some 4 percent of Japan's GNP, and if imports of services were taken into account.)

In the spring of 1992, Vice President Dan Quayle hinted that the United States might withdraw substantial numbers of troops if the EC did not moderate or abandon their Common Agricultural Program (the glue that has held the Franco-German agri-industrial relationship together) and work to resolve the Uruguay Round of the GATT agreement in regard to disputes over agriculture and aerospace subsidies (among other issues involving exchange rates, intellectual property rights, U.S. banking access in the EC against EC banking access in the United States).[38] By November 1992, the United States threatened sanctions (initially threatening $300 million, but potentially $3.7 billion) and demanded that the EC and Germany pressure France into an agreement. NATO Secretary-General Manfred Wörner stated that a full-scale trade war would strain alliance unity. The EC and U.S. subsequently reached an agreement in the Blair House accords, but Paris threatened to derail the EC decision until a last minute compromise—brokered by Bonn—was concluded in December 1993. (Disputes over financial services, among other issues, were not resolved, however.)

The last minute conclusion of the GATT talks, establishing a World Trade Organization (WTO), should help mitigate trends toward regional blocs and assist the development of Russia and other CIS states (assuming trade benefits spread globally *and soon enough*) by generating as much as $100–$200 billion yearly in global trade. (Russia and China have been pressing to become observers in GATT and associate members of the European Community—as has Ukraine.) But the process of forging a political-economic entente with the world of former Soviet republics and Chinese "capitalist roaders" will not be an easy task. The instabilities already generated by sectoral and regional restructuring and adjustment, particularly in the former Soviet Union and PRC, but to some extent within the United States, EU, and Japan, combined with fierce political-economic and military-technological competition in the subsequent economic upswing, may exacerbate the chances of conflict.

7

Arms Rivalries and the Quest for Parity

THE SOVIET AND RUSSIAN QUEST FOR PARITY

The Soviet Union did obtain a rough nuclear "parity"—and perhaps a questionable conventional superiority over NATO in the 1970s (resulting in a loss of allied confidence in the U.S. deterrent); but the equipoise of nuclear and conventional war-fighting capabilities began to shift away from the Warsaw Pact in the 1980s, as the United States began to win out on the level of "emerging technologies" which threatened Soviet tank and aerial defenses, for example. Moscow was consequently faced with the choice between a major high-tech modernization and cutting its liabilities and retrenching. It chose the latter.

Whereas Mikhail Gorbachev accepted substantial unilateral and asymmetrical cuts in intermediate-range nuclear weapons (IRBMs) and conventional forces in Eastern Europe as part of a Soviet retrenchment, he refused to accept similar asymmetrical cuts in Soviet central strategic nuclear forces, in particular heavy, land-based missiles with MIRVed warheads capable of launching a first strike. The Soviet military believed that the SS-18 and SS-19 provided deterrence against American first-strike weapons such as the MX and Trident D-5. Hence Gorbachev expressed the refusal to accept "possible disparity" before his 1990 meeting with the U.S. Senate.

In his June 1992 summit with George Bush, Boris Yeltsin radically altered previous Soviet policy even before the START I treaty had been ratified. Yeltsin's position flipflopped in the mere space of a week (from 11 June to 18 June 1992) once Yeltsin stated that he would depart from the position of "ominous parity." He agreed to the elimination of all heavy, land-based MIRVed SS-18s as well as mobile MIRVed SS-24s by the year 2003—a position previously regarded as heresy. Then, by December 1992, Yeltsin rushed the United States into forging a START II agreement, in part to head off the Ukrainian threat to retain nuclear weapons.

In addition to promising radical nuclear cuts (but cuts that would sustain the American offensive potential of its eighteen Trident SLBMs), the Bush administration also promised to study the feasibility of including the new Russia in a joint ballistic missile defense (BMD) project and to consider the possibility of joint military exercises. Here, the spread of dual-use, nuclear and ballistic missile technology led to efforts to find a "technological fix" through "Star Wars," Bush's "Global Protection Against Limited Strikes," and then Clinton's "Ballistic Missile Defense Organization." Initially, joint U.S.-Russian cooperation (plus U.S. allies) would involve development of missile-launching detection mechanisms; more intensive defense cooperation would involve stationing interceptor missiles in several sites—thus requiring a controversial revision of the ABM Treaty.

Through disarmament and the sharing of BMD technology, for example, the new Russia hoped to obtain an entente or alliance with the United States. Whereas the old Soviet leadership hoped to *impel* Washington into an entente—thus Foreign Minister Andrei Gromyko's insistence on sustaining the "principle of parity"—the new Russian leadership has thus far hoped to entice the United States into a defense relationship. If Yeltsin can forge a secure entente or alliance with the United States, then the relinquishment of the "principle of parity" should become a dead issue.

The North Atlantic Cooperation Council (NACC), plus the Clinton administration's Partnership for Peace initiative of November 1993, have been depicted as an "evolutionary process of expansion" in which Central and East European states, Ukraine, and Russia, can all be drawn into a new defense and economic community of nations. At the same time, however, the Partnership of Peace initiative (adopted at the January 1994 NATO summit) does not provide mutual security guarantees. Eventual membership in NATO is to be determined by the nature and scope of a particular state's participation in the partnership (which could entail considerable defense expenditure)—subject to approval by NATO itself. From this perspective, the Partnership for Peace initiative seeks to counter-balance the conflicting interests of former Soviet bloc states and does not necessarily include or exclude any one state from eventual membership in NATO's integrated command.

This fact, in itself, will keep a state leadership guessing as to which side (if either) NATO will take in any specific conflict.

From this perspective, the effort to counter-balance the conflicting interests of former Soviet bloc states could result in the alienation or exclusion of some states to the advantage of others. NATO could not so inadvertently exacerbate regional rivalries. The intent to harmonize equipment, for example, might alienate arms producers from states whose equipment is not chosen, for example. On a deeper level, as U.S. forward strategy that was designed to contain Russia—as well as U.S. allies—has yet to be altered, new forms of allied military cooperation with Russia need to be worked out—if Russia is not to be alienated. Proposals include joint military planning to deal with nuclear proliferation; joint operating procedures to deal with Stealth aircraft and other forces viewed as "threatening" by Moscow; joint naval maneuvers and other confidence- and security-building measures. On the other hand, the Pentagon has feared that Russian calls for close sharing of military technology, doctrine, and operations could permit Russia to obtain a rough parity with the United States in areas in which the United States has traditionally possessed a qualitative advantage.

Concurrently, emerging third powers—either concerned with lack of U.S. or former Soviet security supports or else with the prospects of a U.S.-Russian double containment—may intensify efforts to develop political-military independence (if economically feasible), if not forge new alliances potentially in conflict with U.S. and/or Russian interests. Accordingly, in order to contain Kiev's threats to retain an independent nuclear deterrent, for example, the United States and Russia signed in January 1994 a disarmament pact with Ukraine, mandating that Ukraine eliminate its nuclear arsenal over a seven year period. Should Kiev fail to carry out its pledge to dismantle all nuclear weapons and ratify the NPT, however, the arms reductions promised by START II could well be jeopardized.

DYNAMICS OF THE NUCLEAR ARMS RACE SINCE NIXON

Following the 1968 global recession, President Richard Nixon decided in 1969 to alter U.S. war-fighting doctrine from the ability to fight two and one-half wars to only one and one-half wars, in effect, for war against the Soviet Union, not the PRC. Nixon's calls for greater allied "burden sharing" (following NATO's 1967 adaptation of flexible response) coupled with U.S. military-technological innovations and the nature of the Single Integrated Operations Plan (SIOP) forced greater and greater defense expenditure on the part of Moscow.

Nixon's policy deviated from the tacit U.S.-Soviet security relationship established in 1964, when the two powers discussed the possibility of joint military action against the PRC—resulting in Chinese contingency planning for a major or nuclear war in 1964–65. By 1969, however, when the Soviets took "soundings" as to the possible U.S. response to a Soviet military action, if not a preemptive nuclear strike against China, the negative response led the Soviets to conclude that there was some form of Sino-American collusion.[1]

Following the Soviet build-up of ICBMs and SLBMs in the aftermath of the Cuban missile crisis, Moscow had, in essence, achieved nuclear strategic "parity" with the United States. Nixon and Kissinger still hoped to sustain a relative paramountcy over the Soviet Union—in the area of qualitative and relatively less expensive military-technological advances. Kissinger did not act to ban Multiple Reentry Vehicles (MRVs) and Multiple Independently Targetable Reentry Vehicles (MIRVs). The latter system Moscow shortly developed. Consequently, because of the new MIRV technology and the U.S. intent to circumvent the issue of "forward bases," as well as the desire to prevent British and French forces from being counted in SALT I totals, the Soviets were permitted a larger number of launchers than the United States. Moscow was also permitted 308 offensive SS-18 missiles. SALT I thus limited quantitative launcher deployments: The issues of qualitative innovations were not confronted; and respective forces were counted in terms of launchers. (These issues were not addressed until the START I talks.) As Raymond Garthoff put it, the MIRV decision "was, in retrospect (and to many at the time), a short-sighted judgment."[2]

Consistent with the calls for "burden sharing" was the Nixon administration's decision in 1973 to support secret U.S.-French nuclear collaboration, and to push for greater Anglo-French nuclear cooperation. Presidents Kennedy and Johnson opposed support for French nuclear systems (fearing a Soviet preemptive strike, if not French efforts to draw the United States in a nuclear defense of French interests); Nixon, however, believed that the French *force de frappe* would create greater "uncertainty" in Soviet planning. U.S. assistance to France would also make the French nuclear program more survivable, less expensive (so France could spend more on conventional forces). U.S. nuclear support was also intended to cool French fears of a U.S.-Soviet condominium arrangement following the June 1973 Prevention of Nuclear War and SALT I agreements.[3] In addition, French nuclear weapons could be considered less threatening to the Soviet Union than nuclear weapons in West German hands and could serve to contain German demands for nuclear independence.

Following Nixon's tilt to China, closer NATO and Japanese links with the PRC put the kiss of death on détente in the period 1975–77. The Carter administration's decision to establish full diplomatic relations with the PRC overruled the Joint Chiefs of Staff's recommendation to make the PRC renounce the use of force in the Taiwan Straits as a precondition for establishing diplomatic relations. By forging an alliance with the PRC, Washington hoped to draw off Soviet forces to the east, and thus reduce pressure on NATO. PRC leader Deng Xiaoping argued that Moscow would try to avoid fighting a war on two fronts—but must be prepared to do so.[4] Presidential Review Memorandum (PRM) 24 had warned against the tilt to China and argued that Moscow would strengthen its resolve. PRM 10, however, exposed Soviet weaknesses in Asia, but stated that the United States might not be able to defend the east-west German border. The United States would meet Warsaw Pact forces along the Weser-Lech rivers, losing almost one-third of West German territory, including the cities of Hamburg and Munich.[5] Once the latter fact was revealed to the press—coupled with Carter's decision to cancel the B-1 bomber and the neutron bomb—political pressure for a NATO high-tech build-up augmented.

The decision to forge a strategic relationship with China also necessitated a closer U.S.-Japanese alliance, as the Soviet build-up in the Far East—plus concerns with a potentially stronger PRC—meant a "forward defense" of Japan. Washington thus signed a military cooperation agreement with Japan in 1978, which extended that signed in 1969. The pact asked Japan to uphold mutual defense obligations, particularly vis-à-vis South Korea and Taiwan; it stated (for the first time) that if there were a war in the Pacific, the U.S. and Japanese navies would cooperate (see Chapter 5). By 1979, Moscow was prepared for the possibility of a two-front war with the establishment of a wartime command for the Far East alone; and by May 1980, the Chinese tested their first ICBM.

U.S.-Soviet détente began to thoroughly break down following President Carter's attempt to significantly lower Vladivostok II guidelines, originally agreed to by President Ford in 1974. (The SALT I interim guidelines were to expire in October 1977.) Soviet Premier Brezhnev denounced Carter's proposals to radically reduce land-based MIRVed missiles as "deliberately unacceptable" and argued that American "forward base systems" would be able to threaten the Soviet Union if Moscow were to permit deep cuts in heavy land-based ICBMs. (Not affecting submarine or cruise missile technology, Washington was to forgo development of the MX missile in exchange.) Although Carter and Brezhnev did sign SALT II in 1979, Carter was unable to obtain Senate approval. The refusal of the Senate was not merely a consequence of the Soviet invasion of Afghanistan: The Senate saw the treaty as inherently flawed, as it appeared to give the Soviet Union a significant advantage in heavy land-based MIRVed missiles.

In open opposition to the Nixon Doctrine, the Reagan administration claimed not to restrict itself to any two-, two-and-a-half, or one-and-a-half war strategy. In the spring of 1981, Reagan's Nuclear Weapons Employment and Acquisition Master Plan followed by National Security Decision Directive (NSDD)-13 set the ground work for SIOP–7 (1989). The latter emphasized the contingency of a prolonged nuclear exchange and increased spending on command, control, communication, and information systems (C^3I) to improve reliability and survivability (to last at least 180 days of nuclear warfare). It also emphasized the ability of U.S. weapons systems to survive a first strike. Most provocatively, it sought the capability to strike Soviet command and control systems *at the initiation of a strategic nuclear attack.* These new goals contrasted with the Carter policy, which had previously altered U.S. strategic planning through Presidential Directive (PD)-59 and NUWEP-2 in an effort to deemphasize economic targeting and reemphasize Soviet military capabilities including both nuclear and conventional forces, as well as war-supporting infrastructure. Both Nixon and Carter strategic planning had left an attack on Soviet command and control centers as an open option possibly to be pursued at the later stages of nuclear warfare.[6] Reagan's NSDD-13 remained in effect through the Bush administration—but is to undergo a "fundamental" Nuclear Posture Review by the Clinton administration.

By 1983, the Reagan administration hoped to obtain the largely utopian goal of eliminating the threat from ballistic missiles, through a "vision of the future"—or Star Wars (see discussion below). Star Wars was to be accompanied by a new first-strike capability. The Minuteman with multiple Mark IV warheads, the MX ICBM, and the Trident D-5 SLBM, equipped with earth penetration aids as a means to destroy Moscow's ABM systems, were to be accorded counter-leadership and counter-command and -control capabilities. Cruise missiles were also considered crucial for follow-on-forces attack. Stealth bomber technology and cruise missiles were to be developed in order to attack or retaliate against mobile Soviet systems, such as the land-mobile, single-warhead SS-25s and rail mobile ten-warhead SS-24. Soviet first-strike weaponry included the multiple-warhead SS-19 and SS-18, and the Typhoon nuclear submarine. While the United States began to fear the "window of vulnerability," Moscow concluded that its land-based missiles—which made up 75 percent of its deterrent force—could become vulnerable to a U.S. first-strike attempt once all systems were deployed (particularly if coupled with a Star Wars defense shield). A 1983 CIA estimate stated that Moscow was planning to augment delivery capability by 13–25 percent. By 1993 the Soviet Union was estimated to have produced some 45,000 nuclear warheads—significantly above previous U.S. estimates.

Following the November 1985 U.S.-Soviet summit, which proposed to reduce nuclear arsenals by 50 percent, the terms of the unratified SALT II agreement expired. Although both sides agreed to voluntarily keep within SALT limits, Washington alleged that Moscow had purportedly violated the treaty on several occasions in 1984 and 1985, and thus proposed a policy of "proportionate responses." Thus by May 1986, Reagan decided to exceed SALT II limits—to respond "tit for tat" to purported Soviet violations. Without taking its complaints to the Standing Consultative Commission set up by SALT I to address purported violations, by November 1986 the United States broke out of SALT II by deploying cruise missiles on modified B-52s.

In effect, the threat to break out of SALT II, the NATO nuclear build-up, including Cruise missiles and the Trident SLBM, Star Wars, the expansion of SIOP plans, high-tech conventional arms modernization, plus alliances with China and Japan, were intended to stretch Soviet defenses to the maximum. Yet Moscow initially refused to capitulate: Star Wars in particular was regarded as a major stumbling block to a strategic arms agreement. By the mid-1980s, 80 percent of Soviet ICBM forces with 95 percent of the nuclear warhead inventory of the Strategic Rocket Forces and one-third of Soviet SLBMs were on permanent alert. (The latter contrasted with only 15 percent of SLBMs on alert in the 1960s and 25 percent in the 1970s.) The Soviet Union continued to improve large-phased array radars, harden targets, develop air-, sea-, and land-launched cruise missiles, and other emerging military technologies. Some 4,000 Soviet targets were mobile in 1984.[7]

The START I agreement (finally signed by Moscow in November 1992 prior to ratification by the U.S. Senate) eased tensions somewhat, but still raised the prospects of an arms race in high-tech "gray areas." On the former Soviet side, the START I treaty forced an asymmetrical 33 percent reduction; on the U.S. side, a 19 percent reduction. The treaty permitted modernization of air-launched cruise missiles and short-range nuclear weapons, but cut SLBMs and ICBMs. Both sides continued to possess thousands of tactical nuclear weapons. Unlike the specifications stated by the INF treaty, warheads and missiles could be reutilized.

This fact made missile technology available for use in BMD systems, for example, and thus permitted reuse of missiles for launching into space or for use as targets. In addition, the START I agreement did not cover Stealth technology (see below for START II).

AN UNBALANCED U.S. AND SOVIET RETRENCHMENT

Nixon's China policy was key to meet domestic demands for a cutback in defense expenditure without giving up U.S. commitments to Europe and Japan. From 1966 to 1974, Senator Mike Mansfield had called for 50 percent cuts in U.S. spending for NATO. Congressional demands for NATO cuts led to the Mutual Balanced Force Reductions talks, which continued to stall until the late 1980s for lack of political support. The advent of the Conventional Force in Europe talks (CFE) in the late 1980s finally led Moscow to accept asymmetrical conventional force reductions.

In effect, there were three distinct, but interrelated, rationales for "burden sharing": Senator Sam Nunn's demands for Europe to do more to increase conventional forces to reduce reliance on nuclear weapons, and hence reduce the risks involved in the U.S. commitment to Europe; second, Congresswoman Pat Schroeder's support for burden sharing as "burden shedding" so as to reduce apparent strains on the U.S. economy; third, Zbigniew Brzezinski's views that the retraction from Europe would permit the United States to intervene more readily in peripheral regions, particularly in the Persian Gulf and Middle East.[8]

The issue of burden sharing raised a number of troubling questions. In addition to the question of whether a reduced American defense budget would adequately reassure American allies, another key issue was whether U.S. force reductions would actually result in long-term economic gains if defense cut-backs were accompanied by reduced strategic leverage and access to European and Japanese markets—including arms exports. A third issue related to the reaction of the Soviet Union to "encirclement" should allied military-technological capabilities improve to the point that Europe and Japan could obtain greater political-military independence. (At the same time, both Europe and Japan appeared reluctant to build up forces—in deference to both domestic opinion and Soviet concerns.)

By 1985, President Reagan and Soviet leader Mikhail Gorbachev signed an agreement to eliminate nuclear war as an option; concurrently, significant security- and confidence-building measures were implemented through the Stockholm Conference on Confidence and Security Building Measures in Europe from January 1984 to September

1986. By 1987–89, Gorbachev promised a "Christmas present" involving the reduction of 500,000 troops and 10,000 tanks in Eastern Europe. At the same time, Moscow achieved a rapprochement with the PRC: Gorbachev's July 1986 Vladivostok speech promised the withdrawal of 13,000 troops and 250 tanks, and to pull back 80–90,000 troops from the Sino-Soviet border. China was to cut the PLA by one million troops, and did remove at least 100,000 from the border.

The 1989–90 Conventional Force in Europe (CFE) Agreement (signed November 1990) limited NATO and the Warsaw Pact forces west of the Ural mountains. Moscow made a significant concession by accepting the principle of asymmetrical U.S.-Soviet troop reductions in Europe—235,000 for the United States; 195,000 for the Soviet Union. (The French had initially agreed to CFE talks because if such talks ended with no positive result as did the Mutual Balanced Force Reductions (MBFR) talks, neutralist or pan-nationalist sentiment could augment in Germany—ending the "double containment.")

The CFE agreement also significantly increased the warning time in case of attack from a few days to at least six months, making it structurally impossible to rapidly reintroduce significant quantities of military equipment into Central/Eastern Europe. On the other hand, a rapid attack in the northern theater—NATO's Greenland-Iceland-UK defense gap (GIUK)—was still considered feasible; and Moscow was still regarded as exerting pressure on NATO's southern theater as well in Northeast Asia. At this point, NATO began to revise its strategy of forward defense, and opted for a more "multilateral" approach in which U.S. allies would remain dependent upon U.S. logistical capabilities.[9] After German unification, Bonn discovered secret road and rail networks linking Soviet bases, and seized documents indicating advanced Warsaw Pact contingency planning for a fourteen day offensive throughout all Europe—perhaps most reminiscent of the Imperial German Schlieffen Plan (but utilizing nuclear arms).

The July 1990 NATO pronouncement to use nuclear weapons as a "last resort" in case of U.S.-Soviet conventional force confrontation, then marked a major modification of NATO's strategy of flexible response and "forward defense." The complete review of NATO's strategy in June–July 1990 called for a brand-new U.S.-Soviet political and security relationship involving cooperation between the NATO members and former members of the Warsaw Pact (lobbied for by Bonn). Thus, in the wake of the Malta summit, the Bush administration took some steps, such as inviting Soviet Foreign Minister Eduard Shevardnadze to NATO headquarters, joint inspections of the MX and Trident, Soviet SS-18 and SSN-23 missiles, and proposed an "Open Skies" initiative.

By late 1990, the disintegration of the Warsaw Pact led Moscow to reconsider the CFE agreement. Signs of such a backlash were revealed in allegations of Soviet "cheating" on the signed CFE agreement (moving additional forces behind the Urals), and stalling on the START I accords in 1991. That summer, however, NATO accepted the "legitimacy" of Soviet troop changes as the CFE agreement had been signed before the demise of the Warsaw Pact. Moscow then gave no advanced notice of troop maneuvers during the crackdown on Vilnius and Riga in January 1991—violating CFE regulations and raising serious questions about the ability of weak international regimes to sustain peace. Concurrently, Washington and Moscow both threatened to seek bilateral security pacts with newly independent Eastern European states (the Soviets looked to Romania, for example).

Following the failed August 1991 putsch, questions were raised as to whether former Soviet republics would uphold the CFE agreement. By July 1992, the CFE agreement was signed by former Soviet republics (to be implemented by January 1996), but it left very high limits. Russia was permitted 1,450,000 troops; Ukraine, 450,000; Belarus, 100,000; the United States, 250,000; France, 325,000. Concurrently, the 24 March 1992 Treaty on Open Skies represented a major step for confidence- and security-building in that CSCE member territory (including the United States, Canada, and Russia) is open to overflight—and other nonmember states are invited to join. By October 1993, however, Russia hinted that it wanted to raise force ceilings of the CFE agreement in order to police the Caucasus—angering Turkey among other regional actors.

The situation in Asia was less clear, however, and has resulted in Senate demands to retain and build up military bases in Alaska, despite projected cuts in military spending. In August 1992, Japan estimated Russian troop strength east of Lake Baikal at 320,000; Moscow stated its troop strength to be 120,000. In 1991–92, the United States was initially to cut 135,000 service personnel based in Japan and South Korea. The intention to cut 40,000 U.S. troops from South Korea under a mutual security pact then led South Korea to seek the "Koreanization" of its armed forces and to look closer to Europe for defense ties; South Korea considered developing its own independent military capabilities, including fighter jets, missiles, and submarines to counter potential threats from North Korea, the PRC, and Japan. Secretary of Defense Dick Cheney then postponed most cuts until the question of North Korea's nuclear weapons program was resolved. The American decision to remove tactical nuclear weapons from South Korea (as part of a worldwide stand-down of tactical nuclear arms announced in September 1991) and invite North Korean representatives to inspect U.S. bases, plus

Japanese pressures to link aid to International Atomic Energy Agency (IAEA) inspections, plus the South Korean promise not to manufacture, possess, store, deploy, or use nuclear weapons, were all intended to entice North Korea to abandon its nuclear weapons program and to enter into a new reassociation with South Korea.[10] But by 1993, North Korea threatened to drop out of the NPT. In November 1993, President Clinton warned that "North Korea cannot be allowed to develop a nuclear bomb," but concurrently looked toward possible compromises to avert conflict, including U.S.-Japanese-South Korean aid, the cancellation of U.S.-South Korean Team Spirit military exercises, coupled with U.S. recognition of Pyongyang (see Chapter 9). The option of a preemptive strike against North Korean nuclear facilities was ostensibly ruled out because of Pyongyang's high state of conventional force readiness and ability to rapidly strike, if not seize, Seoul.

TOWARD RADICAL NUCLEAR ARMS REDUCTIONS

Despite the political-military effects of Gorbachev's declaration of "reasonable sufficiency" and significantly advanced warning time given by promised troop withdrawals from Eastern Europe, the Bush administration refused to cut back U.S. defense spending. Secretary of Defense Cheney cited "instability" within the Soviet Union as the major threat to U.S. security; by December 1991 he accused former Soviet republics of continuing to build against the United States. In addition, the August 1991 putsch raised unanswered questions as to who was really in charge of Soviet strategic nuclear forces. At this point, U.S. nuclear contingency plans aimed at more than 9,000 targets with approximately 12,000 warheads. Moscow probably targeted about 7,000 sites in the United States, with about 11,000 warheads. By mid-1992, Kiev threatened to renege on its previous May 1992 agreement to unilaterally destroy all nuclear weapons located on its territory by 1994 (for analysis, see Chapter 8). Ukraine possessed between 2,000 and 4,000 tactical nuclear weapons and 176 long-range strategic nuclear weapons with 1,240 warheads. Of these, 130 launchers had been scheduled for destruction under START I. Kiev also possessed 168 warheads on its 101 heavy bombers. Kazakhstan had 1,040 warheads on 104 launchers, and 320 warheads on its 40 heavy bombers. Belarus had 54 warheads on its ICBMs. Russia had 4,278 warheads on 1,064 ICBM launchers, 2,804 warheads on its SLBMs, and 367 warheads on 122 heavy bombers.[11]

These concerns led the Bush administration to take a number of ostensibly "unilateral" steps designed to reduce some of the nuclear pressures on the former Soviet Union, and to seek to influence the former Soviet republics with promises of financial assistance. In September 1991, the Bush administration took steps to remove nuclear weapons from naval ships (something the navy had wanted for a number of years). The Bush administration also decided to eliminate land-based MIRVed warheads. In 1992, under the Soviet Union Demilitarization Act, Washington also earmarked $303 million (out of $800 million) to help former Soviet republics scrap nuclear weapons. Washington promised Ukraine an additional $175 million—if the latter would ratify the START I protocol and accede to the NPT as a non-nuclear weapons state; Kiev threatened to retain weaponry if it did not receive additional funds. (Russia, Belarus, and Kazakhstan are all vying for limited disarmament funds!) By March 1993, roughly $25 million had been spent in dismantling former Soviet weapons, in part because of Pentagon resistance to a Congressionally-mandated program (using funds originally allocated to the Pentagon) and once administrative costs had been substracted. Furthermore, exactly how Russia planned to dismantle its warheads and store its fifty tons of plutonium in "fort plutonium" remained a Russian military secret.

In January 1991, the Bush administration stated its intention to cut the defense budget by $50 billion over five years by curtailing or cancelling programs such as the B-2 bomber and Seawolf submarine, and by suspending production of most new models after the development of prototypes. Money would go into research, but not as much into development. Further U.S. nuclear arms reductions—such as elimination of MIRVed MX systems and cuts in the Trident D-5 program—were to be made contingent upon efforts made by each of the former Soviet republics to eliminate its multiple warhead capabilities.

While negotiating to eliminate all nuclear weapons in Ukraine, Kazakhstan, and Belarus, the United States also insisted that Russia eliminate all its heavy land-based SS-18s. Initially, Boris Yeltsin, reflecting military fears of losing strategic "parity" by giving up too much offensive capability, stated that Russia would reduce SS-18s by 30 percent, or more, if it obtained concessions regarding American SLBMs. By February 1992, the United States proposed a limit of 4,700 warheads; Yeltsin proposed 2,500, and to halt patrols by missile subs (if the United States would do the same). In effect, the rationale for reducing warheads was as much technical as political: as "Circular Error Probability" increased, fewer warheads were needed to strike targets, down from 4–5 warheads to 2–1.

In his June 1992 summit with George Bush, Boris Yeltsin reversed himself and promised the elimination of all heavy, land-based MIRVed

SS-18s, SS-19s, as well as mobile MIRVed SS-24s, by the year 2003. In effect, such cuts leave Russia without an offensive capability—the SS-18 and SS-19 being primarily offensive, the SS-24, retaliatory. Russia was left with a single-warhead, rail-mobile SS-25. In exchange, the United States agreed to eliminate its fifty offensive land-based MIRVed MX missiles and to cut the number of its MIRVed warheads on SLBMs to 1,750. Both sides promised to reduce the total number of warheads to between 3,000 and 3,500 by the turn of the century. The make-up of respective forces gave 15 percent ICBMs to both sides; 25 percent bombers for Russia and 33 percent for the United States; and 60 percent SLBMs for Russia and 52 percent for the United States.

In October 1992, Russian hard-liners demanded retention of SS-18 missile silos and some SS-19s. Though passing the START I treaty, the Russian parliament expressed misgivings over the agreement, arguing that Russia would lose its cheaper MIRVed first-strike capability (cheaper relative to single-warhead missiles), particularly as Russia was unable to improve its more expensive submarine capability to counter that of the U.S. Trident. By December, Bush and Yeltsin ratified the START II treaty—largely to head off Ukrainian demands to retain nuclear weapons. (Since MIRVed SS-18s and SS-24s are largely produced in Ukraine, their elimination pressures Kiev and eliminates Russian dependency on Ukrainian production; the main facilities for producing single-warhead missiles are in Russia.) By January 1994, the United States, Russia, and Ukraine signed a disarmament pact in which Kiev promised to dismantle all Ukrainian nuclear weapons in a secret step-by-step process over a seven year time-table (Kiev will most likely retain some of its forty-six advanced SS-24s for as long as possible). In addition, Kiev must ratify the NPT treaty (see Chapter 8).

Throughout 1992-93, Russia promised sharp cuts in defense spending, largely in response to economic depression. The former Soviet army of 3.9 million was to be cut by 1.5 million by 1995. (Fears of unemployment and discontentment among army officers and their families helped to delay cuts, however.) The new Russia has, in effect, been using a "disarmament race" as a tactic to achieve an entente with the United States; yet Moscow still intends to retain significant nuclear "defensive" capabilities to counter U.S., European, and Chinese capabilities and is expected to test its own Stealth tactical fighter, for example. The new Russian military doctrine (November 1993) refused to rule out the "no first use" of nuclear weapons. It also stated that Russia could use nuclear weapons against states that did not sign the NPT, or against states that are allied with a nuclear power. As Ukraine had yet to ratify the NPT, it interpreted Russia's new military doctrine as a direct threat. Similarly, the PRC interpreted the Russian nuclear doctrine as "hegemonist" and potentially directed against China's more populous but poorly equipped forces—an interpretation in part aimed at obtaining U.S. defense assistance.

The Bush administration's SIOP (which, in April 1991 was believed to reduce targeting on Central and Eastern Europe by about 1,000 targets) continued to target the Russian leadership. President Reagan's NSDD-13 continued to remain in effect—but to be reviewed by the Clinton administration's Nuclear Posture Review to determine precisely which states should be targeted. By mid-1993 in the effort to shave $88 billion off the defense budget by 1997, the Clinton administration proposed a defense plan permitting the United States to win two nearly simultaneous regional conflicts or "half wars"—ostensibly eliminating Russia as the primary enemy. Critics attacked the plan as not affordable given budget restraints, and as either differing very little from Bush's 1991 plan or as spreading U.S. defenses too thin— particularly if global peacekeeping responsibilities (in regard to Iraq, Somalia, Bosnia, and Haiti) must also be sustained.

Despite cutbacks, European nuclear systems were still considered significant threats to the new Russia. Boris Yeltsin asked for British and French nuclear reductions on his trip to Western Europe in early 1992. In January 1992, French President François Mitterrand proposed that the French and British nuclear deterrents should be extended to cover "all of Europe." By the year 2000, British systems are to increase from 200 to roughly 300 strategic warheads. France is to build down from 524 to roughly 465 warheads. Depending upon finances, Britain is to replace its Polaris missiles with as many as sixteen Trident D-5s on four Trident subs (tying British forces to the United States). France planned to refit six submarines with the M-5 missile (similar to the Trident D-5). Paris also deployed eighteen MIRVed IRBMs in central France. If implemented, the June 1992 Yeltsin-Bush agreement to lower U.S.-Russian nuclear warheads to 3,000–3,500 should reduce some pressure on France and Britain—unless both fear a U.S. or Russian BMD system

States reluctant to trust the security guarantees provided by either the United States, Russia, or else by cooperative international agreements are likely to develop (or retain) their own nuclear systems, if economically feasible. China has shown no willingness to reduce its 300 strategic and 150 tactical nuclear weapons systems. Israel purportedly possesses 50–300 nuclear warheads; India and Pakistan may also possess small numbers of warheads; North Korea, Iraq, and Iran all possess nuclear weapons programs. Both Germany and Japan possess the technological capability to build ballistic missiles and nuclear weapons, but have thus far abided by constitutional restrictions reinforced by the (weakening) double containment. The success or failure of the January 1994 U.S.-Russian disarmament pact with Ukraine could well determine the extent to which nuclear capabilities proliferate on a global scale.

NAVAL AND SUBMARINE POWER

Attempting to fill the geostrategic "void" created by the British withdrawal "east of Aden" and the Gulf region from 1967 to 1971, Moscow sought a shorter naval connection between European Russia and the Far East. (On land, the western and eastern reaches of the Soviet Union were linked by the less efficient and strategically vulnerable trans-Siberian railway, which was double-tracked by 1986.) In addition, the Soviet concern with sea passage through the Suez Canal (blocked after the 1967 Arab-Israeli war), and via the Indian Ocean, meant that the northern sea passage played an increasingly vital part in maintaining Soviet sea lines of communication (SLOC). Concurrently, Moscow intensified its efforts to guarantee naval passage around the Cape of Africa, enhancing the importance of pro-Soviet regimes in Africa. In order to pass through open waters, the Soviet navy has to pass through nine natural "choke points" which made it vulnerable to U.S. forward deployment; in the late 1970s, for example, the Soviets began to build a Sea of Okhotsk–Sea of Japan "maritime province complex" capable of launching submarines without fear of being tracked by the U.S. Seventh Fleet. Moscow also sought to establish bases and *points d'appui* by which it could counter advanced U.S. weapons systems, NATO's position in Turkey, Israeli capability to deny access to the Suez, the Diego Garcia base in the Indian Ocean, among others.

By the 1980s, the Reagan administration argued that in its effort to hurdle the "containment barrier" from the Near East to the Middle East, Moscow had been attempting to encircle Turkey not merely in the Caucasus, Bulgaria, and the Black Sea, but also by means of Syria, the Soviet Mediterranean fleet, ties to Libya, Algeria, and Iraq. Soviet strategy included both sticks and carrots such as increased aid and technical assistance to Ankara. The Reagan administration accordingly exerted its "rights" to penetrate the Black Sea within twelve miles of the Soviet coast to test Soviet naval defenses in March 1986. American "forward deployment"—in part designed to reassure and hence contain U.S. allies—threatened a major confrontation. (Did U.S. actions raise questions in Kiev as to Moscow's ability to defend Ukraine?)

Prior to its collapse, the Soviet Union had been particularly keen on revitalizing its navy in response to the U.S. Navy's forward deployment strategy, and the threat posed by air- and sea-launched cruise missiles, which have made "every major U.S. surface vessel . . . a potential threat to [Moscow's] inner strategic core."[12] The Reagan administration's forward strategy ironically helped to save Admiral Sergei Gorshkov's navy. Thus despite the "new thinking" rhetoric of the Gorbachev regime, Soviet naval commanders pursued the development of aircraft carriers (which Kiev considered selling to the PRC or India). In the late 1980s, Moscow reduced the number of out-of-area exercises and long-range naval sorties to the Indian Ocean. It also reduced aid to states such as Vietnam and Cuba. Russia thus negotiated to remove combat troops from Cuba in September 1992, but retained its electronics intelligence station at Lourdes which provides Moscow with about 75 percent of all strategic information from the east coast to Cape Canaveral. Soviet Northern Fleet operations in the Norwegian Sea were cut by 75 percent from 1985 to 1987. But ironically, in so doing, Moscow tended to concentrate its naval forces closer to Japan and the GIUK defense gap.[13]

The Soviet navy had been regarded as becoming leaner but meaner; the new Russia, however, promised in November 1992 to stop submarine production for military purposes in two-to-three years (perhaps contingent on U.S. Trident cutbacks). The Soviet navy's protective capabilities included longer-range SLCMs, advanced communications, and air-borne early warning systems; they were specifically designed for icy conditions. Soviet advances in cruise missile technology also threatened U.S. seaboards. The Soviet Union had 61 percent of its warheads on ICBMs and 29 percent on SLBMs; the United States had 18 percent on ICBMs and 43 percent on SLBMs; the rest were on cruise missiles, which are harder to detect (particularly if equipped with Stealth defenses), and which are more usable than MIRVed defenses because of their high accuracy (except for the highly accurate Trident II missiles with a payload of 8–15 warheads).[14]

Economic measures took their toll, however, in the 1990s. Sea time was cut; no Russian warships were deployed in the Middle East, Persian Gulf, or Indian Ocean. And no new construction was started in 1992. New Russian naval plans envisioned deploying 45 percent of the Russian fleet in the North Sea, 40 percent in the Pacific, 8–9 percent in the Baltic, and 6–7 percent in the Black Sea. The latter fleet would only possess a minimum defense capability.[15] On the other hand, in early 1992 and April 1993, U.S. and Russian submarines collided in areas purportedly within CIS territorial limits. Though downplayed, the collisions illustrated the point that U.S. forward strategy had not yet been altered. In 1993, the U.S. Navy drafted plans to cut its fleet from 457 ships to 340, but still preserving 12 aircraft carriers (it may be forced to cut to 10)—a far cry from President Reagan's call for a 600-ship navy.

Soviet collapse has largely broken up its integrated military command and SLOC. Former Soviet republics have been in a disputes over control of the former Soviet fleet in the Baltic region, the Black Sea, the Caspian Sea; the port of Vladivostok could become a free port city. Russia had begun to pull out significant parts of its Black Sea Fleet to prevent it from being seized by Ukraine—Russian military insistence on a unified and indivisible nuclear and naval command may result in conflict with Ukrainian efforts to form a more independent fleet not limited to coastal defenses (see Chapter 8). In the Baltic—Tallinn and Paldiski, Estonia (the latter a site of a nuclear submarine training base), Liepaja, Riga, and Ventspils, Latvia (the latter a site of a satellite listening post), are no longer Russian home ports. By November 1993, Russia proposed to leave all its military bases in the Baltic (including its naval base at Liepaja); but it hoped to hold onto an early warning system in Skrunda, Latvia, until it completes a similar system in Belarus. At the same time, however, the military still considers the region part of its integrated command: Hard-line Russian naval commanders have urged an expensive build-up of Kaliningrad—where more than 100,000 troops plus equipment remain.

Despite Russia's promised retrenchment, planned naval forces of China, Japan, South Korea, and India (and other Asian states) appear to be on the rise. A potential conflict of interest may be brewing as the PRC and Japan expand their fleets. As China develops, a larger and more modernized navy has been wanted to protect its offshore oil resources, the economic zones on its coast, and to deter the possible interdiction of its sea lines of communication. China is still largely a continental power; the modernization of its navy had been largely delayed by the Cultural Revolution. Prior to the Iranian revolution, the Chinese had supported the Shah of Iran's naval build-up to counter that of India and the Soviet Union. The collapse of the Shah may have provided an additional impetus for the Chinese to back up Pakistan and Sri Lanka against Soviet and Indian encroachment as New Delhi had begun to assert its regional hegemony from Sri Lanka to the Malacca Strait. Following its rapprochement with Moscow since 1982, Beijing has given priority to air and naval modernization and has redeployed conventional submarines from the North Sea fleet to patrol the South China Sea. As the Chinese navy has thus far maintained a limited "blue water" capability—and has completed only one XIA-class nuclear submarine—its "threat" is primarily regional.

China has possessed the capability to blockade Taiwan—the primary sea line of defense that links Japan to the Persian Gulf. Japan, on the other hand, has thus far lacked protection of larger ships to defend its diesel subs and destroyers to make its self-defense forces more offensive. To effectively be able to counter China's "encirclement," the PRC's navy must be in position to guard the approaches to the Strait of Malacca. In the long term, if Beijing ultimately obtains an adequate second-strike capability, it could take more assertive risks. It has purportedly sought use of naval bases at Myanmar (formerly Burma) and pressed London to retain its naval base in Hong Kong. (London, however, sold the base in 1993 for commercial development—a "unilateral decision" angering Beijing.) In the short term, by extending its logistical capabilities, China will most likely attempt to demonstrate its effectiveness as arms supplier and its reliability as a provider of diplomatic security.[16]

The breakup of the Soviet Union made China's 3.2 million army the world's largest; Beijing has concentrated on high-tech modernization, naval and air power. China's defense budget has increased 50 percent in the period 1989–92, but China's public defense budget represents roughly one-half of all defense spending. It does not include financing for new equipment, or research and development. It also does not include profits derived from arms exports or consumer industries owned by the PLA. China has looked to significant levels of defense cooperation with both the new Russia and Ukraine—creating a rivalry between the two for China's allegiance.

The collapse of the U.S. geostrategic position in the Philippines could also affect the geostrategic relationship between China and Japan—the latter has quietly supported Britain in Hong Kong and has warned against Chinese efforts to obtain an aircraft carrier from Kiev or Moscow. Washington subsequently negotiated with Singapore as a partial substitute for its loss of bases in the Philippines; the United States has also looked for closer military ties to Indonesia and other ASEAN states. Asian states began to seek a new security system in fear that China, Japan, or India (which has hoped to neutralize the U.S. base at Diego Garcia) may seek to fill the strategic no-man's-land created by U.S. and former Soviet retrenchment.

THE INF TREATY

The 1987 INF treaty, followed by significant conventional force reductions, symbolically ended tacit U.S.-Soviet collaboration in keeping Germany divided, even if efforts to double-contain German military capabilities within NATO did not entirely come to an end. Once the United States and Soviet Union had achieved central strategic nuclear parity, both NATO and the Warsaw Pact began to focus on the balance of forces at the so-called theater level. In 1977, Moscow began to deploy SS-20 IRBMs in both Europe and Asia in order to target forward-based systems—such as U.S. lighter delivery aircraft, which were regarded as most capable of delivering nuclear weapons against Soviet targets—and to update SS-4s and SS-5s. In addition, the SS-20 was intended to target European and Chinese nuclear weapons and medium-range bombers as well as U.S.-Japanese forward-based systems.

Concurrently on the NATO side, the year 1977 saw the introduction of "AirLand Battle" strategy which would integrate conventional, nuclear, chemical, and electronic war-fighting capabilities of NATO against the Warsaw Pact. This new strategy involved high-tech and outer-space technology and would utilize a "forward defense" against the quantitative advantage of the Warsaw Pact and the forward deployment of Soviet troops.[17] New "emerging technologies" and "deep-strike" weaponry of the Western forces began to challenge traditional notions of Soviet defenses, deemphasizing the role of tanks, for example, leading Soviet Marshall Nikolai Ogarkov to demand an expensive high-tech build-up. In addition, the 1978 decision to establish formal diplomatic relations with the PRC and to permit the sale of European arms to China was, at least in part, a response to the deployment of Soviet SS-20s in 1977.

By 1979, after the urging of German Chancellor Helmut Schmidt in October 1977, NATO decided upon a "dual track" system of the deployment of 108 Pershing and 464 ground-launched cruise missiles, if U.S.-Soviet negotiations did not result in the withdrawal or destruction of the SS-20. It was argued that the establishment of the U.S.-Soviet central strategic nuclear "parity" had in effect cancelled out the U.S. deterrent; the deployment of the SS-20 was regarded as giving an advantage to the Soviet Union in European and Asian theaters.

After the failure of the 1983 "walk-in-the-woods" proposal of Paul Nitze to reach a compromise, Washington began to deploy cruise and Pershing II missiles. The failure to reach a compromise angered Helmut Schmidt, as Germany had not been consulted. He feared that the United States was not bargaining in good faith, as President Reagan had appointed opponents of détente in arms control and negotiating teams. The Germans were then further angered by the ease with which Reagan and Gorbachev came to a general agreement to eliminate INF missiles in Europe at the Reykjavik summit in December 1986—after having suffered the sociopolitical consequences of U.S. deployment.

Prior to the December 1988 Soviet offer of radical Warsaw Pact conventional arms reductions, the removal of INF forces was seen to hurt NATO's flexible response strategy and erode the principle of extended deterrence. Thus the removal of INF missiles played a role in leading the NATO Monterey meeting in November 1987 to demand the deployment of a new fighter aircraft; add ACLMs to the B-52 and F-111 bomber; modernize Lance nuclear missiles; and deploy cruise missiles on surface vessels and subs. These factors—plus decisions to deploy additional British and French nuclear forces in 1987—raised fears of a build-up of "gray area" systems not covered by the INF treaty.[18]

Fears of an ultimate withdrawal of U.S. forces in response to Congressional budget cuts, and the feared German "drift toward the East," resulted in French efforts to strengthen the British and German participation in all-European defense efforts. In 1987, Bonn and Paris moved to create a joint Franco-German brigade and sought to assure that extended French nuclear coverage would be "automatic" once the Elbe was crossed. Bonn also asked to be informed of French nuclear objectives and hoped that Paris would boost its conventional forces; instead France put more money into its SLBMs.

In April 1987, France opted for a major defense build-up, including four nuclear subs capable of destroying 50–70 percent of Soviet infrastructure, the Hades "neutron bomb," and the mobile S-4 comparable to the Pershing II missile, which had all been scheduled for deployment in the 1990s. Furthermore, by December 1987, France and Britain planned a joint development of a cruise missile (later cancelled). Britain also bought the Trident nuclear submarine from the United States raising Soviet objection to nuclear weapons transfers to U.S. allies. Britain then planned to limit its acquisition to four Tridents. (By 1993, U.S. defense cuts raised fears in London that the Trident program may prove more expensive, forcing cutbacks in Britain's own nuclear program.) Following the razing of the Berlin Wall, many of the European defense programs were delayed or cancelled. But changing perceptions of Russian or Ukrainian intentions—plus the issue of BMD defenses—could alter European plans.

Initially growing confidence in its conventional forces and tactical fighter jets, as well as the development of ALCMs and SLCMs, in addition to the development of the SS-25 and SS-24 deployed in 1987, helped to provide the military (though not political) rationale to bargain away SS-20s and short range systems in return for the elimination of Pershing and cruise missiles. On the U.S. side, the deployment of sea-based and air-based cruise missiles more than made up for land-based IRBMs removed from European turf. Hence the INF agreement was largely a result of political pressures. (The INF treaty only represented 3 percent of the total nuclear arsenals of the two superpowers.) Reagan also used the INF treaty to press the Europeans toward greater "burden sharing" and a conventional defense build-up; the United States was to concentrate on SDI. Unable to sustain the competition, however, Gorbachev decided to head off a high-tech conventional force build-up by cutting Soviet liabilities.

As the "double-zero" option resulted in total German dependence upon short-range tactical nuclear weapons for defense, even the Christian Democratic government of Helmut Kohl officially opted for a "triple-zero" option, which had originally been proposed by East Germany. Short-range nuclear weapons were regarded as weapons of allied strategy to use Germany as a battleground, and "for Germans to kill Germans." Contrary to U.S. and British efforts to sustain the double containment, the Kohl government would not permit the modernization of the Lance tactical nuclear weapon until a new comprehensive defense concept had been worked out by NATO.

As late as February 1988, Reagan Defense Secretary Frank Carlucci urged Bonn to modernize short-range nuclear weapons or else risk the removal of U.S. troops from Germany. By 1990, the Bush administration, in deference to Bonn, finally cancelled the follow-on-to-Lance program and modernization of U.S. artillery shells, in effect, abandoning the U.S. ground-based nuclear deterrent. France, on the other hand, initially decided to produce the Hades short-range tactical nuclear weapons, until deciding against production in June 1992, under German pressure and financial restraints.

On the eastern flank, the 1987 Soviet decision to eliminate SS-20s in Asia was announced only after President Reagan had acquiesced publicly to Moscow's demand that 100 SS-20s remain in Asia as a deterrent against U.S. nuclear forces stationed in Japan and the Pacific, as well as against China's burgeoning nuclear capabilities. (Moscow's unilateral concessions may have resulted from Defense Secretary Caspar Weinberger's threats to station INF missiles in Alaska; President Reagan had already publicly acquiesced to Moscow's demand in May 1987. The Soviets dropped the demand in July 1987.[19]) The Soviet unilateral decision to remove all SS-20s in Asia subsequently tended to weaken U.S. credibility and reassurance in the eyes of both Japan and China, particularly following President Reagan's initial acquiescence and as the SS-24 could substitute for the SS-20.

It was thus by no accident that Beijing decided in late 1987 not to follow the "Japanese model" and begin steps toward greater military spending and political centralization. Following the Soviet decision to dismantle SS-20s in Asia (and on the verge of obtaining border agreements with Moscow), and in response to the Japanese decision to participate in Star Wars and enter into a closer strategic relationship with the United States, Beijing opted to revamp its People's War concept, and adopt a more modern strategy of "flexible response" that integrated tactical and strategic nuclear weaponry with modernized conventional and maritime forces.

THE INF TREATY AND NEW MISSILE STATES

Ironically, the INF agreement meant that China maintained a "quasi-monopoly" on intermediate-range ballistic missiles. And by the turn of the century, it has been projected that some 15–20 emerging powers will possess a ballistic missile capability. Moreover, at least sixteen states may want to enter the missile and high-tech market. Cruise missile technology has become more available and can be developed under the cover of aircraft development; ballistic missiles can be developed under cover of satellite launchers. Guidance systems for cruise missiles could be easier to obtain after 1992, when a global positioning system of twenty-four satellite markers is to start operation.

Hence, in an agreement that corresponded with the 1987 INF agreement, the G-7 countries announced the 1987 Missile Technology Control Regime (MTCR). In the May–June 1990 summit, the United States and Soviet Union subsequently affirmed their support for the objectives of the MTCR. They announced that they were taking measures to restrict such proliferation and would investigate regional initiatives to reduce the dangers of missile proliferation. At that point, the Soviet Union indicated that it would unilaterally abide by rules compatible with those of the MTCR, but then neither the Soviet Union nor the new Russia fully agreed with U.S. policy.

In 1987–88, for example, Moscow had transferred missiles to North and South Yemen, and in 1988–89 it had transferred hundreds of Scud missiles to Afghanistan.[20] Yet despite its own missile sales to the Middle East, Russia has been more vulnerable to missile deployment in that region than China and is particularly vulnerable to attack by former Soviet republics! Ukraine possesses two of the largest missile production facilities in the former Soviet Union (producing SS-18s and SS-24s). (Kiev has considered converting the SS-18 for commercial purposes; Russia has considered the sale of converted SS-20s to South Africa for use in satellite launches.)

In May 1992, a Russian sale of long-range cryogenic engines to India was regarded by the U.S. Senate as a violation of Russia's promises to abide by the MTCR. The U.S. Senate placed a rider on the multilateral aid package for the CIS that threatened sanctions that would make Russia ineligible for U.S. aid. Congress also pressed for sanctions against Indian organizations involved in the proposed transfer of aerospace technology. On his trip to India in early 1993, Yeltsin stated that he would not permit any third power (i.e. the United States) to interfere in the Russian-Indian aerospace relationship—but then backed down under G-7 threats not to provide aid, in effect humiliating Yeltsin, and angering Russian hard-liners (and moderates) who stated that the United States was attempting to sustain a monopoly in aerospace technology.

Lack of PRC membership in the MTCR regime meant that Beijing could sell its East Wind missile to Saudi Arabia in 1988. China was also purportedly involved in missile projects in Pakistan (the M-11 missile), Egypt, Iran, and North Korea. (Ironically, Israel secretly helped modernize the guidance systems of Eastwind missiles sold by China to Saudi Arabia!) By 1992, China "promised" not to augment missile sales, but retracted its promise after the October 1992 U.S. sale of F-16s to Taiwan. North Korea opposed the MTCR regime, and stepped up efforts to export missiles—purportedly to Syria and Iran. A North Korean IRBM could strike Osaka, Kyoto, Hiroshima, Fukuoka, and Kagoshima, and aid in a surprise attack on Seoul. In addition, the Chinese monopoly on IRBMs intensified India's efforts to develop its Agni IRBM and Prithvi short-range missile projects. New Delhi's Agni missile can hit targets in Pakistan from southern India beyond the range of Pakistani nuclear-capable F-16 aircraft and missiles. The Agni missile can also reach key Chinese military and industrial centers and hit Beijing (if deployed in Arunchel Pradesh). Its intent is to dissuade Beijing from assisting Pakistan in case of renewed Indo-Pakistani conflict, as China has deployed missiles in Xinjiang, Tibet, and near Kashmir. Tokyo is scheduled to launch the H-2 long-range missile, which could port nuclear warheads, but has promised to abide by the MTCR regime.

RAMIFICATIONS OF EU STRATEGIC INTEGRATION

From August 1990 to January 1991, Washington removed half of its troops deployed in Germany for deployment in the Persian Gulf. By May 1991, NATO designed a "New Look" strategy stating that two-thirds of more than 300,000 troops were to be withdrawn from West

Europe, and sought to deploy a new 100,000 man-ACE Rapid Reaction Force (ARRF) by 1995—to be capable of rapid deployment within fourteen days. The problem with NATO's new strategy, however, was more political than military: The goals of NATO's intervention force have been ambiguous in "out of area" scenarios in which NATO members are not directly threatened by Russia or third states.

At its Rome summit in November 1991, NATO stated that the new global environment did not require a change in its basic mission. At the same time, however, under heavy pressure by Bonn, NATO also formed the North Atlantic Cooperation Council (NACC), which has attempted to forge greater military, technological, and economic cooperation between NATO and former Warsaw Pact states. (NACC first met in December 1991.) By June 1992, NATO offered to make its forces available to the UN or CSCE for out-of-area peace-keeping and peace-making operations.

In addition, at the December 1991 Maastricht conference on European unity, European states stated their intention to develop the West European Union (WEU) into a force that could "complement" NATO. (A relatively small Euro-force would not pose a problem to NATO-dominated communication, supplies, intelligence, and leadership.) The WEU coordinated European naval forces during the Iran-Iraq war after 1987 and organized forces for the August 1990 conflict with Iraq. Like the Suez and Cuban missile crises, as well as the 1973 Arab-Israeli War, the Persian Gulf War also served as a catalyst for greater European unity.

As the United States was expected to withdraw land-based nuclear and conventional forces from Germany/Europe (decreasing from 225,000 to 100,000—as suggested by President Bill Clinton—to even as much as 50,000–30,000 sometime after 1995), the continental states of France and Germany continued to push for a more autonomous 35,000 troop Franco-German force (discussed since 1987)—derogatively referred to as a "language school"—to be operational by 1995. Here, Paris sought a cross-stationing of armed forces, with German troops stationed in Alsace! France argued that the purpose of the force was to ultimately form an all-European army; Germany stated the purpose was to bind France closer to NATO. Franco-German demands for greater defense autonomy were counterbalanced by the essentially maritime states of Britain and Italy, who sought to assure that any WEU actions must be "compatible" with European obligations to NATO.

In addition, France signaled a willingness to participate in NATO nuclear consultations (on the same grounds as Spain), even though not being a member of NATO's integrated military command. Paris also hoped to participate in NACC. By January 1993, thirty years after the 1963 Franco-German treaty, NATO accepted the integrity of the Franco-German force as a single unit, and Belgium, Spain, and Luxembourg stated the intent to join. Concurrently, the United States formed its own bilateral U.S.-German force, arguing it was more ready for deployment than the Franco-German brigade.

In June 1992, the WEU hoped to bring Greece, Denmark, and Ireland into full membership and to grant Turkey, Norway, and Iceland associate membership. (Like NATO, mutual security guarantees in the WEU cannot be invoked in case of conflict between two members—such as Greece and Turkey. Turkey has been hesitant to join the WEU—seeking guarantees for its regional and economic interests.) The Bush administration opposed the expansion of WEU membership to all EC members by warning that such a development would create a European caucus within NATO that might isolate the United States—and draw European states into new conflicts.

Conflicts of interest have thus begun to emerge within NATO: The question of the constitutional legality of using forces outside NATO defenses plagued both the ARRF and the Franco-German force. In January 1993 the German decision to cut the Bundeswehr from 370,000 to 300,000 troops by 1995—because of the excessive costs of German unification—raised NATO's concern. The decision could cut into NATO's force goals and came at a time when German troops were wanted for UN out-of-area peace-keeping operations. Additionally, U.S.-Russian plans to stage joint military maneuvers on German territory were strongly protested by an ostensibly uninformed Bonn in November 1993.

Moreover, efforts by the former Soviet bloc states to join the EU opened up a potential clash between the EU, United States, and Russia in regard to states within the no-man's-land of former Soviet spheres of influence and security. If permitted to join the EU, Central and East European states would expect to establish a tacit defense relationship with the WEU, and indirectly with NATO. The latter in turn would have to extend its defense capabilities to protect these states. (President Bush, for example, had blocked the sale of advanced aircraft and military technology to Central and Eastern Europe—so as to avert a potential conflict of interest.)

In 1993, Russia warned Poland and Ukraine against forming defense ties; former Vice President Rutskoi proclaimed a Russian version of the Monroe Doctrine—implicitly warning the United States and EU. In late September 1993 at the time of the dissolution of the first Russian parliament, Boris Yeltsin likewise warned against East European states joining NATO—after having hinted that Moscow might accept Polish membership in NATO in August. At the same time Yeltsin did not rule out a NATO partnership with Russia (see also Chapter 8). In November 1993 the chief of the Russian Foreign Intelligence Service, Yevgeni M. Primokov, stated that a NATO expansion eastward would result in a fundamental reappraisal of Russian defense concepts; a restructuration and relocation of the Russian military; increased military expenditure (potentially breaking the budget); plus a related exacerbation of anti–Western sentiment. (Concurrently, an expansion of NATO security guarantees eastward could entail a provocative forward defense.)

In November 1993, the WEU agreed to strengthen ties to Central and East European states, but rejected a Franco-German proposal to offer associate membership. Likewise in November, and in part to contain the possibility of EU expansion, the Clinton administration proposed a Partnership for Peace initiative as a substitute to earlier proposals to enlarge NATO membership. Joint military exercises, political-military consulting and planning, were open to all former Soviet bloc states—but no security guarantees would be granted. Then, in an effort to compensate for the European quest for parity within NATO (and likewise to forestall efforts to forge a separate European defense grouping), the January 1994 summit formally adopted the concepts of a Combined Joint Task Force (CJTF) and of a European Security Defense Identity (ESDI) that are to create "separable but not separate" forces. Immediately after the January 1994 NATO summit, however, Germany announced plans for joint naval and troop maneuvers with Denmark and Poland to be held in September 1994—depicted as contingency planning for a resurgent Russian threat to Lithuania. Concurrently, Washington also announced plans for joint military maneuvers with Poland. Romania, Lithuania, Poland and Hungary were among the first East European states to request membership in the Partnership for Peace initiative. Moscow stated its intention to join in early 1994—but could pose "some basic conditions."

Prior to the crackdown in Tiananmen Square, the WEU sought out defense linkages with the PRC. The WEU had sent three delegations to China prior to 1986. (It has also been purported that France had supplied China with tactical nuclear weapons in the mid-1960s.[21]) If the United States cannot provide the EU adequate reassurance, a tacit Sino-European alliance may come about precisely because of the inability of Europe to develop a more coordinated defense policy in face of a nuclear-armed yet instable Russia—or Ukraine—despite the fact the PRC itself may be instable. Or, more likely, if strong Sino-European ties cannot be forged, then the EU could forge a "plutonium alliance" with Japan. In November 1993 German Defense Minister Völker Rühe called for regular German-Japanese defense consultations.

FROM OUTER- TO INNER-SPACE WEAPONRY

After a heated national debate throughout the 1980s over whether Ronald Reagan's "vision of the future" (which was really initiated in the Carter years) was truly feasible,[22] the Bush administration sought a scaled-down version of SDI called Global Protection Against Limited Strikes (GPALS). The Clinton administration then renamed the project the Ballistic Missile Defense Organization. Initially, the Reagan administration sought a leak-proof defense shield; yet as technological feasibility and cost factors ruled out such a system, a more limited land-based BMD has been envisioned, which has been concerned with the possibility of accidental nuclear strikes or third-party threats. (It is furthermore not clear that BMD systems can effectively counter cruise and Stealth technology, once the emerging powers prove capable of developing such high-tech defenses.)

The Warner-Nunn Missile Defense Act of 1991 called for deployment of a Limited Defense System (LDS), plus provisions for a Theatre Missile Defenses by the mid-1990s for U.S. forces deployed abroad and for use by U.S. allies. In the short term, this meant upgrading the Patriot system (despite its debatable performance in the Persian Gulf War); in the long term, the Warner-Nunn act called for Theatre High Altitude Area Defense by the turn of the century. At the same time, however, the Pentagon may be planning a dual capable system in ground- or space-launched weapons: The 1991 Missile Defense Act called for the deployment of an ABM compliant defense (100 ABM interceptors) as a single system which could expand if the ABM treaty is revised. The GPALS system (expected to be deployed by 1997) was to include an early warning system, and a global anti-missile center to serve as a command post for interceptor missiles. In December 1993 Congress allocated $3 billion for BMD systems—in effect shifting strategy from a unilateral defense of the continental United States under the SDI concept toward a global forward-based defense of U.S. allies and troops abroad.[23]

After August 1991, the new Russian leadership withdrew its overt opposition to SDI. In a UN speech in February 1992, Boris Yeltsin called for a merging of the SDI technology with Russian technology. In effect, Yeltsin's plea represented a call for a U.S.-Russian military alliance (that could incorporate other states such as the EU and Japan). Russia hoped to provide space-scanning radars for the U.S. system. The June 1992 Yeltsin-Bush summit promised to research the feasibility of joint defenses, but Russia still did not commit to amending the ABM treaty. At the same time, the United States did not absolutely renounce its threat to withdraw from the 1972 ABM treaty and to deploy anti-missile weapons without constraints in an effort to force Russian compliance.[24]

Prior to the Soviet breakup, Moscow had been investigating direct energy weapons, lasers and particle beams, and dual-use missile and anti-ballistic missile systems, but it still feared the military and technological spill-over effects that the U.S. SDI program might generate, in addition to the fact that such a system might make Russia's predominantly land-based missile deterrent highly vulnerable. Not able to develop a "Star Wars" system, Moscow threatened to expand its land-based Galosh ABM system beyond the point permitted by the ABM treaty, and also accused the United States of violating the ABM treaty by upgrading early warning systems in Thule, Greenland, and Fylingsdale Moor, Great Britain. In October 1989, Soviet Foreign Minister Shevardnadze admitted that the Krasnoyarsk radar system was a violation of the 1972 ABM treaty; yet Moscow hard-liners stalled on the issue. Secretary of State Baker then granted a measure of legitimacy to the Soviet claim against the two "legal" U.S. radars in Greenland and Britain.[25] After 1991, Moscow has been in a much weaker position. The infrastructure supporting Russia's nuclear deterrent and defense network has been broken up among the former Soviet republics: early warning systems (phased array radars in Latvia, Belarus, and Kazakhstan); facilities for low-frequency communications with submarines (Sevastapol and the Baltic coast); and space-tracking stations (in the Crimea, Kazakhstan, Tajikistan, and Georgia).[26]

The Europeans were generally skeptical as to the feasibility of SDI in averting a theater or tactical nuclear assault on Europe. They believed the expense of the program would result in a division of labor: as the United States spent more money on SDI, Europe would have to concentrate on conventional forces. Europeans also complained that new technologies could probably be obtained through civilian research and development more effectively. The United States also insisted that European firms employ their strengths (lasers, microcomputers, and aerospace technology), thus not helping to develop European technological weaknesses. Europeans tended to see SDI and U.S. technology transfer policy as a means to restrict European capabilities and exports—a form of double containment. This fact forced states such as Germany to opt for alternative security strategies, and led Germany/Europe (despite British skepticism) to develop its own EUREKA program (emphasizing dual-use technologies such as robotics, information processing, telecommunications, biotechnology) and push its own Ariane space program. German Defense Minister Manfred Wörner called on Europe to develop its own SDI program.

Japanese corporate participation in Star Wars since 1986 began to cloud the Sino-Japanese-U.S. relationship even further. Japan's defense spending ($30 billion) was technology intensive and roughly equal to spending by the UK, West Germany, France, and Italy. As it was feared that Japanese links to SDI might ultimately be directed against China (as was the case with the ABM treaty), Beijing thus began to side with the Soviet Union in its denunciation of Star Wars. At the same time, China hoped to benefit from SDI advances through the backdoor of the European EUREKA project—representing an potential link between Europe and China. In the 1980s, China sought to develop nuclear and laser weapons platforms for space. More feasibly, the acquisition of Russian S300 surface-to-air missiles in 1993 could help China develop a comprehensive land-based missile defense system, providing a possible shield either for defense or for attack.[27]

Politically, the Bush administration's limited land-based GPALS system appeared less controversial than the former SDI system, but still raised suspicions. The first major problem was, in order to be effective, the system would necessarily violate the ABM treaty, as the Pentagon admitted. In addition, critics argued that domestic pressure might force such a system to become nationwide, as states other than those protected would seek coverage. Moreover, as Moscow would need to protect itself against more numerous threats from former Soviet republics, Russia would need a more expansive system: thus "even a limited ABM system inevitably would undermine mutual deterrence between Moscow and Washington."[28]

Margaret Thatcher had originally supported the SDI program as a means to gain a technological advantage, and undermine the Soviet ability to compete, but she did not support U.S. efforts to gain strategic superiority. (Both Britain and France feared that Soviet counteractions to adopt a nationwide system would undermine their own nuclear deterrents.) In regard to the more limited land-based concept, the UK argued that it was too early to bring Russia into the new program. London believed that such an offer would strain NATO unity, at the same time that it would transfer high technology to Russia before it was clear that there was no resurgent Russian threat.[29] France, which boycotted SDI, stated the need for disarmament, but also preferred to develop its own European program. Already stung by SDI, Bonn feared that the new Bush proposal would not bring major subcontracts or technology transfer. The Clinton administration's proposals to develop BMD defenses with Japan raised concerns of Japanese techno-nationalists that the U.S. efforts were intended to gain access to Japanese high-technology—complaints similar to the FSX controversy.

The fact that even American allies were not thoroughly integrated into technology sharing through SDI contracts raised questions as to how thoroughly Washington would be able to integrate the new Russia into the Bush administration's BMD program. Some Russian observers argued that the United States had been trying "to isolate [Russia] technologically" and that Washington wanted Moscow to share in the blame for the revision of the ABM treaty in such a way that it would work for a U.S. unilateral advantage.[30] It was argued that the United States and Russia could join in joint maneuvers in space and in some sharing arrangements, but Russia should not delude itself: the United States has never placed its forces under international controls and there was no reason to expect a change. Moreover, in April 1992, when the United States lifted restrictions on imports of former Soviet military technology, including the Topaz-2 space nuclear reactor, the sale of the latter was opposed by Russian critics as potentially aiding the U.S. BMD program.

Furthermore, despite the focus on a limited BMD system, General Colin Powell and Air Force General Donald Kutyna stressed that the primary purpose of SDI systems was to defend against a first strike. As long as either Russia or the United States continues to fear the first-strike potential of the other, negotiations upsetting the ABM treaty and setting new limits on anti-missile deployments may prove difficult, in part because of differing geostrategic considerations, as well as significant differences in U.S. and Russian military-technological capabilities (which largely favor the United States).[31]

Not only was it not clear if the major powers could cooperate in designing such a system, but the issue of U.S.-Russian collaboration thus raised questions as to precisely which third states did, in fact, represent potential threats. In February 1992, Ukrainian President Kravchuk questioned whether the intent of U.S.-Russian collaboration was to defend "against Britain, France, or Ukraine?" States with actual or potential ballistic missile capabilities have accordingly viewed the possibility of U.S.-Russian defense collaboration as a double containment.

8

The U.S-Russian Courtship (1991-?)

THE COLLAPSE OF THE SOVIET ROLE IN THE FIVE-DIMENSIONAL DOUBLE CONTAINMENT

After decades of preaching the necessity to contain—if not roll back—the Soviet empire, U.S. national security managers appeared to be at a loss as to what strategy the United States and the G-7 powers should pursue once the Iron Curtain so suddenly—but not so unexpectedly—came down. Should Washington maintain a general détente with Moscow, or should it forge a more far-reaching entente or alliance? Should the United States support the "democratic experiment" in the new Russia, or should it continue to put pressure on the Russian military-industrial complex, for example? Should the United States sustain a "Russia first" strategy, or should it pursue a more even-handed approach among the CIS states, "counterbalancing" Ukraine and Russia, for example?

The Bush administration tended to take a minimalist approach, giving greater emphasis to security issues, and, as argued in Chapter 6, was slow to press for significant political-economic assistance. The Bush administration's failure to deftly manage U.S.-Soviet relations was best revealed in Secretary of State James Baker's confession to Mikhail Gorbachev in September 1991: "It is only now—after the putsch—that we really understand the difficulties and dangers with which you were confronted daily, as well as the reasons for your tactics, which had disconcerted and alarmed the West, but which were justified in the effort to neutralize the conservative forces in your country."[1]

In March 1992, former President Richard Nixon offered a severe critique of the missed opportunities of Bush administration policy. Nixon thus threatened to raise a debate as to who lost "democratic

Russia" if Russian revanchists ultimately did seize power.[2] While Bush could have taken more decisive steps, steps should have also been taken much earlier to gradually devolve Soviet controls. Nixon himself missed a number of opportunities and is responsible for the tilt to China. The roots of the crisis, however, lie in the failure to think through a truly long-term strategy, particularly in regard to how German unification would ultimately affect the Soviet empire. In short, the breakdown of the former bipolar world order has challenged U.S. national security managers with profound dilemmas: The outbreak of regional conflicts in no longer clearly demarcated spheres of influence and security has tended to aggravate disputes between "minimalists," "activists," and "interventionists" among the elite in major and minor states.

THE UNITED STATES AND HUMPTY DUMPTY (THE FORMER SOVIET UNION)

Ironically, in the aftermath of the August 1991 coup, the American leadership began to look for new ways to piece the former Soviet Humpty Dumpty back together again. Following Gorbachev's failed efforts to form a "federal" New Union Treaty both before and immediately after the August 1991 putsch attempt, the major former Soviet republics attempted to form a new confederal Commonwealth of Independent States (CIS) in December 1991. Initially Washington supported Gorbachev's New Union Treaty. Prior to the botched coup, in the intent to carefully balance the Soviet center and republican aspirations, President Bush warned that the United States would not support the "suicidal nationalism" of Ukraine in his 1 August speech in Kiev. Critics, however, dubbed the speech "Chicken Kiev" because of its ostensible kowtowing to Moscow.[3] Then, even after the botched coup of 19 August 1991, Washington still clung to the New Union Treaty until the president of the Russian Federation, Boris Yeltsin, rejected it and forged his own confederal Commonwealth agreement.

The new CIS did not, at least initially, seek to establish an absolute "equality" or "parity" among the four major founders—the three former Soviet Slavic republics (Russia, Ukraine, and Belarus), later joined by Kazakhstan. In effect, Moscow sought to pressure the former Soviet republics into acquiescing to Russian primacy (as "the first among equals") within the CIS. Ukraine, on the other hand, tended to see the CIS as a "civilized way to divorce." Kiev argued it was best to thoroughly break up the old regime, and then move back toward reconciliation at a later date. It thus pressed for greater political-military-economic independence from Russia itself. (Belarus largely played a role as mediator between Russia and Ukraine—but its policy was split between those who sought to retain tight links with Moscow and the "democrats" who sought greater autonomy. Minsk has tended to fear Kiev more than Moscow—in part because of Stalin's division of Polish territory between the two.)

Kazakhstan was not originally part of the first 8 December 1991 treaty at Minsk among Russia, Ukraine, and Belarus—the states of the "Slavic union." Alma-Ata, along with former Soviet republics except Georgia and the Baltic states, then joined the CIS in late December 1991. Kazakhstan generally remained suspicious of Russian intentions: Northern Kazakhstan is 47 percent Slavic and was claimed by writer Alexandr Solzhenitsyn as part of Russia. On the other hand, Alma-Ata is more fearful of China's irredentist claims to Kazakh territory (which include Alma-Ata itself). The latter has been seen by Beijing as supporting pan-Turk movements (or Uighur independence) in Xinjiang province—some 60 percent of Xinjiang's inhabitants are Turkic Moslems.

Accordingly, the December 1991 agreement of the CIS ostensibly "guaranteed" former inter-republican borders; at the same time, Russia used its strategic leverage to pressure Ukraine, Belarus, and Kazakhstan back into closer accommodation. The new Russian republic attempted to use its economic leverage (cheap oil and other raw materials, nationalization of gold reserves, plus its large domestic market) in an attempt to hold the economic aspects of its former empire together. The Russian leadership sought a stronger political-economic union with Ukraine; the Russian parliament declared the transfer of the Crimea to Ukraine (ceded by Khrushchev in 1954) illegal. In effect, Moscow threatened the use of military force, border revisions, economic sanctions, and the threat of a preemptive nuclear strike against Ukraine if the latter did not comply with its demands.[4]

In addition to roughly three and one-half centuries of Russian predominance (Ukraine originally turned to Russia for protection against Poland), plus the shift of trade from Germany, Austria-Hungary, and the Ottoman empire to Russia from 1914 to the 1930s, the issues that have driven a wedge between Russia and Ukraine include disputes involving nationalization of former Soviet armed forces and materiel, control over former Soviet Black Sea naval forces, claims to the Crimea and the southeast Ukraine, responsibility for the Chernobyl nuclear disaster, prices of oil and raw materials, disclosure and sharing of Soviet assets, Russian nationalization of gold reserves, the formation of separate currencies and issues of foreign debt repayment, "dual-key" nuclear weapons power-sharing arrangements, and Ukraine's long-term determination to build a costly 200–450,000 man army, navy, air force and national guard. In arguing that Soviet defenses formed a strategic whole, Russian military commanders generally opposed any effort to divide their integrated nuclear, conventional, and naval forces.

On the other hand, by promising not to raise energy prices too rapidly throughout 1992, Yeltsin had, in effect, promised to maintain peace with Ukraine and other states that depended upon subsidized Russian energy resources. Concurrently Yeltsin risked the reform process and continued G-7 assistance. The January 1993 bilateral Russian-Ukrainian summit dealt inconclusively with aforementioned issues, including tensions over START I and II. The multilateral Minsk summit then resulted in a two-tiered CIS—with Russia, Armenia, Belarus, Kazakhstan, Kyrgystan, and Uzbekistan as the inner core; Ukraine, Turkmenistan, and Moldova formed the outer core. By June 1993, the former Soviet republics gave up the pretense of maintaining a joint command. Azerbaijan departed from the CIS; Tajikistan and Georgia were in the midst of civil war. (Moscow's "divide and rule" tactics, however, brought the latter states back to the CIS by January 1994.)

On the level of foreign policy, Ukrainian diplomatic recognition of Croatia and Slovenia (in December 1991, prior to official German recognition) already indicated a break with the foreign policy of the Russian Federation, which has had historical ties to Serbia. In February 1993, Kiev opposed Russian efforts to either lift sanctions on Serbia or impose similar sanctions on Croatia. On the other hand, both states appeared to possess a joint policy toward the Dniester republic (constituting Ukrainians and Russians), which has sought autonomy or independence from Moldova. (The latter wants to unite with Romania.)

As an integral aspect of Russian efforts to sustain CIS primacy, Russia also sought to sustain a monopoly over the control of former Soviet nuclear weaponry—with overt American backing. U.S. national security managers regarded it as essential to forestall Ukraine, Kazakhstan, and Belarus from actualizing their threat to retain nuclear weapons. Here, the United States threatened not to grant full diplomatic recognition to those states which did not accept Secretary of State James Baker's "principles." Formal U.S. recognition of Ukraine, for example, was ostensibly dependent on whether Ukraine would live up to the Conventional Force in Europe (CFE) agreement, agree to repay its share of Soviet debts to the West, ratify the NPT, and either remove/destroy nuclear weapons or accept a single, centralized command with Russia in the CIS in a way that would live up to the START treaty, as well as accept CSCE and human rights conventions.[5]

Under joint U.S.-Russian pressures, Ukraine, Kazakhstan, and

Belarus finally did agree in May 1992 to sign the Lisbon Protocol to the START I treaty. The fact that five nuclear states—Ukraine, Belarus, Kazakhstan as well as the United States and Russia—all signed the START I Protocol meant, in effect, that the former three states were able to gain quasi-legitimacy as "nuclear" powers. These states also promised to eliminate nuclear weapons on their territory by the end of the decade, and to abide by the NPT and CFE treaties. (It was not clear, however, that signing the NPT treaty would necessarily mean the adoption of full-scope safeguards.) But here, U.S. diplomatic recognition was extended in December 1991, prior to formal ratification of the NPT treaty by the Ukrainian parliament. At the same time, little was said about adherence to the ABM treaty or even to the MTCR regime.

Ukrainian actions in particular led to concern. In March 1992, Ukraine "temporarily" halted the return of tactical nuclear weapons to Russia, ostensibly in fear that the weapons would not be immediately destroyed and might fall into "hostile" hands. Kiev stated that it would ask for greater international financial assistance to destroy weapons on its territory. Rather than unilaterally cutting all nuclear weapons on its territory by 1994 as originally promised, Ukraine then stated its intent to negotiate with other republics first. Second, Ukraine insisted on technical means to prevent Russia from firing the nuclear weapons deployed on its territory. Third, Kiev wanted to assume jurisdiction over the personnel assigned to strategic nuclear forces on its territory. (In September 1992, Marshall Yevgeny Shaposhnikov, commander of the joint CIS forces, stated that Russia alone should take control over all CIS nuclear weaponry—an action ostensibly achieved by May 1993, but opposed by General Konstantin Morozov of Ukraine; Ukraine counter-claimed that it held the ennabling codes, and owned all nuclear weapons on its soil.)

Unlike Kazakhstan, Ukraine refused to sign a defense pact with Russia. In May 1992 Moscow was able to forge a security pact with Armenia, Turkmenistan, Uzbekistan, Tajikistan, as well as Kazakhstan. As the latter feared Chinese claims to its territory, it moved closer to Russia; it has thus far sought out Russian protection despite its own fears of Russian irredentist claims. On the other hand, Ukraine, Azerbaijan, Kyrgystan, and Moldova all refused to sign a defense pact with Russia. (Belarus argued that the pact violated its constitution, but promised to revise its constitution to join at a later date.)

After ostensibly agreeing to eliminate its nuclear forces, Ukraine continued its search for security guarantees to check Russian claims—looking to NATO, the CSCE, and WEU—as well as Poland and the PRC. Kiev hoped to show that it alone, among the former Soviet republics, was worthy of joining the EC. By signing a friendship treaty with Paris in June 1992, Kiev could avoid accusations of a German-Ukrainian axis; concurrently, Paris could counterbalance both Bonn and Moscow. Ukraine also began to look to the PRC for security cooperation. In early November 1992, in his trip to the PRC, Ukrainian leader Kravchuk stated that he was "ready to start cooperation with China in the military field" (at the same time that he denied intent to sell an aircraft carrier to Beijing). Here, China did not pressure Ukraine to sign the NPT or START I treaties—Ukraine has been regarded by the PRC as counterbalancing both Russia and the West. By September 1993 China gave its diplomatic support for the Ukrainian position on the Crimea and the Black Sea fleet. In return, Ukraine supported the PRC's goal to reunify Taiwan with the mainland—to the opposition of some Ukrainian officials.[6] These actions set the basis for a Kiev-Beijing axis.

The fact that the United States supported Russian efforts to retain a single integrated command under CIS command over nuclear forces thus did not preclude efforts by the newly independent former Soviet republics to gain tacit U.S. and EC/EU support against Russia in exchange for giving up their nuclear deterrent—if they could not obtain joint security guarantees. In effect, threats to retain their nuclear weapons for as long as possible were intended to retain an independent means of defense as well as press their own regional interests; such threats were also intended as a strategic lever to pressure Washington into granting these states greater financial assistance to convert military facilities, as well as to obtain overt security guarantees against potential Russian aggression. Not being able to obtain an overt alliance with the United States did not prevent Ukraine and Kazakhstan from hoping that large scale Western investment in their states would provide a *tacit* security guarantee in case Russia did begin to assert its territorial claims. In addition, President Nursultan Nazarbayev of Kazakhstan stated that Secretary of State Baker had reaffirmed in writing the U.S. commitment to defend the security of NPT signatories in event that the latter were threatened by a nuclear power.[7] Secretary of State Baker subsequently denied that the United States had unilaterally guaranteed Ukrainian or Kazakh security in case of military conflict with Russia. Washington (under German urging) had been willing to consult with CIS states and former Warsaw Pact states through NATO's new North Atlantic Cooperation Council (NACC), but it appeared reluctant to engage in greater defense cooperation with individual CIS members. This fact left individual CIS and East European states uncertain as to whose interests the United States or the EC/EU would support in time of conflict. (After stalling, the Kazakh parliament finally signed the NPT in December 1993, in part due to Russian military contingency plans stating the threat to use nuclear weapons against states that did not sign the NPT.)

In September 1992, prior to the U.S. elections, Moscow threatened to retain some first-strike SS-18 silos and some SS-19s (despite Yeltsin's June 1991 promises for a follow-on-to-START agreement). Moscow also stated that it might call into question its nuclear agreements if Kiev did not sign the NPT. In late December 1992, Russia urged the United States to sign the START II pact—radically reducing nuclear weapons—largely as a means to forestall Ukrainian demands to retain a nuclear capability. In addition, the June 1993 U.S. cruise missile attack on Bagdhad—not authorized by the UN—provided a pretext for Kiev to rationalize retention of its missile force. The same U.S. unilateral action was supported by Moscow to rationalize its own unilateral interventions, but opposed by Beijing.

In January 1993, Yeltsin promised Kiev a guarantee against a Russian nuclear attack if it would ratify the START I accord; yet Ukrainian parliamentarians remained skeptical. As attention given Russian interests tended to alienate Kiev, the Clinton administration vowed to fend off attacks that his administration had offended Kiev more than President Bush did. The fact that Moscow attempted to obtain special authority from the UN to police conflicts (Moldova, Georgia, Tajikistan) in the former Soviet Union in March 1993, plus efforts to block Poland and Ukraine from forging stronger defense and economic ties (a Russian version of the Monroe Doctrine), appeared to justify Secretary of Defense Les Aspin's decision to "turn the page" in U.S.-Ukrainian relations. The U.S. hoped that June 1993 promises of U.S. aid for Ukrainian conventional force modernization and mediation in Ukrainian-Russian security disputes would compensate the storage of nuclear warheads and materials under UN supervision on Ukrainian territory at the same time that such actions counter-balanced Russian pressures. Moscow, however, saw the effort as resulting in closer U.S.-Ukrainian military ties; and argued that UN supervision would release former Soviet nuclear secrets. An angry Moscow then demanded unconditional surrender of all Ukrainian warheads to Russia.

In September 1993, Russian pressures and strategic leveraging, including May–June steps to raise oil and gas prices to world levels, threats to cut off supplies, hyperinflation, and heavy international debt ($2.5 billion to Russia)—plus purported threats of war by Russian Defense Minister Pavel S. Grachev—led Ukrainian leader Kravchuk to acquiesce to a tentative deal with Moscow. The deals involved selling both the Ukraine's share of the former Soviet fleet—as well the return of its 1600–1800 nuclear warheads to Russia, plus Russian leasing of Sevastopol for its navy. Kiev was also to acquiesce to a military union in the Black Sea. In addition to financial and technical difficulties involved, Kravchuk feared that Ukrainian retention of nuclear weapons could provoke a Russian preemptive strike and result in a loss of G-7 supports. Kravchuk stated that Ukraine would retain its forty-six SS-24s, but destroy its SS-19s after START I is signed. In November 1993, the Ukrainian parliament "ratified" the START I treaty—but with thirteen strings attached in essence making full implementation contingent upon cooperative security guarantees. Here, Kiev has hoped to draw Washington, Moscow, and London into a cooperative security pact which would guarantee Ukrainian territorial integrity—once (and if) Kiev signs the NPT as a non-nuclear power. (Washington did promise security "assurances," but not formal security "guarantees.")

Joint Russian and American pressures accordingly led to the January 1994 U.S.-Russian-Ukrainian executive agreement promising total Ukrainian nuclear disarmament. Ukrainian warheads are to be dismantled over a seven-year period and shipped to Russia. The enriched fuel extracted is to be sold by the U.S. Enrichment Corporation and proceeds are to be divided over a twenty year period. Part of the commercial value of the enriched fuel is to be swapped to pay Ukrainian debts to Russia. In addition, Russia is also not to engage in acts of economic warfare against Ukraine as part of the agreement. Kiev is to resubmit the START I protocol and NPT treaty for potential ratification once the new Rada is elected in March 1994. The parliamentary debate is likely to be intense, particularly as Ukraine's very political-economic viability is in question: The feared secession of the eastern or western Ukraine (or the Crimea) could jeopardize Ukrainian stability and promises of total nuclear disarmament—if not the START II pact.

Between July and October 1992, at the same time that the "Civic Union" led by General Alexandr Rutskoi pressed for a Cabinet reshuffle, rumors of a new coup were repeated publicly at the highest level in the Russian government: These fears were based upon the activities of the "Russian Unity" and, in particular, the National Salvation Front, which threatened a "constitutional coup"—unless Yeltsin shuffled his cabinet.[8] In essence, Yeltsin's legitimacy and ability to rule were increasingly being questioned—all the more so as his tsarist-like decrees were ignored by parliament. Parliament threatened to impeach Yeltsin in response to Yeltsin's threats to dissolve the parliament. By December, Yeltsin threatened a national referendum (finally implemented on 25 April 1993) in exchange for sacking the reformist Prime Minister Yegor Gaidar (demoted to presidential adviser) in an effort to dissolve the

Communist-dominated legislature—originally established under Gorbachev. (Former-Communist Party members [86 percent] predominated in the Congress of People's Deputies, which was divided into roughly three blocs: Coalition for Reforms, Civic Union, and Russian Unity.) In the following months, parliament also took control over the Defense and Interior Ministry and demanded formation of an Interdepartment Security Council Foreign Policy Commission designed to coordinate defense, foreign affairs, and intelligence.

At the mid-December 1992 CSCE conference, Foreign Minister Kozyrev issued a scare tactic, warning the West that the new government could ultimately renounce its pro-Western cooperation. By March 1993, the Clinton administration purportedly hinted that the United States would not formally object to Yeltsin's decision to dissolve parliament, but would draw the line at a military crackdown. By April 1993, emergency G-7 assistance promised before the national referendum was intended as a "strategic investment" to help a pro-Western leadership sustain power; at the same time, Yeltsin ironically obtained support from Ukrainian leader Kravchuk, who, in essence, saw Yeltsin as the lesser of evils—despite the unresolved disputes between Kiev and Moscow. The April 1993 referendum, which gave Yeltsin a 58.7 percent vote of confidence with 53 percent backing radical reforms, helped provide a certain measure of legitimacy to Yeltsin's government.

In September–October 1993 Yeltsin moved to crackdown on a recalcitrant Russian Parliament using former KGB forces to smash former Vice President Rutskoi's *pronunciamento*. Concurrently, on 30 September, Yeltsin and Foreign Minister Kozyrev warned NATO against its expansion eastward to include Poland, the Czech Republic, and Slovakia, if not the Baltic states and Bulgaria. Having hinted in August 1993 that Moscow might accept Polish membership in NATO, Yeltsin ostensibly flipflopped and argued that NATO expansion would not be in conformity with the 1990 Russo-German Treaty of Good Neighborliness, Partnership, and Cooperation dealing with German unification (see Chapter 5). But he also stated that NATO should consult with Moscow first before drawing third partners into new security arrangements. In January 1994, Foreign Minister Kozyrev then called for a NATO-Russian "system of overlapping security guarantees."

The general unpopularity of Yeltsin's government was shown following the December 1993 parliamentary elections which gave a coalition of anti-reformists a majority of seats in the Duma. Yeltsin subsequently promised to delay cutbacks in military personnel, increase state credits to industries, sought to place controls over banks to stall capital flight (which increased significantly after the December 1993 elections) and intensified steps to dampen claims to regional autonomy. Yeltsin called for greater unity among the four major reform-oriented parties to check a "red-brown" coalition.[9] In asserting Russian primacy/hegemony (if not dominance over lesser states), Moscow began to press its interests over former Soviet spheres of influence and security in an effort to preclude both Western "encirclement" *and* prevent the disaggregation of Russia itself—concurrently drawing the Russian military into the domestic and international policy-making process.

GERMANY/EUROPE

German-Russian relations are really a mix of conflict and cooperation. On the one hand, Russia needed German finance, technology, and investment; on the other hand, Russia feared that German/European competition might "annex" former Soviet spheres of interest and security. Here, Bonn overtly supported demands for Ukrainian and Kazakh independence; and after the Soviet collapse German Foreign Minister Hans-Dietrich Genscher visited both Kiev and Alma-Ata before visiting Gorbachev in October 1991. Gorbachev consequently warned Genscher against an early recognition of the former Soviet republics because of the lack of legally defined borders (such as the Donbass and the Crimea) fixed by the local Soviets; Gorbachev viewed Genscher's actions as "negligent."[10] Moscow continued to be concerned with perceived German irredentist claims to Kaliningrad as well as political-economic ties to Ukraine.

Bonn promptly recognized Baltic state independence and pushed for Slovenian and Croatian independence, contrary to the more cautious U.S., Russian, and EC policy. It was feared that premature recognition might encourage other secessionist movements, if not result in a generalized Balkan war. By August 1992 (following Genscher's retirement), Germany opted to provide a destroyer and three reconaissance planes to assist a WEU naval blockade of Serbia without settling the constitutional question of whether German forces could legally be deployed in out-of-area operations. The opposition Social Democrats questioned the constitutionality of the action, and opposed the "sneaking movement toward combat missions by German military around the world."[11] Ironically, while initially in support of maintaining the Yugoslav federation, France, for example, subsequently advocated a more interventionist stance to halt Serbia, largely in order to assert political-military leadership over Germany and the extension of German influence in the Balkans.

By December 1992, Germany expressed willingness to send troops to Somalia, but it was initially reluctant to send Germans for UN missions in the former Yugoslavia in deference to Russia, and fear of provocating accusations of renewed German militarism. By April 1993, however, German blue helmets were sent to Bosnia. Russian pan-nationalists argued that Germany (through Hungary) was supporting Croatian interests against pro-Russian Serbia, and that Germany was seeking maritime outlets in the Adriatic. From Bonn's perspective, German participation in UN actions was intended to prove German "parity" as a future member of the UN Security Council.

German actions taken after the December 1991 Maastricht Conference on European unity indicated a willingness on the part of Bonn to go it alone without U.S. or European political backing. As Germany had become Europe's economic motor and political driver, it appeared that the rest of Europe had to follow the German lead; concurrently, it was feared that Germany itself might become increasingly reluctant to drag Europe along because of crises resulting from rapid unification. By November 1993, the United States stated its opposition to EU and German dealings with Iran. Also in November, German Defense Minister Völker Rühe stated that Bonn and Tokyo should start regular defense consultations at roughly the same time that Bonn concluded a subsidized multibillion dollar trade deal with Beijing, in addition to pressuring Washington to permit Central European states to enter NATO.

NO-MAN'S-LANDS

The East European no-man's-land (plus the former Yugoslavia and the Caucasus) has begun to converge with conflict in the Middle East/South Asian regions (including Turkey). In addition to the fears of Russian revanche and of German revisionist claims to Polish and Czech territory as well as Kaliningrad (fears raised by burgeoning acts of neo-Nazi terrorism inside Germany)—there were also significant disputes among East European states themselves. Both Belarus and Ukraine possess irredentist movements that look toward Polish support. Here, however, as Belarus is more pro-Russian than Ukraine, Polish leader Lech Walensa discussed defense ties with Ukrainian President Kravchuk. An instable Ukraine has been split between pro-western pro-Polish movements in the western regions (Lvov); pro-Russian movements in the southeast; plus demands for independence in the Crimea, for example. Belarus has voiced irredentist claims to Lithuania (the latter backed by Poland). Conflict in Moldova over the secessionist Dniester republic has threatened to bring in Russia, Ukraine, and Romania. Conflict between Armenia and Azerbaijan has threatened to bring in Russia, Turkey, or Iran. The fissure of the Czech and Slovak republics eliminated a key buffer state in Central Europe. Hungarian irredentist claims could play a role in destabilizing the region because of claims to Slovakia and Transylvania—plus the Hungarian presence in former Yugoslavia. The refugee crisis of Albanians and former Yugoslavians trying to enter Italy, Austria, and Germany (combined with roughly over one million emigrants yearly trying to enter Europe from the former Soviet bloc) has raised the prospects of a general xenophobic backlash.

In the case of the former Yugoslavia, U.S. and Soviet/Russian policy refused to recognize the breakaway republics of Slovenia and Croatia (declaring independence on 25 June 1991)—which took steps toward independence after Soviet troops left Hungary. Germany, on the other hand, moved to recognize Croatia and Slovenia (but took effective action only after Serbia took Vukovar). The United States still opposed recognition largely in fear that civil war would spread to Bosnia-Herzegovina, Kosovo, and Macedonia. The latter two regions could become the focal point of conflict among Bulgaria, Serbia, Albania, and could also drag in NATO members Greece, which fears Bulgarian hegemony over Macedonia, and Turkey, which formed an alliance with Albania to protect Kosovo. Also in January 1993, the Islamic Conference Organization offered to assist Bosnian Moslems through UN and CSCE channels. Iran also threatened to end the arms embargo to the former Yugoslavia if no action was taken to assist Bosnian Moslems, who had called for UN forces to be deployed the previous year.

Only following actions taken by Serbs in Bosnia-Herzegovina did the United States take steps, in April 1992, to isolate Serbia. The Serbian leadership consequently threatened to widen the war throughout the Balkans. In August 1992, the Bush administration moved to officially recognize Slovenia, Croatia, and Bosnia-Herzegovina; Croatian actions of "ethnic cleansing" against Bosnian Moslems were largely overlooked (as were Bosnian counter-actions). Despite the implementation of economic sanctions in mid-1992, and imposition of a naval blockade and no-fly zone by the WEU and NATO, initially divisive American and German policies, and reluctance to intervene in the mountainous "porcupine" of Serbian defenses, resulted in a capitulation to pan-Serbian expansionism. Secretary of Defense Dick Cheney opposed a Desert Storm-like intervention; but NATO and the WEU repeated promises of stronger actions. In December 1992, the first UN preventive war force was deployed in Macedonia (supported by NATO)—in an effort to delimit Serbian claims and forestall potential

Greek and Bulgarian conflict over the region. In addition, NATO called for deployment of UN preventive war forces in Kosovo—an action opposed by Russia in the UN Security Council. The Bush administration consequently threatened unilateral action if Serbia itself entered Bosnia. (U.S. calls to intervene in Bosnia were, in part, derived from the effort to prevent Ankara or Teheran from unilateral intervention.)

Newly elected President Clinton likewise threatened either unilateral action or to end the UN arms embargo on Bosnia—both options opposed by Russia. Only following the 25 April 1993 referendum did Yeltsin promise joint action if Bosnian Serbs did not obey the still-born Vance-Owen peace plan. Here, Yeltsin supported peace-keeping actions but threatened to oppose NATO air strikes. (Moscow argued that U.S. threats tended to strengthen Bosnian intransigence and unwillingness to negotiate.) In the April 1993 Vancouver summit, Clinton promised not to act on the Bosnian question in such a way as to hurt Yeltsin's chances to win the April referendum. Clinton did, however, threaten intervention two days before the Russian referendum in response to Serbian actions.

Deteriorating Soviet controls over the Caucasus, Central Asia, and Afghanistan opened the vulnerable Islamic underbelly to the rival claims and interests of states such as Turkey, Iran, Saudi Arabia, Pakistan, India, as well as China. Following the Persian Gulf War and collapse of the Soviet Union, Turkey's strategic position became pivotal in regard to maintaining continued pressure on Iraq, and in countering Iranian penetration in the former Soviet Central Asian republics and the Caucasus. Concurrently, Turkey asserted its interests in regard to the Serbian thrust into Bosnia-Herzegovina, and vis-à-vis Greece. Ankara also sought new relations with Central Asian states of Turkish origin. (Potentially, Turkey could establish links with Tartars in the Ukrainian Crimea, Russian Kazan, if not Siberian Sakha [Yakutia]. In addition, China is more susceptible to pan-Turk movements in Xinjiang than it is to Pakistan-based or Iranian-based pan-Islamic movements.)

On the other hand, Turkish conflict with the Kurdish PKK revolutionary movement (purportedly given support by Iraq, Iran, and Syria until the 1993 U.S.-Syrian rapprochement) threatened to polarize Turkish society. Ankara feared lack of NATO and WEU support for its regional and domestic interests, at a time in which Ankara sacrificed its own interests (loss of Iraqi markets and trade) to check Baghdad in the Persian Gulf War. In addition, Turkey hesitated before accepting a European offer to enter the WEU, as Turkey hoped to gain European supports for its own regional interests, and check those of Greece. In effect, Greece and Turkey have engaged in a renewed arms race—as each seeks to sustain "parity" with the other. In November 1992, after a sale of German military equipment was blocked by domestic German opposition, Turkey became the first NATO member to purchase Russian military equipment including Mi-17 helicopters and armored personnel carriers. (Turkey could also decide not to extend U.S. basing rights for a no-fly zone over northern Iraq and relief operations for Iraqi Kurds.) Whether Turkey will enter the EC-WEU (and the possible ramifications if it does not) remains to be seen.

In rivalry with Turkey, Pakistan, Saudi Arabia, Iran sought closer ties with Tajikistan and Turkmenistan, as well as northern Afghanistan, and forged a cooperation agreement with Azerbaijan. By 1993, civil war in Tajikistan, in which Russia has supported a neo-Communist (or Russified) regime against pan-Islamic movements, threatened to drag Russia into another quagmire, potentially undermining Russian controls over Uzbekistan. (Both India and Russia fear the potentially destabilizing affects of Uzbek pan-nationalism.)

But despite their ostensible rivalry in Central Asia, both Russia and Iran have hoped to check pan-Turk ambition, and keep Azerbaijan divided. It is feared that an oil-rich unified Azerbaijan could threaten Iranian territorial integrity and further undermine Moscow's containment of Central Asian states, if not India's Kashmir. In checking Azerbaijan (which initially refused to join the CIS), the new Russia forged an alliance with Armenia. Turkey, on the other hand, largely in fear of Armenian irredentist claims, tended to back Azerbaijan against Armenia. Concurrently, Washington was tempted to back its NATO ally, Turkey. Initially, Moscow feared Iranian pan-Shi'ia movements in Afghanistan and Tajikistan, but increasingly, Moscow has opposed pan-Turk interests. Moscow accordingly tilted toward Iran *against* Turkey, but simultaneously trying to coopt both.

On 20 May 1992 Marshall Yevgeny Shaposhnikov, warned that the world "will be on the edge of World War III" if a third party (i.e. NATO's Turkey or Iran) intervened in the conflict between Armenia and Azerbaijan over Nagorno-Karabakh and Nakhichean. While a rough equipoise existed among Russia, Iran, and Turkey (and Russia has been establishing greater diplomatic, trade, including arms sales, with both Turkey and Iran), Moscow feared that a sudden change in the regional balance could result in major power intervention.[12] Ankara subsequently assured Moscow that it would not intervene. By September 1993, as Armenian forces seized as much as one-fifth of Azeri territory, Iran brought its troops to the Azeri border.

Iran (much like Iraq before the Gulf War) hoped to become the major regional power, in part by obtaining advanced Soviet weaponry (purportedly obtaining tactical nuclear weapons and nuclear know-how at bargain basement prices from "mafias" of former Soviet republics)—in addition to significant purchases of high-tech from Germany/Europe and Japan (who sold against U.S. counsel). Russian arms sales to Iran were intended to strengthen Iran against U.S. pressures, at the same time that they counterbalanced pan-Turk ambitions; Russian sales to Iran may also have been intended to check oil links between Ukraine and Iran if not counterbalance Kazakh interests—as the latter contested the Russian nuclear monopoly. The strong Russo-Iranian rapprochement raised fears that Moscow wanted to pressure U.S. interests in the Persian Gulf—after losing the former Soviet ally, Iraq, which purportedly had rebuilt some 80 percent of its military capabilities by 1993.

In addition to acquiring former Soviet weapons, Teheran, in August 1992, purportedly began to press its claims to islands shared with the United Arab Emirates. At the same time, Kazakhstan did not want to be seen favoring Turkey over Iran, and thus forged oil, transport, and finance agreements with the latter. Iran and Saudi Arabia have also been competing for control over Islamic movements in Algeria and the Sudan—if not over the fate of the pivotal Egyptian state; Iran, with Pakistan, also supports Kashmiri secession. Accordingly, Israel sent diplomatic missions to the newly independent Central Asian republics in an effort to prevent anti-Israeli alliances from being forged—in addition to reaching out for a rapprochement with India, Syria and the Palestine Liberation Organization (against pan-Islamic movements.)

As the Indo-Soviet system of supply and financing (and tacit Soviet nuclear umbrella) dissipated, India has become the world's largest importer of arms, and started development of its Prithvi and Agni ballistic missiles to counter the military capabilities of China and Pakistan. (India began to assert its regional hegemony by intervening in Sri Lanka in 1985 and by suppressing a coup in the Maldives and blocking the Nepal border—after sale of Chinese weapons and trade disputes—in 1988.) In February 1993, Yeltsin assured India that Moscow would resolve India's military debts to Moscow by changing the rupee-ruble exchange rate, and would deliver cryogenic engines for India's space program despite U.S. objections. Yeltsin also envisioned the prospect of India, China and Russia forming a bridge of stability in Eurasia against pan-Turk, pan-Iranian, and pan-Mongolian movements. Although Moscow and New Delhi dropped the security clauses of the 1971 Indo-Soviet friendship treaty, Boris Yeltsin also stated that "truth was on the side of India" in Kashmir. (U.S. pressure—including the threatened loss of G-7 assistance—however, dissuaded Moscow from selling high-tech that would permit India to manufacture missile technology. Yeltsin's flipflop outraged Russian hard-liners—as well as moderates.[13])

Since the Indo-Pakistani wars of 1948 and 1965, Pakistan and India have been engaged in a proxy war of mutual subversion in Kashmir and the Sind. In May 1990, the United States defused a crisis in which Islamabad purportedly threatened to use nuclear weapons (on modified F-16s) against New Delhi. Widespread disorder in Jamma and Kashmir in May 1991 followed by the destruction by Hindus of the Babri Masjid Mosque in Ayodhya in December 1992 led to violent clashes throughout India (where there are 120 million Moslems). Hindu militants of the Bharatiya Janata Party (BJP) continued to pressure the ruling Congress Party to take a stronger stance against Pakistan. Protesters in Pakistan, Bangladesh, and Afghanistan called for *jihad* (holy war). Washington once again stepped in to quell tensions. Continued Indo-Pakistani conflict could result in the first open war between two nuclear-weapons states (not counting the 1969 Sino-Soviet border clashes), particularly as the defeat of the pro-Soviet Najibullah Afghan government heightened Indian fears of pan-Islamic encirclement and encouraged demands for Kashmiri independence, or increasingly, linkage with Pakistan.[14] In September 1993 India and China signed border agreements dealing with Chinese claims to Kashmir and Indian claims to parts of Xinjiang and western Tibet. With the shift in the global and regional equipoise, Beijing began to tilt toward New Delhi—in opposition to its perceptions of U.S. backed secessionist movements in Tibet, Xinjiang, and Kashmir.

THE FAR EAST

In the Far East, the rise of a more independent Mongolia, which has sought closer ties with the United States, South Korea, and Japan, has reopened Russian and Chinese fears of pan-Mongolian claims vis-à-vis the Russian federation as well as Chinese control of Inner Mongolia and the Xinjiang provinces of China. Though the PRC and Soviet Union resolved border disputes that led to the 1969 clashes by mid-1991, the collapse of the Soviet Union opened up new territorial disputes. On the one hand, in March 1989, Beijing formally recognized Mongolia's territorial integrity and its new multi-party democracy in 1990. On the other hand, Beijing sustains a sweet and sour approach: It has not totally renounced its irredentist claims vis-à-vis Mongol and Kazakh territories (including claims to Alma-Ata and all the Mongolias, plus the Russian Federation republic of Buryatia).[15] Though Russian troops were to be removed by 1992, and the Soviet base at Ulaan Orhon was handed back to Mongolia, Soviet/Russian-Mongolian relations soured in 1991 when Moscow cut back subsidies and demanded hard currency, and likewise sought to renegotiate the debt. Accordingly, China augmented its trade, opened the port of Tianjin for Mongolian use, and sought to influence the fledgling democracy. Beijing wanted to make certain a pro-Chinese leadership stayed in power in Mongolia.

Russian strategic and military ties with the PRC have been symbolized by the Chinese acquisition of S300 surface-to-air missiles and supersonic all-weather Su-27 aircraft. The latter, if provided with in-flight refueling capability (purportedly provided by Iran from leftover U.S. equipment), can threaten Taiwanese, Indian, and Vietnamese air capabilities. Chinese fighter pilots have received Su-27 training in Moscow. In addition, Russia has sold other advanced military and nuclear technology to Beijing. By December 1992, Yeltsin signed new trade agreements with the PRC, demarcated disputed border areas, and established a relationship deemed "no alliance, no confrontation" (in my view, a neo-Rapallo pact).

Initially, the Russian foreign policy elite appeared to be split between those who wanted to sustain good relations with Beijing (and other non-Western nations) against those who would prefer to isolate the last major hard-line Communist regime. Both interests have been assuaged by maintaining strong relations with Beijing while opening unofficial ties with Taipei. On the one hand, Russia recognized China's claims to Taiwan as an inalienable part of China (confirmed in Yeltsin's December 1991 message to PRC Chairman Yang Shangkun); on the other hand, the new Russia since September 1992 has sought out "unofficial" economic, scientific-technical, and cultural ties with Taipei.[16] At the same time, Beijing has warned Moscow against opening air links with Taiwan and engaging in arms sales.

Beijing has not yet renounced its claims to hegemony over the far eastern littoral, including Thailand, Burma, Cambodia, Vietnam, both Koreas, and Taiwan. In February 1992, China formally reaffirmed its claim to the potentially oil rich Spratly and Senkakku Islands. The breakup of the Soviet Union made the Chinese elite ever more vigilant against China's own fissiparous tendencies. The Li Peng leadership continued to fear the ultimate breakup of "Socialist Spiritual Civilization," should Xinjiang (site of nuclear testing), Inner Mongolia, and/or Tibet ultimately break away—reminiscent of the "warring states" period at the turn of the twentieth century. In addition, there has remained the not-to-be excluded possibility of the breakaway of the richer coastal provinces—seen as supported by Taipei. In September 1993, China's White Paper on Defense reaffirmed China's claims to reunify with Taiwan—by force, if necessary.

The breakup of the Soviet empire, forewarned by Chinese

Communist Party hard-liners, reconfirmed the above fears. With more than 1.2 billion people, the danger of China seeking *Lebensraum* (already taking place in Tibet and Xinjiang—as a means to preclude the breakup of the PRC itself—cannot entirely be dismissed. The 1992 Chinese Communist Party Congress continued steps toward integrating PLA military leadership into the power structure at the same time that it retired certain octogenarian leaders. These moves were made to coopt younger party members; the drawing of the PLA in the decision-making power was meant to repress social dislocations caused by its new market orientation, if not to prepare for self-prophesied confrontation.

Concurrently, as China found itself caught between fears of Russian instability, and fears of renewed Japanese militarism, it ironically opposed the withdrawal of U.S. forces from the Far East. China feared that Japan would ultimately fill in the strategic-economic no-man's-land once Russian interests withdrew, and if the U.S. military presence no longer served as a "cork in the bottle" to moderate Japanese behavior. In addition, as North Korea's nuclear program could provoke a South Korean and Japanese nuclear build-up (and make Russia less likely to reduce forces in Asia), China ostensibly attempted to use "quiet diplomacy" to influence North Korea, but concurrently sought U.S. military assistance as a reward for its diplomatic efforts.

In order to gain China's assistance for Korean "unification," South Korea and the PRC established formal relations; South Korea accordingly downgraded diplomatic ties with Taiwan. Concurrently, as South Korea feared both Chinese and Japanese pressures, it looked to Germany/Europe for defense supports following the (postponed) decision to reduce the U.S. military presence. In addition, in November 1992, Boris Yeltsin promised to drop the old Soviet alliance with North Korea—despite pressure from Russian geostrategists who preferred that Moscow retain influence in that country. Russian insistence that North Korea pay for oil in hard currency helped to destabilize the country at a time when the successor to Kim Il Sung was still in question.

Soviet collapse also reopened the question of the Sakhalin and the Kurile Islands between Russia and Japan, in addition to that of Siberia. Calls for independence by Sakha (Yakutia), for example, have raised Russian fears of a loose confederation of Sakhalin Island, the Russian Far Eastern Republics and Mongolia—backed by China or Japan. In addition to fears of losing access to warm-water ports in the Baltics (and control over the Black Sea to Ukraine), the Russians have also been afraid of losing strategic access to the Kurile Islands, which are also rich in fish and minerals. Ironically, the new Russian defensive-oriented strategy resulted in the concentration of naval forces near Japan, reinforcing a sense of Japanese vulnerability.[17] Japan insisted upon the return of all Kurile Islands possibly in exchange for aid and larger investments in Russia and to help the reconversion of the Russian military-industrial complex—including a reduction of the Russian military and naval threat in the North Pacific. Russian refusal to "sell out" to Japan reflected its refusal to accept an entirely land-locked status. For Japan, the Kurile islands would be difficult to defend but would still help track Russian submarine movements.[18]

In early 1992, Germany and France both made overtures in an effort to broker a compromise. Japan, however, stated its intention to settle the dispute bilaterally without U.S. or European interference. Boris Yeltsin suddenly cancelled two trips to Tokyo in 1992–93; however, Yeltsin's October 1993 Russo-Japanese summit did not raise the issue of the Kurile Islands. In April 1993, Japan promised Russia $1.8 billion in aid. Tokyo regarded aid to Russia as a trade-off for U.S. trade concessions, as it would generally prefer to invest in the PRC and Vietnam. (Japanese corporations have sought to modernize Russia's petroleum and gas industry, in part to reduce Japan's dependence upon the Middle East; but Japan prefers to look to China.)

On the surface, Japan appeared to be the country most willing to placate China, but only up to a certain point. Japan argued that the West should resume foreign assistance to China, both as a means to check Soviet/Russian influence in the Asian Pacific region and as a way to wean China away from dangerous "instability." At the same time, Japan increasingly feared the vulnerability of its sea lines of communications (SLOC) from the Persian Gulf to the South China Sea, particularly after the loss of U.S. bases in the Philippines. Japan did not want China to develop an air or naval capability that could threaten Japan itself. China has complained that Japan has refused to sell high technology that China needs to become globally competitive. Using threats to Taiwan, and support for North Korea, as well as threats to block its access to the China market, China has hoped to pressure Tokyo into a *quid pro quo* to gain finance and high technology. At the same time, it is not clear that a unilateral Japanese decision to resume financial assistance (of up to $5.4 billion in 1993) will necessarily dissuade China from withdrawing its claim to regional hegemony and to Taiwan.

Japan also hoped to use its financial leverage to shore up states, such as the Philippines (supporting a "mini-Marshall Plan"), South Korea, and Indonesia, which are key to the protection of its SLOC. In late 1992, Japan also promised $8 billion to Kazakhstan, Turkmenistan, Uzbekistan, Kyrgystan, and Tajikistan, officially to counter growth of potential pan-Islamic movements that could destabilize the Gulf and imports of oil. Japan also decided to invest heavily in Vietnam—not only to profit, but also to counterbalance burgeoning PRC influence and Taiwanese investment. By November 1992, Japan formally agreed to aid Vietnam ($369 million on concessional terms)—*even before* Washington provided aid or began the process to normalize relations with Hanoi. (Washington had tried to hold back Japan from going ahead with assistance three times in 1992.) George Bush eased curbs on trade with Hanoi by December 1992. The Clinton administration then permitted Hanoi to obtain World Bank loans—and opened the door to greater U.S. investment in January 1994 as a possible step toward normalization.

Japan has been generally respectful of the political implications of Asian fears of a rebirth of Japanese "imperialism." Japan does not yet possess the international legitimacy to play an effective role as the globally paramount power—should the United States move into greater isolation. Hence, Japan, much like Germany's support for UN and CSCE "blue helmets," sought cooperative security approaches to conflict resolution (promising to underwrite the over $2 billion costs of the UN mission in Cambodia, for example, and concurrently demanding a place as an "equal" on the UN Security Council). In July 1992, Japan's parliament enacted legislation permitting the deployment of up to 2,000 Japanese troops in UN peace-keeping missions.

In addition to containing Russia, a strong U.S.-Japanese alliance and Japanese military buildup had been regarded as a strategic lever to pressure the recalcitrant PRC back into a closer defense relationship with the West, if not break up closer Sino-Soviet ties.[19] If China could not be drawn back into a positive strategic relationship with the West and Japan, then the United States would tend to look to Japan alone to check both Russia and China. At the same time, however, Japan became increasingly suspicious as to whether the U.S. ultimately intended to defend its interests. Tokyo feared that a U.S. retrenchment in Asia might lead to American isolation. Burgeoning trade, monetary, and high-technology disputes tended to exacerbate U.S.-Japanese tensions, as did U.S. demands for greater "responsibility sharing" without granting Tokyo effective decision-making authority or "power sharing." (The United States pressed Japan to pay up to 73 percent of cost of U.S. military deployment.) Tokyo then threatened a possible accommodation with Beijing (to cooperate with the latter vis-à-vis North Korea and concurrently to draw Beijing away its "Rapallo pact" with Moscow). Tokyo also threatened a "plutonium alliance" with London and Paris.

After Brent Scowcroft's secret mission in June 1989 and the Soviet Valentin Falin mission in December 1989 (in which the United States and Russia sought to confirm relations with the PRC after Tiananmen

Square), Japan pushed for a new opening to China, followed by Germany. Secretary of State Baker then effectively reopened U.S. relations with Beijing in November 1991. The EC considered lifting sanctions imposed after Tiananmen Square, and stated that it would revive defense cooperation, ostensibly if China ultimately improved its human rights record. By November 1992, Germany had effectively normalized relations with China. France, on the other hand, moved into a period of confrontation with China, by looking to Taiwan for arms sales and a more developed market. In January 1994, Paris formally capitulated— promising Beijing not to sell more arms to Taiwan in exchange for commercial contracts with the PRC.

Prior to the Bush administration's decision to sell 150 F-16s to Taiwan in September 1992, China hoped to muffle Western criticism of its repression of the Chinese democracy and Tibetan autonomy movements, and to end its diplomatic isolation and gain Western financial assistance. China ostensibly pressured North Korea to halt its nuclear program and sought to compromise with the United States over issues such as the NPT and MTCR. It promised to limit arms and missile sales abroad and to compromise over significant trade disagreements and human rights violations. On the other hand, the PRC's support for Algerian, Pakistani, and particularly Iranian demands for conventional weaponry and nuclear infrastructure, suggested an alliance between China and pan-Islamic movements. (The PRC-Israeli rapprochement has sought to deflect Chinese support for pan-Islamic movements.[20])

The Russian sale of at least twenty-four Su-27s (equivalent to the U.S. F-15) coupled with other Russian offers to transfer production facilities for jets and other hardware to aid Chinese military modernization, plus South Korea's decision to recognize China in order to curry the latter's acceptance of Korean unification, at the expense of downgrading relations with Taiwan, plus French efforts to sell Mirage 2000-S jets to Taiwan, then led the Bush administration to justify the sale of at least 150 F-16s and 12 anti-submarine helicopters to Taiwan in September 1992. In addition to tough bargaining over trade, this latter action broke the Sino-American 1982 accord signed by the Reagan administration phasing out arms sales to Taiwan. Though the sale was timed to obtain election support, the decision initially appeared to overturn the U.S. "appeasement" of PRC claims to Taiwan evident since the Nixon administration. China responded that the sale represented interference in its domestic affairs and threatened not to cooperate with U.S. efforts to stem sales of missiles and missile technology to states such as Pakistan, Syria, and Iran. Concurrently, China threatened sanctions against European states, particularly France, that supply Taiwan with arms.[21] President Bush did, however, seek to counterbalance sales to Taiwan with the sale the Cray supercomputer (which could assist nuclear weapons development) and aid to modernize Chinese fighter jets; Bush also sought to compete with Russian and European arms sales.

Despite his initial campaign promises, President Clinton then began a new rapprochement with Beijing. To fend off a militant Chinese reaction and in the attempt to wean Beijing away from supporting North Korea (and to establish a line of communication through China to North Korea), President Clinton announced a "constructive engagement" initiative in October–November 1993. This strategy was also based upon an effort to expand defense and high-tech sales (possibly including the Cray supercomputer) against Russian arms sales and German-European high-tech rivalry. Ostensibly, the initiative was still dependent upon Beijing's promise to improve its human rights record. (These actions have also been rationalized as a way to counter burgeoning Japanese military-technological capabilities.)

In October 1992, the Emperor of Japan—upon China's request—visited China in an effort to stem swelling anti-Japanese sentiment. U.S. retrenchment and apparently closer Sino-Japanese relations have led to fears of a pan-Asian alliance or a "re-Asianization" of Japan. Japanese leaders argued that they have played a role as a "bridge between Beijing and Washington" but it still not clear where that bridge is leading, as Japan and China have begun to reassess their relationship with the United States (and to one another). While Sino-American relations have declined since 1987, so too have Japanese-American relations, expressed by the neologism *kenbei*, or aversion to Americanism (this term has been coupled with more extreme derogations).[22]

The defeat of the Japanese Liberal Party in August 1993, which had ruled Japan for four decades, opened a new phase in Japan's foreign relations. The new Prime Minister Morihiro Hosokawa promised to oppose "great power ambitions," shun ostentation, reduce Japan's current account surplus, and indefinitely sustain membership in the NPT (the previous government had opposed an indefinite extension of the NPT at the July 1993 G-7 summit). Initially, the Hosokawa government took a tougher line on China's nuclear testing, weapons exports, and human rights abuses—but moved to a more pro-Chinese stance by 1994 as U.S.-Japanese relations continued to sour. The combined defeat of the Liberal Party and of the Socialist Party in the Diet meant the relative rise of an unstable coalition of techno-nationalist forces that support rearmament and a defense policy more independent of Washington. In September–October 1993 Japan (with U.S. participation) engaged in its largest military exercises since World War II—raising fears throughout Asia.

9

Toward a New Global Concert? Or End of the U.S.-Russian Courtship?

THE CHALLENGE

As the world enters a period of transition from a loose bipolar to an "uneven polycentric" global system, three interrelated questions appear crucial. What steps can the United States take to foster an evolution toward a more cooperative, pluralistic, and pacific global system? What is the best policy to manage the fissiparous collapse of the Soviet empire without promoting dangerous new rivalries among the former Soviet republics? What steps must be taken to prevent a revanchist Russian reaction, a more militant Chinese foreign policy, new German/European or Japanese alliances with third powers, while simultaneously keeping regional conflicts limited?

Since the basis of the allied security consensus formerly rested upon a commonly perceived Soviet threat, the initial collapse of that common threat has implied that Washington and its allies may find it increasingly difficult to sustain political-military unity in response to new regional conflicts. German/European and Japanese demands for "power sharing" as compensation for U.S. demands for "responsibility sharing" may not split the NATO and U.S.-Japanese alliances formally, but may make these alliances effectively impotent in response to conflicts or "threats" not directly affecting NATO countries or Japan.

Divergent geopolitical interests, efforts on the part of the former Soviet republics and other states, such as the PRC, to play allied interests against one another, combined with conflicting trade and monetary practices, may make allied interactions less cohesive. Will the United States attempt to deal with intra-allied and intra-CIS disputes by means of a concerted policy, involving active Russian participation? Or will Washington take a more unilateral approach in asserting its interests, for example, expanding NATO to include Central European states (without Russian participation in such an endeavor)—in part in the effort to "double-contain" its own allies? And how will Russia manage its relations with the PRC, India, and Iran at the same time that it attempts to hold Ukraine and other CIS states together under Russian primacy/hegemony—if not dominance over lesser states?

TOWARD A NEW CONCERT OR GLOBAL CONFLICT?

Greater NATO cooperation with the UN and a more effective Conference on Security and Cooperation in Europe (CSCE) have been urged as one path that can help enhance NATO and West European Union (WEU) cooperation and help to integrate the new Russia, Ukraine, and other states into a pro-Western entente. At the same time, the number of potential crises appears to create insurmountable obstacles to the formation of a new system of global security. From this perspective, either stronger international security regimes must be built to provide global security, or else the major powers—including Russia—will need to engage in concerted actions to prevent war or at least limit conflict if international security regimes do not prove to be effective.

UN or CSCE preventive war forces could be deployed in key geostrategic regions—long before the conflict erupts. If given more intrusive powers, the UN or CSCE can help to bring attention to specific areas of potential conflict. The United States has not yet acted on a number of Russian proposals that might help reduce tensions (and which in turn mean an expansion of either UN or CSCE powers). Russia has requested the deployment of UN preventive war units in the Baltic states and in the Kurile Islands, for example, yet neither the Baltic states nor Japan appears keen to accept such proposals. In addition, the belated deployment of the first UN preventive war force (involving U.S. troops) in the former Yugoslav republic of Macedonia in December 1992 represented an effort to prevent the latter from becoming a focal point of conflict. The UN force, in effect, serves to symbolically delimit Serbian expansionism by drawing the line at Skopje—and serves to deter Greece, Bulgaria, and Albania from conflict over the region.

The possibility for joint U.S., Russian, and European action in regard to former Yugoslavia really arose only after the 25 April 1993 referendum in Russia—once Yeltsin's pro-Western policies obtained a certain—though not definitive—measure of legitimacy. In May 1993, Russia began to take a more active stance in the effort to prevent pan-

Serbian "ethnic cleansing" from drawing Russia into a wider conflict. At the same time, however, domestic pressure groups sought to push Moscow into more overt support for pan-Serb goals. Accordingly, U.S., EU, and Russian policies have not been coordinated as Yeltsin has been unable or reluctant to support policies that can be regarded as anti-Serb. Moscow thus argued that U.S. calls to lift the arms embargo to Bosnia (in part in deference to Ankara) enhanced Bosnian intransigence. Moreover, despite its expressed willingness to engage in peace talks with both Serbia and Bosnian Serbs and to join in a UN peace-making mission, Moscow complained that NATO air strikes in Bosnia in April 1994, for example, were not coordinated through the UN Security Council and could perpetuate the conflict—if not jeopardize U.S.-Russian cooperation in general. While waiting until April to engage in air strikes, the United States itself has been reluctant to engage ground troops—policies evocative of isolationism. The UN has feared that NATO air strikes not accompanied by U.S. ground forces will put at risk UN blue helmets.

Ultimately, a concerted policy must work to prevent Serbian and Croatian expansion from exploding into a generalized Balkan war, at the same time that such a policy seeks to actively engage Russia in joint actions and avert a Russian revanchist backlash. On the one hand, unilateral NATO and WEU actions risk more overt Russian support for pan-Serb goals as threatened by Russian revanchists; on the other hand, concerted threats (tacitly supported by Russia) against Serbia must appear credible. Concurrently, political-ethical constraints (opposition to "appeasement") should not be permitted to block a feasible deal reached with Serbia and Croatia to check their further expansion.

Moreover, if a CSCE or UN preventive war forces are to be accepted by Russian military leaders, it might prove necessary to counterbalance CSCE or UN deployments in former Soviet spheres of influence and security with CSCE or UN forces deployed in Western spheres of influence and security—what I have called an "addendum to the Genscher plan."[1] The temporary deployment of UN or CSCE forces in the centrally strategic region of the former East Germany, for example, would help allay Russian fears, that are not entirely exaggerated, of a NATO-WEU "forward deployment"—or of a resurgent Germany—and thus double-contain Germany in an international security regime in which Russia would maintain a political-military presence. Such a deployment may help mitigate Russian pan-nationalist concerns; it may also assist in the socially dislocating consequences of German unification. (The risk might be the rise of a thus far more containable German neo-Nazi movement in response to a UN "occupation"—albeit temporary.)

If both the UN and CSCE are to be truly effective, both may have to be restructured to incorporate the new changes in the global equipoise; and a bloated UN administration would have to become much more efficient if it is to take on risky peace-making (in addition to peace-keeping) operations. U.S. Senator Joseph Biden's call for a "standing army" for UN use and a Presidential directive intended to commit the United States to a rapid expansion of UN peacekeeping operations and financing may change the U.S. relationship with the UN if not blocked by domestic U.S. opposition. As proposed above, preventive war units (which can be trained by the U.S. Partnership for Peace initiative) could be deployed in key buffer areas such as the Baltics, eastern Germany, Central European states, and the Kurile Islands, for example. Since unilateral military efforts by the United States or EU could provoke global conflict (depending on the geostrategic "nexus" of the region), concerted efforts—involving Russia as well as Ukraine—must be pursued. (On the other hand, UN or CSCE reluctance to engage forces in the Caucasus region—an action in part blocked by Russia itself—has granted Moscow a *de facto* sphere of influence.)

On the political level, a CSCE security council could be established that would incorporate such states as Germany, France, Russia, the United States, Sweden, Italy, Poland, and possibly Ukraine.[2] (Yet would Russia accept the membership of Ukraine in such a council?) The UN Security Council could ultimately be restructured according to the "Brazilian proposal" to include the United States, Russia, the EU (joining France, Britain, and Germany together), Japan, and China; or alternatively Germany and Japan could join a seven permament member Security Council. In 1992 Tokyo demanded action by 1995; Germany likewise signaled its intent to join the Security Council (despite second thoughts, following its domestic crises resulting from unification and difficulty in controlling neo-Nazi terrorism). Initially, Japan and Germany would not enjoy veto rights. At a later stage (it is hoped, in a more stable global environment), new permanent members could be added, such as India, Brazil, Nigeria, and Indonesia. Here, it will be impossible to stall German and Japanese membership on the Security Council forever—if both states sustain a positive political and economic role in the support of UN missions. Membership on the UN Security Council may also help dampen their drive for more politically independent policies. (Temporary deployment of UN preventive war forces in eastern Germany and the Kuriles—combined with a new U.S.-Russian-EU-Japanese defense relationship—could be the condition for eventual Japanese and German membership on the UN Security Council.)

The process of bringing new powers into UN decision-making

may initially raise tensions (particularly with Russia and/or China)—or else result in indecision and inaction. States would need to forge new strategies and new behind-the-scenes coalitions to help carry through UN unanimity and prevent vetoes. There is likewise a danger of overextension: UN humanitarian assistance and defense of buffer zones in Cambodia, the former Yugoslavia, Somalia, and elsewhere, have proved extremely costly. Impotence in the face of combat has raised questions as to their effectiveness, as combatants have ignored or opposed UN mandates. Both the United States and Russia have been behind on regular and peacekeeping dues. Accordingly, if the UN decision-making process *does* prove ineffective (depending on the situation), then the United States, EU, and Russia (plus other states that join) may need to carry out joint actions *outside* the UN framework.

The United States, Russia, and the EU through the North Atlantic Cooperation Council (NACC) and the CSCE process, and other means of mediation, should seek preventive steps as much as possible so as not to have to deal with each crisis as it arises. (The Clinton administration has accordingly sought to jointly train U.S. and Russian heavy combat units for peace-making operations.) The U.S. political presence in the CSCE should also help guarantee that the United States will not become isolated from European affairs. At the same time, should Russia ultimately drop out of the CSCE, preventive war forces would still be in place. In addition to maintaining an adequate presence in Europe, NATO (at least until Russian stability can be assured) would still maintain its role to guard and maintain European sea lines of communication (SLOC) and strengthen U.S. air- and sealift-capabilities in case of the "new" worst case scenario of "long war uncertainty."[3]

Rather than engaging in a provocative effort to expand NATO membership into Central and Eastern Europe alone (that is, without Russian cooperation in such a venture), the United States should engage in a more cooptive approach utilizing both NATO-Russian defense cooperation and international security regimes, such as the UN and CSCE. (Efforts by NATO or the WEU to incorporate Central European states alone risk isolating not only Russia, but also Ukraine, the Baltic states, and other states not included as well.) At the same time, the United States should encourage the EU to form a much wider union incorporating Russia, the Ukraine, and other powers. The January 1994 U.S.-Russian-Ukrainian disarmament pact could provide a model for future cooperative security pacts—if the pact can be sustained.

In November 1993, the Clinton administration called for a Partnership for Peace—a compromise position which intends to establish closer defense ties with all former Soviet bloc states, but which does not provide mutual security guarantees. As long as such a plan continues to give Russia *primacy*, it will be supported by Moscow; on the other hand, East European states will remain insecure (from potential regional conflicts in addition to the threat of Russian revanche) until an all-European security regime (a neo-Barthou plan) is fully implemented (see five pessimistic scenarios outlined below).

ENDING THE CONTINUING COLD WAR IN ASIA

New systems of security must also be applied to Asia, where the Cold War has not ended. Washington should work to ameliorate tensions between Tokyo and Moscow through a resolution of the Kurile Islands dispute, and continue to formulate confidence- and security-building measures that will reduce the Russian threat to Japan from the Sea of Okhotsk in return for a U.S. *quid pro quo* including a U.S.-Russian-Japanese entente. (Joint ownership, a phased return of the islands, or a UN trusteeship, or protection by an Asian Pacific security force, have all been suggested.) Initially, working to combat piracy in the region might help bring states together into an Asian Pacific security regime.

By reducing tensions between Russia and Japan, the intent is also to prevent the possible rise of a more militarily powerful Japan—and hence sustain the double containment. A U.S.-Russian-Japanese entente would reduce demands for Japanese "burden sharing," as Japanese "power sharing" in cooperation with both the United States and Russia would be granted. In addition, steps should be taken to assure Japanese access to U.S. and European markets, and coordinate G-7 economic policy vis-à-vis Russia and the PRC. Japan has given numerous indications that it reserves the right to say "no" to the U.S. demands; but, despite economic tensions, it is dubious that Tokyo will break out of the double containment unless it cannot get U.S. (and Russian) reassurance in the face of a more militant China or a nuclear North (and South) Korea.

Accordingly, a concerted effort must also carefully manage the prospects of either North Korean isolation or Korean unification which threaten to upset an already precarious Asian equipoise. A step-by-step approach involving confidence- and security-building measures, International Atomic Energy Agency (IAEA) inspections, U.S., South Korean, and Japanese aid, plus U.S. diplomatic recognition for Pyongyang can hopefully ameliorate tensions if the appropriate negotiating formula can be found. Ultimately, the best option is to find a compromise between South Korean demands for a limited commonwealth and North Korean demands for a close confederation—rather than move toward German-style absorption and reunification. (A Korean compromise, however, largely depends upon a possible succession crisis following the death of the "Great Leader" Kim Il Sung.)

Washington, Tokyo, and Moscow must determine not to assist Beijing's pursuit of its irredentist claims. Should China ultimately obtain Taiwan (it will be absorbing the important financial enclave of Hong Kong in 1997, and claims both the Spratly and Senkakku Islands), such a strategic position would, in effect, grant China strategic denial capability, control over sea lines of communication in the South China Sea and Pacific, as well as access to deep water in the Pacific for its SLBMs. Although the threat to end China's MFN status can be utilized as a form of strategic leverage, it is better to put pressure on China for violations of specific trade issues and arms sales—and not to link human rights issues to MFN status. Much as trade restrictions worked to militarize Japanese behavior before World War II, a decision to rescind Chinese MFN status might work to militarize Chinese behavior; and it may not work if China obtains closer economic ties with Japan. Any economic incentives to nudge China toward democratic reform must be accompanied by a tough geostrategic and selective geoeconomic policy designed to foreclose Chinese irredentist claims in the Pacific Basin region. On the other hand, Beijing's threats to support Pyongyang have, in part, impelled Washington toward closer military ties with the People's Liberation Army (PLA) ostensibly in order to sustain lines of communication with the military leaderships in both Beijing and Pyongyang. The ostensible need to rely on the PLA, however, can be mitigated should Washington finally recognize Pyongyang.

In order to forestall Moscow from forging a stronger Sino-Russian "Rapallo" agreement, a joint U.S.-Russian policy will need to pressure Beijing on specific issues (and indirectly keep Moscow and Beijing divided). The Clinton administration's January 1994 decision to lift the embargo on Vietnam should also represent a means to counterbalance burgeoning Chinese influence, and give the green light for U.S. investment in Vietnam to counterbalance that of Tokyo and Taipei. As the new Russia is "in no haste" to leave Cam Ranh Bay, U.S.-Russian naval and diplomatic cooperation could counterbalance Chinese pressures and Japanese political-economic influence. U.S. diplomatic recognition of Hanoi can ultimately help secure a U.S.-Russian entente in Asia, and symbolically help to reconcile U.S. relations with states that were alienated from the United States during the Cold War.

A concerted strategy would also seek compromise over issues of oil and the Spratly Islands and a mutual renunciation of the use of force in the Taiwan Strait, at the same time that cultural and economic ties between Taiwan and the PRC should be encouraged. (Here, however, Taipei fears that the loss of Taiwanese investment to the PRC might undercut Taiwan's economic growth.) A U.S.-Russian-German/European-Japanese entente would seek to defend Taiwan's "independent" status. The fact that Russia and other CIS states have decided to exchange "unofficial" permanent missions with Taipei appears to support this option. (Officially, Russia, like the United States, still regards Taiwan as part of China.) In addition, the significant share of U.S. investments in Hong Kong should permit the United States (and other states, such as Japan and Britain) to apply pressure on Beijing to sustain Hong Kong's civil liberties and rule of law once Hong Kong returns to the mainland in 1997—if the democratic powers of Hong Kong's Legislative Council cannot be expanded. One way is to link these issues to China's membership in GATT rather than with MFN status.

A U.S.-Russian-EU-Japanese entente should work to prevent Russian isolation and the possibility of a Sino-Russian alliance, as it seeks to check Beijing's claims to regional hegemony. Such a policy would provide incentives for Russia not to play a "double game" with Beijing by pressuring China in some areas, but also supplying significant arms and military supports. A joint U.S.-Russian effort to resolve Sino-Indo-Pakistani tensions may help to counterbalance China (perhaps looking toward Tibet/Kashmir autonomy guaranteed by the major powers). In addition, such a policy would seek Russian help in isolating both Iraq and Iran at the same time that the United States seeks to restrain pan-Turk linkages in the former Soviet Central Asian republics if not within Russia itself. Washington and Moscow will need to sort out their strategy if their support for conflicting regional allies is not to draw them into conflict. The dilemma, however, is that Washington may need to "appease" some Russian demands in order to prevent Russia from giving even greater support to the PRC or other states; at the same time, such a policy assumes that Russia will remain extroverted and not become embroiled in domestic strife.

A U.S.-Russian-EU-Japanese entente should also meet China's legitimate demands for social and economic modernization and international developmental assistance. Accordingly, the United States and Russia should announce an "Alternative Technology, Resource Conservation, Ecology, and Energy Program for Global Peace and Development" in which the PRC, Ukraine, and any other state could join. In addition to developing alternative, ecological, and decentralized technologies, such a program would represent an international effort to deal with contamination related to both the "peace" and "war" atoms, as well as the problems stemming from military-industrial and nuclear plant reconversion to consumer-oriented industries. Helping to reduce China's critical dependence on oil would be one goal. NACC has taken some steps in this direction with the CIS states, involving defense conversion, environmental controls, and scientific research, as have the 1992 Safety, Security, and Disarmament (SSD) talks. In addition, the replacement for COCOM should not concern itself with negative sanctions alone; it must also point in a positive direction toward alternative technology for global development if North-South tensions are ultimately to be ameliorated.

A concerted irenic diplomacy should concurrently mitigate tendencies toward both instability and revanche in the former Soviet Union; actively mediate between Russia and Ukraine; Russia and Japan; Russia and Turkey in Central Asia; at the same time that it is hoped that successful Russian reforms will provide China with an alternative model to single-party rule. Using both carrots and sticks, this new global strategy would attempt to prod China toward substantial human rights, multiparty democratic, and federalist reforms (which may include some measures of regional autonomy or confederation), without resulting in destabilizing collapse or militarization.

POLITICAL-ECONOMIC ISSUES

The G-7 countries need to forge a long-lasting defense and economic relationship with the new Russia in such a way as to help sustain a viable working relationship among all states of the CIS—but without alienating Moscow. As the debate over "shock therapy" or "shock without therapy" indicates, the failure of the West to provide at least $6 billion to help stabilize the ruble (plus lack of CIS monetary coordination) is, in part, responsible for the continuing political economic crisis. As important as aid, is also the need to develop a free trade association among Eastern European states and Russia with the United States and a much *wider* EU.

While Russian ties with surplus "oasis" countries such as South Korea and Taiwan could benefit Russia, such links are not sufficient. Former President Richard Nixon, for example, had urged President-elect Clinton to press for a rescheduling of Russia's roughly $80 billion foreign debt for fifteen years; to grant substantial bridge loans to help Russia through the winters and move toward a free market economy; and to press for massive private investment—up to $300 billion over five years. More feasible proposals include expanding the Overseas Private Investment Corporation's insurance program and programs involving swapping debt for ownership in Russian enterprises. In addition, as Moscow claims the former Soviet Union is owed some $250 billion, debts can be renegotiated. Greater G-7 assistance, plus investments in former oil, natural gas, and other resource industries, will be needed to help create a "freer" and "richer" world in Nixon's words. Aid *plus* trade must stimulate a self-sustaining recovery at the same time that Russia is brought into the defense and economic community of nations.

To accomplish the above, more teeth will need to be pulled. As argued, the high costs of German unification and Germany's general reluctance to draw the CIS into a free trade association with the EU or else establish full membership in GATT (a process that might take more than ten years); Japanese reluctance to provide major assistance until the issues of the Kurile Islands and Japanese security are resolved; the burgeoning U.S. debt and deficit crisis, coupled with competing global demands for development assistance; plus political-economic instability within Russia and the CIS itself—all represent factors that block greater finance and trade with Russia and the former Soviet bloc.

THE QUESTION OF STRATEGIC ARMS REDUCTIONS

At the historic June 1992 summit, Boris Yeltsin promised to radically change former Soviet strategy by dropping Moscow's claim to strategic parity. At the same time, however, Moscow threatened not to ratify the START II pact (or follow through with START I) if Kiev refused to ratify the Lisbon Protocol to the START I agreement eliminating nuclear weapons, or else if Kiev refused to sign the NPT. By November–December 1993, Kiev's pseudo-ratification of the START I treaty, and non-ratification of the NPT, risked full implementation of the START II treaty. Among other items, Kiev demanded joint U.S.-Russian-French-British security guarantees if it was to renounce nuclear weaponry altogether. By January 1994, the United States, Russia, and Ukraine signed a disarmament pact—the latter still hoped for a collective guarantee of Ukrainian security once (and if) Kiev follows through on its pledge to eliminate all nuclear weapons over a seven year period and to ratify the NPT treaty as a non-nuclear state.

Without a significant reduction in U.S.-Russian nuclear-strategic capabilities, France, Britain, and, even more, China will not necessarily be dissuaded from upgrading their nuclear stockpiles. Other states, such as Japan (confronted with the possibility of a nuclear North or unified Korea), Germany, or lesser powers, however, may also not necessarily be deterred from developing their own nuclear or ballistic missile defenses, if these states are not reassured by NATO, WEU, and Russia. As the U.S. emphasis on reducing land-based nuclear systems in the START talks enhanced the importance of naval and submarine nuclear forces, Japan is particularly concerned about U.S. security guarantees and confidence measures. Yeltsin's November 1992 promises to withdraw nuclear forces in the Far East, and eliminate production of all submarines for military purposes in two to three years, should ultimately help reduce Russo-Japanese tensions—if carried through and aided by a U.S.-Russian-Japanese entente.

As roughly 300 nuclear warheads are sufficient to wipe out each side, the United States and Russia could reduce the number of nuclear warheads even further; but such reductions would eliminate the still bipolar U.S.-Russian nuclear predominance relative to other nuclear weapons states. U.S.-Russian reductions to roughly 1500 warheads each, for example, would create a rough parity between the United States, Russia, France and Britain, China (and Ukraine, if it should retain a nuclear capability). If these major nuclear states can forge a truly concerted relationship, a rough parity of nuclear weapons would not create a problem. However, without the formation of a concert of the major nuclear powers, shifting alliance formations could change the global equipoise of nuclear and conventional power capabilities, political intent, and international norm. States may accordingly refuse to disarm to "equal" levels, for once states have disarmed it is easier for third states to build up to "parity."

Radical disarmament issues can possibly be addressed by ultimately extending the START talks to include Britain, France, and China. (START talks have indirectly been extended to include Ukraine, Kazakhstan, and Belarus.) One risk, however, is that these states may not accept proposals which sustain U.S.-Russian predominance. A second risk is that nonnuclear states such as Germany and Japan, which are dependent upon the U.S. or European nuclear deterrent, may be alienated by multilateral talks. Suggestions such as banning anti-satellite systems, slowing down or banning some forms of technological innovation, if not ultimately eliminating tactical nuclear weapons, if not a ban on ballistic missiles themselves, should all be considered.[4] These steps can be accomplished only as part of a concerted strategy—symbolized by the January 1994 U.S.-Russian disarmament pact with Ukraine. On the other hand, such cooperative security pacts will be difficult to sustain—

if states continue to harbor revisionist or irredentist claims.

The removal of nuclear arms from surface ships and attack submarines (in peacetime), including Tomahawk cruise missiles, has represented a significant step in that these actions helped to reduce pressure on Russian naval forces defending naval choke points against U.S. forward deployment. Controls over cruise missiles on naval ships are in the U.S. interest as, in many ways, the United States is more vulnerable to cruise missile attacks than is Russia. The United States should also seek out naval talks with the CIS to ensure greater confidence- and security-building measures. The dilemma here is that positive efforts may be stalled should Russian-Ukrainian disputes over the Crimea and Black Sea naval forces continue.

Clinton administration defense plans involve the U.S. ability to win two nearly simultaneous major regional conflicts, and only appear to represent a significant shift in American global strategy. The Clinton administration initially debated the possibility of shifting away from a forward naval deployment toward "defensive sea-lines-of-communication protection," in part, so as to reduce the dangers of Russian preemptive strikes against forward deployed anti-submarine forces.[5] Pentagon strategy, however, has not yet moved in this direction: As the strategy of forward deployment involves the double containment of both Russia and U.S. Allies, a fundamental reform in U.S. global strategy must involve concerted efforts: Washington should gradually strengthen Moscow's participation in allied military and naval exercises so as to build confidence and attempt to forestall a Russian backlash (REGT).

CONTROLLING THE SPREAD OF DUAL-USE HIGH-TECH, CONVENTIONAL, AND NUCLEAR WEAPONRY

Since 1964, Washington and Moscow had cooperated closely in the International Atomic Energy Agency (IAEA), including confidential bilateral meetings twice a year.[6] Ironically, Moscow—more so than the European allies—generally supported U.S. efforts to control nuclear proliferation, after initially aiding China's nuclear program. Yet because of its financial crisis, the Soviet Union cut back on its $20 million annual contribution to the IAEA safeguard budget in 1991. The paltry IAEA safeguard budget (which goes mainly to inspect Western countries) was then cut by 13 percent. Russia's own efforts to ban trade in strategic dual-use technology may also prove difficult to enforce. Whether Russia and the other CIS states will continue to fund the IAEA remains to be seen.[7] In addition to Iraq, inspection problems may confront the IAEA in

Iran, Libya, Algeria, among other states—including former Soviet republics. Kazakhstan possesses a fast breeder reactor at Ust-Kamenogorsk; and Ukraine possesses a complex of chemical plants at Dneprodzerzhinsk, capable of producing materials for nuclear weapons. Neither is under international inspection.[8] Ukraine postponed ratifying the NPT; Kazakhstan and Belarus ratified the NPT in late 1993. For these reasons, the IAEA should be given more intrusive rights of inspection and access to intelligence information—if states will agree! In March 1993, North Korea threatened to drop out of the NPT, in part as a means to gain U.S. diplomatic recognition: The nature, location, and process of IAEA inspections became a stumbling bloc to ameliorating tensions—until (and if) an acceptable formula can be negotiated.

China formally signed the NPT treaty in March 1992, but Beijing may have already helped to initiate several nuclear programs. Unless the NPT is revised in 1995, NPT countries themselves may designate the sites they want to be inspected. Though not permitted warheads, NPT states (i.e., those not possessing nuclear weapons before 1967) are permitted to be part of nuclear alliances and nuclear delivery systems, and can be involved in nuclear warfare planning and preparations. On the other hand, states such as India complain that Clause 3 of Article IX of the NPT should be revised: It permits a state such as China to become a member in the NPT as a nuclear weapons state, but not India, which exploded its first "peaceful" bomb after the "deadline" of January 1967. Pakistan will not sign the NPT until India does. Here, much like the interwar debate, tensions between demands for "security" against demands for nuclear "disarmament" plague global policy-making.

The United States needs to restore its credibility by extending greater credits to reward nonproliferation efforts and it must exercise greater self-restraint in nuclear-oriented sales. Recruiting new members for the nuclear suppliers group would help place controls on exports; the creation of internationally managed plutonium storage should also be considered. A revised NPT needs to ban the recovery of plutonium, promote international waste disposal, as well as prevent the spread of technology that produces plutonium.

Efforts to at least limit the number and size of nuclear tests should likewise be pursued, if a comprehensive test ban will not hold. In 1992, France and Russia initiated a nuclear test ban; Beijing, however, initiated a series of major tests in May 1992. China then opted out of the informal test ban in October 1993—in symbolic opposition to Japanese military maneuvers. (The EU-Japanese plutonium alliance plus Chinese nuclear testing may make it more difficult to restrain both North and

South Korean nuclear plans.) In August 1992 the U.S. Senate pressured the Bush administration to accept a nine-month moratorium, arguing that France and Russia will continue testing if the United States does, and that U.S. testing will make it more difficult to dissuade North Korea and Iran—as well as Ukraine—from opting for nuclear development. President Clinton proposed a comprehensive test ban to go into affect in 1996, but then stated that a test ban would be extended from July 1993 to September 1994 as long as no other nation tests. In the meantime, the post–Cold War U.S. Strategic Command began to develop new strategic nuclear contingency plans aimed at select nuclear "terrorist" states. The Clinton administration accordingly began a fundamental review of U.S. nuclear strategy—to decide precisely which states are to be targeted and whether new confidence- and security-building measures can be achieved with Russia. The largely symbolic January 1994 U.S.-Russian nuclear accord promised that neither the United States nor Russia would aim nuclear weapons at the other or its allies—but both states can retarget their ICBMs in a matter of minutes.

Efforts to prevent the spread of conventional weaponry have also faced difficulties. The October 1991 arms trade protocol between the United States, France, China, Britain, and the former Soviet Union sought to avoid weapons transfers that would "aggravate an existing armed conflict . . . increase tension . . . or introduce destabilizing military capabilities," but the protocol is non-binding and does not include weapons sales by emerging semiperipheral states.[9] "National security" interests, demands for hard currency, or efforts to maintain a highly skilled sector in employment and technological leadership, may all provide rationale not to enforce binding limitations.

In 1991, the United States led the world in arms sales (51 percent), in part because of sales to the Middle East before and after the Persian Gulf War. The former Soviet Union was second, but sales dropped from around 40 percent throughout the 1980s to about 20 percent in 1991 after ending sales to Afghanistan, Angola, and North Korea. Demands for hard currency have consequently led the new Russia— unlike the old Soviet bloc—to sell top-of-the-line equipment, including advanced SU-27s, MIG-29s, T-72 tanks, and surface-to-air missiles in competition with Germany/Europe and the United States—as well as in rivalry with other CIS states such as Ukraine. (This has led to a PRC-like mixed solution in which, like Beijing, Moscow claims that it cannot regulate the affairs of "private" merchants of death.) CIS and Russian arms markets still include the PRC, Iran, and India, but have been expanding to include states such as Turkey, the Philippines, Indonesia, South Korea, and possibly Taiwan, among others.[10] Russian leaders have consequently argued that $150 billion is needed to convert the defense industry to a consumer orientation. But to raise that money, Russia must export its stockpiles of arms! (The military-industrial complex directly employs 4.4 million and indirectly 12 million.)[11] Russian military industries have actually bartered arms for mango juice and bananas!

Germany became the world's third-largest conventional arms supplier in the world ($2.015 billion) in part because of the sale of stockpiles from the former East Germany, and delivery of submarines and warships contracted in early 1980s. China was fourth with $1.127 billion, surpassing Britain ($999 billion) and France ($804 billion). China's arms sales rose by 20 percent—and took almost 10 percent of the developing world's market. French sales fell by 58 percent; UK sales fell by 37 percent. India, Israel, Turkey, Afghanistan, Saudi Arabia, and Japan represented the world's greatest importers of weaponry. Thailand also substantially increased its arms imports, particularly from China.[12] In addition, Greece and Turkey have engaged in a major conventional arms buildup, absorbing supplies from NATO cutbacks in Western Europe following the 1990 CFE treaty. After Soviet collapse, Japan ostensibly became the second-largest defense spender in the world; yet as only roughly half of PRC spending is publicly reported, Beijing may be striving to match Tokyo. Furthermore, as Moscow has remained the major arms supplier to the PRC (Europe as a whole is second), a policy that seeks to cool the arms race between Taiwan, the two Koreas, the PRC, and other Asian-Pacific states, must include Russia, EU, as well as Ukraine. At present it has proved difficult to channel Russian sales in a friendly direction: Saudi offers in 1992 to purchase diesel submarines contracted by Iran were refused by Moscow on national security, not economic, grounds. And by December 1993, Moscow planned to restructure its arms export industries in an effort to boost sales.

BALLISTIC MISSILE DEFENSES

To counter ballistic missile, nuclear, and high-tech advances of the emerging powers, the Bush administration proposed a more limited version of the Strategic Defense Initiative—GPALS. The Clinton administration renamed SDI the Ballistic Missile Defense Organization, and promised to eliminate the space-based aspects of SDI, except in areas of research. Moscow and Beijing, however, are still suspicious of U.S. efforts to use BMD to obtain a first-strike capability.

As has been the case with U.S. allies, Moscow may not be convinced of U.S. willingness to thoroughly "share" space technology. And there is still opposition in the Pentagon to a limited BMD shield.

The rise of new missile states could either bring the United States and Russia together against a common "threat," thus maintaining the fifth dimension of the double containment, or else it could create further antagonisms if either side wants to adopt an emerging missile state as its ally. Failure to accommodate the Russian quest for technology sharing may well raise new tensions—if both sides abandon the principle of Mutual Assured Destruction by developing land-based nationwide BMD. Moreover, as BMD capabilities have spread, the PRC and other states may be tempted to develop land-based BMD shields—which could be utilized for both defensive and offensive purposes.

If the United States does move toward developing a strategic defense system in partnership with Russia (even a limited system), U.S. allies may fear a lack of U.S. reassurance in the event that their interests clash with those of Russia or other states. If the United States cannot incorporate the defense interests of Western allies with those of new Russia, a U.S.-Russian defense shield could weaken the effectiveness of allied nuclear deterrents and raise tensions with states, such as Ukraine and the PRC, that might not be part of the agreement. One has to ask the question: against whom would such a system operate, in what circumstances, and in whose interests?

There are many barriers to sharing technological know-how with the Europeans alone: National security considerations, regulations and practices of the Pentagon, and competition with U.S. firms, all limit the possibilities of cooperation among U.S. allies.[13] How will these factors be changed in regard to Russia? One idea is to spend less than one percent of the SDI budget to buy Russian technology; another is to share data derived from U.S. early warning satellites. In turn, Russia has hoped to provide space-scanning measures. In effect, issues raised by BMD defenses parallels issues raised by the Stimson Plan, which promised the sharing of atomic technology in 1945. Will Washington go ahead with such a plan—seeing mutual benefits—or will Washington attempt to sustain a largely unilateral advantage?

Moreover, if a strengthened international control mechanism can be established that would be able to thoroughly implement ground inspections (and enforce sanctions), then the apparent need for a limited BMD program can be curtailed. Further pressure (and incentives) should thus be made to get the new ballistic missile states, such as Ukraine, the PRC—as well as Russia itself—to abide by the Missile Technology Control Regime (MTCR). At the same time, the spread of cruise missile technology (and potentially that of stealth technology) raises questions as to the very ability of the major powers to control missile innovations.

An additional issue is the fact that the present MTCR is not a treaty or a legal obligation. It is specifically designed to "control the transfer of equipment and technology that could contribute to *nuclear-capable* missiles [emphasis added]."[14] The United States interprets the MTCR more broadly than France; and both Russia, Ukraine, and China have been reluctant to participate. In regard to Europe, missile technology is freely transferable within EU countries and could find new export outlets through Greece and Portugal—if manufacturers can find weak spots in member states' controls. Austria, Switzerland, and Sweden so far remain outside the regime, as do East European states; some of these states have been involved in technology and expertise transfers. Ukraine can develop nonnuclear missiles. It is additionally not clear how firm U.S. policy is: U.S. export controls have been hurt by a lack of coordination among the State, Defense, and Commerce Departments.

Comprehensive arms control regimes going beyond MTCR and NPT regimes could help enforce restrictions on missile development and deployment, and work to restrict transfer of strategically sensitive technologies.[15] Only concerted efforts by the major powers to pressure states into accepting some limitations on sovereignty, plus mutual efforts to restrict weapons sales and build-ups among the most powerful states themselves, can make these international regimes work. Without aspects of self-abnegation and enlightened self-interest on the part of the major powers, however, prospects appear bleak.

FIVE PESSIMISTIC SCENARIOS

Few in the West heeded Mikhail Gorbachev's warning that a Soviet marshal would take his place once German unification was announced. As the two-plus-four talks resulted in Soviet acquiescence to a reunified Germany's membership in NATO, Gorbachev's statement was largely interpreted as a scare tactic intended to gain Western concessions on other issues. Yet, when the delayed-reaction putsch finally did take place in August 1991, the world reeled in fear for seventy-two hours. Boris Yeltsin subsequently stated that his actions to check the neo-Brezhnev plotters were intended "to save Russia, to save this country, to save democracy, and the whole world, from a Cold war, or a hot war for that matter." Once in power, Boris Yeltsin himself reiterated warnings that a renewed "cold or hot war" could result from the failure of the West to support reforms. Yet rather than having the intended effect of helping to augment foreign assistance, these warnings unfortunately tended to discourage hopes that even more substantial allied assistance will be successful in preventing an anti-Western government from coming to power.

Russian Foreign Minister Andrei Kozyrev subsequently outlined three possible options for future Western-Russian relations: (1) return to confrontation by forces of revanche; (2) alienation and rivalry, specifically in conflict zones such as Iraq and (former) Yugoslavia unless the specific interests of democratic Russia are taken into consideration; (3) friendly and allied interaction, which, however, is not plausible without serious political and economic investment, "Otherwise, the romantic period of Russia's new relationship with the West is over."[16]

The new U.S.-Russian relationship has not yet entered a "honeymoon," as the two have yet to be married in a formal entente. There are dangerous consequences should the two not sustain deeper than cordial relations. One scenario would include another coup attempt— either a "Pinochet" or "Kemalist" pro-capitalist coup designed to eliminate any resistance to market-oriented reforms. A second scenario may involve limited war between Ukraine and Russia—similar to former Yugoslavia. A third scenario may involve a revanchist "red-brown" takeover—possibly by "democratic" means. A fourth may involve the disaggregation of the Russian Federation itself. And the fifth may involve a status quo of continual political-economic instability with dangerous international repercussions.

While another neo-Brezhnev coup could be attempted, it would be unlikely to last long. Without a sound economic program, it would most likely represent another stage in a continual revolution. On the other hand, the fact that the former Communist elite have attempted to take advantage of "capitalism" for themselves has given more credence to the view that a Pinochet or Kemalist coup may take place to accelerate reforms. Present conditions in the former Soviet Union mimic Leon Trotsky's most detested scenario in the *Revolution Betrayed* of the transformation of the Communist *nomenklatura* into a new property-owning class. Such a pro-capitalist coup could take place once the *nomenklatura* has more firmly established itself in power as a new "bourgeoisie." Yeltsin's dissolution of parliament and attack on the Russian White House in September–October 1993 has already been compared to General Augusto Pinochet's attack on La Moneda palace in Santiago, Chile. Yet, unless Yeltsin seizes absolute power, his actions are not at all comparable to Pinochet's dictatorship. Yeltsin has not yet eliminated parliament, though his constitution, much like that of

Weimar Germany, does gives him (or his successor) the power to do so. The populist one party Kemalist government of that in Turkey after the breakup of the Ottoman empire provides a second analogy.[17] But unlike the Turkish elite at that time, the Russian elite still conceive of Russia as a world power. The possibility that Yeltsin will attempt to retain power cannot be ruled out—yet, here again, it is not certain that he (or his successors) can absolutely contain revanchist forces.

The possibility of conflict among the former Soviet states themselves leads to the second scenario—the 1991–92 conflict in former Yugoslavia. If the CIS cannot be sustained, and if Ukraine cannot be drawn back into alliance (or breaks up), or if the Russian-Kazakh defense pact should falter, it seems dubious that the Russian elite will accept the disintegration of the CIS passively. Here, Russia, Ukraine, and Kazakhstan could play roles similar to Serbia, Croatia, and Bosnia respectively. Much as Serbia sought to incorporate Serbian nationals into a greater Serbia, and concurrently attempted to obtain access to the Adriatic, a Russian pan-nationalist movement may claim to protect the Russian "diaspora," concurrently seeking to secure access to the Crimea. In addition to protecting ethnic Russians in northern Kazakhstan and other Central Asian states (such as Tajikistan and Uzbekistan), Russia might seek to secure missile launch sites and operations bases in southern Kazakhstan. Secessionist movements in a bankrupt Ukraine could demand Russian (and/or Polish) intervention. Concurrently, the Ukrainian leadership could threaten the use of nuclear weapons (in an effort to gain Western support) at the same time that Kiev sought to expand its claims to parts of Kouban, Brest, Voronezh, and Belgorod.

On the other hand, the fact that an independent Ukraine (and less likely) Kazakhstan represent powerful nuclear and conventional actors vis-à-vis Russia and their neighbors, however, has appeared to mitigate against the analogy to the 1991–92 Yugoslav conflict. Soviet failure to win in Afghanistan also appears to make the threat of Russian expansion unlikely. At the same time, Russia's conventional/nuclear capabilities remain generally superior in quantitative terms to those of the former Soviet republics, though Ukraine has inherited most of the elite forward-based units as well as almost one-half of the former Soviet capability to manufacture tanks and missiles. In addition, Russia would have to move forces from behind the Urals.[18] Should such a war break out, it might possibly—but dubiously—remain "containable" depending upon the nature of Russian-Ukrainian war aims and if Ukraine, for example, should succeed in gaining the support of states such as Poland. Accordingly, if Ukrainian or Russian war aims begin to conflict with EU, Japanese, or Turkish security interests (among other states), then the United States, which would have to sustain a high level of conventional and nuclear force alert, could become involved.

Much like Hitler at Munich,[19] after having seized power by "democratic" means, a revanchist Russian movement could seek to neutralize Western opinion and gain Western acceptance for Russian territorial "revisions" and seek to test Western security guarantees along the demarcation lines of possible Russian expansion—the third scenario. As some 25 million Russians (plus Russified non-Russians) remain outside Russian territory, Russia may continue to lay claims to defense of their rights. A revanchist leadership may also be concerned with the breakup of integrated Soviet defenses and U.S. pressures to overthrow Iraq's Saddam Hussein, Cuba's Fidel Castro, Serbia's Slobodan Milosevic (plus pressure on Iran and the PRC)—related to the U.S. refusal to grant the new Russia geostrategic "parity" and a capacity for "strategic denial." These factors could lead the Russian elite to utilize more forceful forms of strategic leveraging to impel the United States into a more full-fledged entente/alliance upon the threat of war. The development of more advanced ICBMs and SLBMs, the pressing of Russian revisionist claims into the Baltic states, Eastern or Central Europe, threats against Japan and Germany, efforts to deflect China and/or pan-Islamic movements against U.S. interests represent several possible examples.

Thus, as was also the case at Munich, the following questions would then be raised: what territories/states should come under Russian and Western spheres of influence and security? At what point, if any, will the line be drawn? Poland—as before World War II? And what if Russian revanchist demands proved "unappeasable"? And concurrently, what if the PRC or other states refuse to serve as an active counterweight to Russia, and either remain neutral or seek to expand their claims as well? From this perspective, Pentagon fears of a Resurgent/Emergent Global Threat (REGT)—in which Russia acted alone or in alliance with other resurgent powers—are not entirely implausible. Such a prospect, however, would only become a self-fulfilled prophecy, should allied policy fail to draw the new Russia into the defense and economic community of nations.

A Moscow-led revanchist effort is not inevitable; yet, at the same time, there is definitely a movement to "defend" non-assimilated ethnic Russians living outside the Russian Federation. If defense of Russian—and Russified—ethnic groups continues to require use of economic pressures (as in the Baltic states) or else direct military intervention (as in the case of Tajikistan), then it may become increasingly difficult for Western political elites to sustain their support for a more hard-line Russian foreign and domestic policy. As was the case with Weimar German *Anschluss*, Russian threats to revise borders will remain latent and may serve to pressure newly independent republics in case they step out of line—or until more aggressive political groups take power in Russia. There are accordingly efforts to crack down on the newly emerging autonomous republics, such as the Chechen republic. The March 1992 Treaty of Federation failed to meet regional demands: Will the December 1993 Constitution of the second Russian republic (which has denied the right of regions inside the Russian Federation to declare "sovereignty" in contradiction to Moscow's laws despite the promises of earlier drafts) do a better job?

If efforts fail to hold Russia together, a fourth scenario—the prospect that Russia itself may break up because of its own internal ethnic/class disputes—cannot entirely be excluded. More than 100 nationalities within Russia have been placed into either ethno-territorial republics or regions. Autonomy movements in Chechen-Ingush, Chelyabinsk, Karelia, Tatarstan, Krasnoyarsk, Sakha (Yakutia), and the Sakhalin Island, threaten to splinter the Russian "federation" in part by claiming ownership over valuable raw materials and resources.[20] Ironically, these movements were once given support by Boris Yeltsin in the effort to gain leverage against the first Russian parliament prior that parliament's dissolution by Yeltsin himself. Rather than the hoped for cooperative decentralization of Alexandr Herzen or Leo Tolstoy (in which the central government would attempt to balance regional with central government concerns), such a situation could result in a medieval-like anarchy involving rival "boyar fiefdoms" which compete for political power and economic influence with Moscow—but armed with late twentieth century weaponry. If Russia did break apart, St. Petersburg and Moscow could gravitate toward Europe; the Far East toward Japan and/or China; Central and Southern Russia toward Turkey or Iran—potentially strengthening the strategic leveraging capabilities of these states. (The not-to-be-excluded breakup of Ukraine or China could also exacerbate regional and global rivalries.)

The very uncertainty as to how an instable Russia might react to the very real prospects of disaggregation will continue to generate global and regional tensions. The fifth scenario thus argues that instability in Russia and the CIS in general will continue to generate tremors throughout the Eurasian continent—even if Russia remains relatively "passive" and transfers of power occur without conflict—during the contemporary version of the interwar "twenty-years crisis" or the new Russian "Time of Troubles." Even if the CIS should survive as a consultative forum (and even if Russia does, for example, retain a single command over nuclear weapons), the fact that Russia will always have to look over its shoulder to see what policies Ukraine, Belarus, and Kazakhstan are pursuing at the same time that each one of these states has to deal with its own monumental domestic socioeconomic, ethnic/national, and ecological crises, will tend to perpetrate tensions. Concurrently, Russia will continue to eye relations with states such Germany, Japan, China, and Turkey with suspicion, as each one of these states attempts to influence policies of individual former Soviet republics. Thus even a moderate—but still "tougher"—Russian stance is likely to generate new tensions as Moscow attempts to sustain old interests and then seek out new ones in the effort to sustain spheres of influence and security—particularly following the victory of revanchist political parties in the December 1993 parliamentary elections. In addition, emerging "new" powers (or instable "old" ones)—having either lost Soviet security supports or else in competition for former Soviet spheres of influence—may take independent military action.

Until the collapse of the Berlin Wall, the West prepared for the contingency of a Soviet-initiated two-front war by attempting to build up a NATO-Japanese-PRC alliance. In today's circumstances, reflecting contingency planning for regional, as opposed to global, conflict, the Clinton administration has begun to shift U.S. national security policy toward the ability to win two nearly simultaneous regional conflicts—the possibility of drawn-out conflicts in Eastern Europe, Central Asia, or the Far East—what has been deemed "long war uncertainty." Such conflicts may not necessarily be initiated by Russia. Ukraine or an isolated China could take more militant actions.

What would happen if a clash between Poland, Lithuania, and Belarus, or between Azerbaijan and Armenia, did begin to draw in NATO members or those of an expanded EU membership—conflicts not necessarily initiated by Russia? Or what if Belarus and Ukraine went to war? What would happen if NATO members Turkey and Greece clashed over the Balkans? Here, the United States, EU, and Russia may split over which states deserve security supports. In Asia, what if disputes over the Spratly Islands or over oil in the South China Sea spark more extensive conflict among the regional powers? What if the PRC pressed its claims to Taiwan, Mongolia (including Russian Buryatia), or Kazakhstan? Or conversely, what if Russia and the PRC opted to divide Mongolia between them? (Sino-Russian conflict over Mongolia could provide the basis for Russo-Chinese collaboration or conflict if either side should be regarded as supporting pan-Mongolian claims or else seeks to grab Mongolia's vast, largely undefended, resources.) Or what if diplomacy fails to prevent war between North and South Korea?

What if India, in fear of its disaggregation, attacked Pakistan (or vice versa)? Or what if Iran, perhaps taking advantage of a weakened Iraq, began to assert its regional claims against the United Arab Emirates? Or what if a resurgent Iraq attacked Kuwait? Would the U.S., EU, and Japan still possess the political will and financial resources to check such challenges as they did during the 1991 Persian Gulf War? And finally, what if any of these actions did occur simultaneously with Russian/Ukrainian conflict over the Crimea, or with a Russian refusal to move out of the Baltics, or to isolate a greater Serbia or other states—thus threatening global, not regional, conflict?

The Pentagon, for example, has expected to "prevail" in ninety days in case Russian forces attack along the Polish-Lithuanian border or else if North Korea attacks South Korea. These latter scenarios tend to risk the prospects of a "short war illusion" based on a false sense of optimism. Following the successful forty day intervention against Iraq, future conflict scenarios (as former Yugoslavia has indicated) may well prove much more complex, as combatants may not be as isolated as Iraq.

An additional dilemma involves the prospect that even if both Washington and Moscow attempt to forge a mutual strategy to deal with the emerging powers, the two states may not be able to incorporate other states into their new "concert." U.S.-Russian efforts to sustain nuclear predominance, plus the lack of EU strategic-diplomatic unity, combined with perceived lack of U.S. reassurance and support, coupled with continuing Russian instability, could lead Germany/Europe to revive and strengthen its tacit strategic defense relationship with the PRC that had been established in the 1970s. Closer EU ties with China would represent a means to draw China away from a possible "Rapallo alliance" with Russia and to counterbalance burgeoning Japanese political-military and economic influence. Alternatively, if EU-PRC relations remain tense (because of British support for democracy in Hong Kong, for example), the EU could forge a closer "plutonium alliance" with Japan. Japanese efforts to forge a closer pan-Asian relationship with the PRC may also represent an attempt to prevent the latter from forming a closer entente with Russia, and concurrently attempt to work to forestall Beijing from pressing its claims in the South China Sea.

Thus far Moscow has attempted to maintain strong diplomatic and military relations with the PRC—in part in an effort to counterbalance Japan, and to prevent closer Sino-EU-Ukrainian ties. It is furthermore possible that the U.S.-Japanese alliance plus Japan's plutonium alliance with Europe might drive the PRC into a closer Sino-

Russian alliance (in which China is no longer the "junior partner" as was the case in the 1950s). A "Weimar" Russia and an economically rising, yet socially and politically instable, PRC have already begun to manipulate allied fears of a Sino-Russian re-alliance as a means to gain allied concessions. The new Russia has strengthened its relations with both India and Iran. In addition, Moscow has hoped to draw Germany closer to Russian interests; Moscow has also sought to block the formation of a Polish-Ukrainian and Ukrainian-PRC entente, as well as closer NATO and EU links to Poland and Ukraine.

If new European alliances are formed, the United States could find itself in an ambivalent situation, as it might have to counterbalance Russian interests vis-à-vis a potential alliance grouping, much as pre–World War I Britain did vis-à-vis the Franco-Russian Dual Alliance and Imperial Germany's Triple Alliance. European and Japanese support for non-Russian republics could give the latter more strategic leverage to press their claims against Moscow; it would likewise permit U.S. allies to more easily play individual republics against Moscow. In such a situation, efforts to forge a new "concert" may prove futile, particularly if Russia once again fears the possibility of encirclement by alliances tacitly or overtly linked to the United States. On the other hand, should the United States ultimately be able to pull Russia into alliance with Germany/Europe and Japan, it could still mismanage U.S.-Russian relations with the other emerging powers. Here, Russia might seek to gain U.S. support against Ukraine; and the United States might seek Russian support against China—the dilemma is that neither may be able to agree on a common policy. Or should both Germany and Japan develop an independent nuclear capacity—the United States itself may not be able to sustain the double containment. Such a situation would make a U.S.-Russian entente even more problematic.

Assuming Russia does not move into absolute isolation (or break up), it is also not inconceivable that Moscow and Washington could fight a war on the same side—if both regard a particular emerging power as challenging their mutual interests, and if joint action suits the interests of the ruling party or elite on both sides, so as to prove their alliance commitment. But if conflict does break out—whether between Russia and its neighbors, or among other significant states—it will be necessary to make certain these conflicts do not spread. As in the interwar period, divisive allied foreign policies and the failure to establish and sustain a larger concert of states may well mean—and in the not-so-distant future—having to choose between "supporting," "appeasing," "containing," and "rolling back" radically divergent revisionist or revanchist powers. The right choice will prevent World War III.

Notes

INTRODUCTION

1. My use of the term "double containment" implies U.S. efforts to contain *both* the Soviet Union *and* U.S. allies; yet it also implies tacit recognition of the Soviet role in containing those very allies. At the same time, however, Moscow placed greater emphasis on "double" or "joint" containment than did Washington. My view thus differs from general usage, such as that of Wolfram F. Hanrieder, *Germany, America, Europe* (New Haven, Conn.: Yale University Press, 1989).

2. On the one hand, Gaddis does not emphasize the extent to which the "long peace" was based upon the U.S.-Soviet double containment of emerging powers; on the other hand, his bipolar analysis does not emphasize the ability of the emerging powers to manipulate U.S.-Soviet relations. John Lewis Gaddis, *The Long Peace* (New York: Oxford University Press, 1987), 229–45. See also John Lewis Gaddis, *The United States and the End of the Cold War* (New York: Oxford University Press, 1992).

3. John Mueller, *Retreat From Doomsday* (New York: Basic Books, 1988).

4. For critique of the unit-veto theory, see Hedley Bull, *The Anarchical Society* (London: Macmillan, 1977), 240–43.

5. On these issues, see Geoffrey Blainey, *The Causes of War* (London: Macmillan, 1988), 283. Michael Howard, *The Causes of War* (Cambridge, Mass.: Harvard University Press, 1983), 94. For the view that the nuclear deterrent may be analogous to the failure of British air power to deter Hitler, see Jeffrey L. Hughes "Origins of World War II in Europe," in *The Origin and Prevention of Major Wars*, ed. Robert I. Rotberg and Theodore K. Rabb (Cambridge: Cambridge University Press, 1988). A Pearl Harbor–type nuclear strike by a desperate nuclear weapons state upon one more powerful cannot entirely be ruled out. See Scott D. Sagan, "Origins of the Pacific War," ibid., 349–51.

CHAPTER 1

1. NSC 68, in Steven L. Rearden, *The Evolution of American Strategic Doctrine* (Boulder, Colo.: Westview Press/SAIS Foreign Policy Institute, 1984), 125. All subsequent references to NSC 68 are from Rearden.

2. NSC 68 was not without its critics. See top secret critique of vagueness of NSC 68's long range objectives of "freedom" and "democratization" for the Soviet Union by James Bryant Conant who predicted that Russia may "Balkanize" or "Byzantine" itself. Department of State, *Foreign Relations of the United States, 1950*, Vol. 1 (Washington, D.C.: GPO, 1977), 176–83.

3. Evidence from the Soviet Archives (though not conclusive) suggests that Khrushchev would have accepted a confederal Germany including a free Berlin, *but had hoped for a U.S. offer of compromise.* See Vladislav Zubok, "Khrushchev and the Berlin Crisis, 1958–62," *Cold War International History Project* № 6 (Washington, D.C.: Woodrow Wilson International Center for Scholars, May 1993).

4. McGeorge Bundy, *Danger and Survival* (New York: Random House, 1986), 232.

5. Bertrand Goldschmidt, "A Forerunner of the NPT? Soviet Proposals of 1947," *IAEA Bulletin* 28, 1 (Spring 1986).

6. Paul Nitze opposed "a periodic inspection system to replace the Baruch Plan" and other Soviet offers "superficially" in the U.S. interest. He feared that by publicly rejecting such a plan "we would be increasing the divisive factors in the United States." See Department of State, *Foreign Relations of the United States, 1950*, 192.

7. See Hans Morgenthau, in *Nationalist, Realist and Radical*, ed. Jerald A. Combs (New York: Harper & Row, 1972), 499. See also the proposal for elections including the Vietcong: George Ball, "Dean Acheson," *The New York Review*, 17 December 1992, 11–12.

8. See Lippmann's memorandum regarding the negotiation of a German Peace Treaty (23 September 1948) to John Foster Dulles, in *Public Philosopher: Selected Letters of Walter Lippmann*, ed. John Morton Blum (New York: Ticknor and Fields, 1985), 521–24. Lippmann regretted using the term "neutrality" to describe a confederal Germany.

9. Walter Lippmann, *U.S. War Aims* (Boston: Little, Brown, 1944), 135.

10. Ibid., 136

11. The first Pentagon Defense Planning Guidance (DPG) stated that the United States must "prevent the emergence of European–only security arrangements which would undermine NATO." It also warned against any precipitous withdrawal of U.S. military forces in Asia that might alienate Japan. See *International Herald Tribune (IHT)*, 18 February 1992; *IHT*, 12 March 1992; *IHT*, 25 May 1992. In 1993, Congress approved a 1995–99 defense budget of roughly $1.2 billion.

12. By November 1993, Moscow formulated a new strategic doctrine involving the abandonment of the principle of no first use of nuclear weaponry; opposition to NATO or WEU expansion into former Soviet spheres of influence and security; contingency plans to prevent the breakup of the CIS and to deal with secessionist

movements in the Russian Federation itself. The plan also suggested policies to deal with efforts to limit Russian economic independence; degrade its industrial and technical capacity; restrict access for Russian exports; and block access to new technology. It also suggested ways to control capital and raw material exports. See *Foreign Report* (London: The Economist, 18 November 1993).

13. Walter Christopher, *IHT*, 17 January 1994, 1. Henry Kissinger, *IHT*, 24 January 1994, 5. (U.S. ambassador-at-large Strobe Talbott purportedly reversed the opinion of U.S. Secretary of State Warren Christopher who initially favored the early acceptance of Central and East European states into NATO—U.S. policy accordingly adopted a "go slow" approach. *IHT*, 3 January 1994, 1, 3.) Russian critics of the Partnership for Peace argue Russia must negotiate for "equality" with NATO, and hence *primacy* over third states—if Russia is to participate. See interview with Vladimir Lukin, *Moscow News*, 16 (22–28 April 1994), 4.

14. See Henry Kissinger, *IHT*, 6 July 1992. Zbigniew Brzezinski, "The Premature Partnership," *Foreign Affairs*, March/April 1994. For cases for and against a Ukrainian nuclear deterrent, see John J. Mearsheimer and Steven E. Miller, "Should the Ukraine Stay Nuclear?," *Foreign Affairs*, 72, 3, Summer 1993. For argument that Washington should "contain" Ukraine within U.S.–led regimes *against* Russia, see Patrick Glynn, "Nukraine," *The New Republic* (13 and 20 July 1992), 24.

15. Lippmann, *U.S. War Aims*, 136.

16. See, for example, Charles Krauthammer, "The Unipolar Movement," *Foreign Affairs*, Winter 1990–91.

17. Joseph S. Nye, Jr., *Bound to Lead* (New York: Basic Books, 1990). Nye's analysis does not fully explain why the United States must increasingly look to Germany/Europe and Japan for "burden sharing."

18. On the possibility of a Euro-Soviet (Euro-Russian?) and U.S.-Sino-Japanese axis, see Immanuel Wallerstein, *The Politics of the World-Economy* (Cambridge: Cambridge University Press, 1984), 66, 75.

19. Alexander Dallin, "America's Search for a Policy Toward the Former Soviet Union," *Current History*, October 1992, 322.

20. See Hanrieder, *Germany, America, Europe*, 1–25.

21. See Joan Edelman Spero, *The Politics of International Economic Relations* (London: Unwin Hyman, 1990), 68–71.

CHAPTER 2

1. E. H. Carr, *The Twenty Years Crisis* (New York: St. Martin's Press, 1966).

2. On the classical geostrategic insular, amphibious, continental approach, see George Liska, *Quest for Equilibrium* (Baltimore: Johns Hopkins University Press, 1981). On the modernist political-economic core, semiperipheral, peripheral approach, see Immanuel Wallerstein, *The Politics*, 38. NAFTA represents the insular hegemonic core bloc; the EU is quasi-insular core; Japan is insular core. Russia and China are continental semiperipheral states with some core and

amphibious attributes. The former Soviet Union represented an amphibious semiperipheral state with some core attributes. I intend to develop a synthesis of the two methodologies more thoroughly in a later book.

3. Wallerstein, *The Politics*, 17.

4. On social aspects of the American Revolution, see J. Franklin Jameson, *The American Revolution Considered as a Social Movement* (Gloucester, Mass.: Peter Smith, 1957, 1926). On U.S. reaction to nationalization, see George Liska, *Career of Empire* (Baltimore: Johns Hopkins University Press, 1978), 245.

5. Francis Fukuyama, *The End of History and the Last Man* (New York: Macmillan, 1992).

6. John Mearsheimer, "Back to the Future," *International Security* 15:1 (Summer 1990): 19. See also Kenneth N. Waltz, *Theory of International Politics* (New York: Addison Wesley, 1979), 168.

7. Hedley Bull's definitions of *primacy, hegemony,* and *dominance* appear misleading. (Bull, *The Anarchical Society*, 213–19). Contrary to Bull, states in the position of primacy—"first among equals"—may, in fact, threaten their allies. Soviet rule over Central and Eastern Europe should be defined as dominance—"divide and conquer." U.S. rule over Western Europe should be defined as a mix of primacy vis-à-vis Britain and France and hegemony—"divide and rule"—vis-à-vis West Germany (if not dominance over the latter from 1945–1955.) In addition, once the Soviet Union imploded, Russia sought primacy over the CIS, if not hegemony over Ukraine and lesser former Soviet republics (if not dominance over the latter); the "new" Moscow has thus far sought *primacy* over Central Europe.

8. See Hall Gardner, "Averting World War III," *SAIS Review* 8, 2 (Summer–Fall 1988): 129.

9. In addition, in October 1993 the German Constitutional Court ruled that German law superseded that of European law and that monetary union was not irreversible. Konrad Handschuh, "L'Europe fédérale est morte à Karlsruhe" *Courrier International*, 156 (28 October–3 November 1993): 15.

10. See Louis J. Snyder, *Macro-Nationalisms* (Westport, Conn.: Greenwood, 1984). Russian pan-movements are divided between pan-Slavism, National Bolshevikism, Great Russian chauvinism, among other revanchist variants; Turkish pan-movements are divided between pan-Turkism and pan-Turanism.

11. Hans Morgenthau, *Politics Among Nations* (New York: McGraw–Hill, 1985), 34.

12. Ibid., 351.

13. In Schumpeter's view, wars in the liberal-democratic era can be explained by the continued presence of atavistic elites in power; yet in my view, revanchism is not entirely an atavistic reaction to socio-political-technological innovations fostered by capitalism. Revanchist elites do not necessarily originate from the old ruling classes. They may actually oppose the complacency of old elites and be willing to use aspects of strategic leveraging and techno–innovation to regain lost imperial status and galvanize popular opinion *across* class lines. On atavism, see J. A. Schumpeter, *Imperialism and the Social Classes* (New York: A.M. Kelly, 1951).

14. Karl Polanyi, *The Great Transformation* (Boston: Beacon Hill, 1944), 14.

15. Fukuyama, *The End of History*, 45.

16. Michael Doyle, "Kant, Liberal Legacies, and Foreign Affairs," *Philosophy and Public Affairs* 1, 12 (1983).

17. Ibid., 232–33.

18. On Japanese Taisho Democracy, see Hideo Ibe, *Japan Thrice Opened* (New York: Praeger, 1992), 99–102.

19. Immanuel Kant, *Kant's Political Writings*, ed. Hans Reiss (Cambridge: Cambridge University Press, 1977), 93–97.

20. Jean–Jacques Rousseau, *Rousseau on International Relations*, ed. Stanley Hoffmann and David P. Fidler (Oxford: Clarendon Press, 1991), 93.

21. Richard Ullman, *Securing Europe* (Twickenham, U.K.: Adamantine, 1991), 27.

22. Ibid., 20.

23. On the Dawes and Young Plans, followed by the Hoover Moratorium, see Marshall Lee and Wolfgang Michalka, *German Foreign Policy, 1917–1933* (New York: St. Martin's Press, 1987), 71, 95–99, 106–11, 118–19, 130–135.

24. See my previous arguments: Hall Gardner, "Averting World War III"; "Past, Present and Future Dilemmas of European Security and Identity," *History of European Ideas* 15, 1–3 (August 1992).

25. On appeasement, see Carr, *The Twenty Years Crisis*; George Liska, *Russia and the Road to Appeasement* (Baltimore: Johns Hopkins University Press, 1982); Robert Gilpin, *War and Change in World Politics* (Cambridge: Cambridge University Press, 1986). Paul Kennedy, ed., *Strategy and Diplomacy* (London: George Allen and Unwin, 1983). For an anti-appeasement perspective, see Blainey, *The Causes of War*; and Patrick Glynn, *Closing Pandora's Box* (New York: Basic Books, 1992). For a historical perspective, see R. W. Seton-Watson, *Britain and the Dictators* (Cambridge: Cambridge University Press, 1988).

26. John Zametica, *The Yugoslav Conflict* Adelphi Paper, № 270 (London: IISS, 1992), 63.

27. Michael Walzer raises this question but does not fully explore its implications in, *Just and Unjust Wars* (New York: Basic Books, 1977), 69.

28. Joshua Goldstein, *Long Cycles* (New Haven, Conn.: Yale University Press, 1988), 17.

29. As Jervis has argued, inappropriate historical analogies can lead to misleading policy conclusions. The more thoroughly similarities *and* differences are drawn out at the systemic level, however, the less the chance for erroneous policy. For criticism of historical analogy, see Robert Jervis, *Perception and Misperception in International Relations* (Princeton, N.J.: Princeton University Press, 1976).

30. John H. Fincher, *Chinese Democracy* (New York: St. Martin's Press, 1981). Hall Gardner, "China's Reaction to Western Liberalism and Democratic Values," *La Canard Laqué*, 5 (Paris: Institut d'Etudes Politiques, Spring 1991), 27–29. To adopt democratic procedures to Chinese conditions, Sun Yat Sen, for example, had advocated a five-fold separation of powers in which a system of examinations and censorship would be added to the traditional three-fold separation of powers among the executive, legislative, and judicial branches.

CHAPTER 3

1. For background, see Thomas Bailey, *America Faces Russia* (Ithaca N.Y.: Cornell University Press, 1950). Norman E. Saul, *Distant Friends: The United States and Russia, 1763-1867* (Lawrence, Kan.: University of Kansas Press, 1991).

2. Thomas Bailey, *America Faces Russia*. Tyler Dennett, *Roosevelt and the Russo-Japanese War* (Garden City, N.Y.: Doubleday, 1925), 165. On missed U.S. opportunities to work with Russia in Manchuria and Korea to check Japan, see William A. Williams, *American-Russian Relations 1781–1947* (New York: Octagon, 1971), 35–44.

3. George Kennan, *Russia Leaves the War* (Princeton, N.J.: Princeton University Press, 1956), 23. See also Robert J. Maddox, *The Unknown War in Russia* (San Rafael, Calif.: Presidio Press, 1977), 77–93.

4. George Kennan, *Russia Leaves the War*, 276–77.

5. Ibid., 188–89.

6. Manfred Jonas, *The United States and Germany* (Ithaca, N.Y.: Cornell University Press, 1984), 139–40.

7. William Taubman, *Stalin's American Policy* (New York: W.W. Norton, 1982), 67.

8. Liska, *Russia and the Road to Appeasement*, 7.

9. John Lewis Gaddis, *Strategies of Containment* (Oxford: Oxford University Press, 1982).

10. See Robert L. Messer, *The End of an Alliance* (Chapel Hill, N.C.: University of North Carolina Press, 1982), 90; 105. Messer argues that Byrnes and Truman did attempt "to use the bomb diplomatically, but to preserve the wartime alliance, not destroy it." Certainly, the United States did want to continue U.S.-Soviet cooperation—but only as long as Moscow accepted U.S. aims!

11. William S. Borden, *The Pacific Alliance* (Madison: University of Wisconsin Press, 1984), 169.

12. Alvin Z. Rubinstein, *Soviet Foreign Policy Since World War II* (New York: HarperCollins, 1992), 77. Thomas Alan Schwartz, *America's Germany* (Cambridge, Mass.: Harvard University Press, 1991), 89. Neal Ascherson, *The Polish August* (New York: Viking, 1980), 44–51. Vyacheslav Molotov believed control of Poland was crucial: "We cannot lose Poland. If this line is crossed they will grab us, too." See *Molotov Remembers*, ed. Felix Chuev (Chicago: Ivan R. Dee, 1993), 54.

13. London and Washington supported a "federal" Germany; Moscow sought centralized control; France sought a confederal approach, but "would support [the United States] against the Russians if faced with an exclusive choice." See Anne Deighton, *The Impossible Peace* (Oxford: Clarendon Press, 1990), 247. Only two states favored a "confederation type of approach" according to Lucius D. Clay, *Decision in Germany* (New York: Doubleday, 1950), 142. In addition to U.S. opposition, Molotov's view that Soviet troops would have to be deployed in each region of a confederal Germany helped kill France's proposal in September 1945.

14. Thomas G. Paterson, *Soviet-American Confrontation* (Baltimore: Johns Hopkins University Press, 1973), 248.

15. Melvyn P. Leffler, *A Preponderance of Power* (Stanford, Calif.: Stanford University Press, 1992), 77–78. Howard Jones, *"A New Kind of War"* (New York: Oxford University Press, 1989), 8–9.

16. Ivo Banac, *With Stalin against Tito* (Ithaca, N.Y.: Cornell University Press, 1988), 31.

17. H. W. Brands, *Inside the Cold War* (New York: Oxford University Press, 1991), 254.

18. See George C. Herring, *Aid to Russia* (New York: Columbia University Press, 1973), 274.

19. See Michael M. Yoshitsu, *Japan and the San Francisco Peace Settlement* (New York: Columbia University Press, 1983), 4. The northern territories are referred to as Kurile Islands throughout the text.

20. See Paul H. Nitze, *From Hiroshima to Glasnost* (New York: Grove Weidenfield, 1989), 49.

21. See Yokokawa Shoichi, in Gilbert Rozman, *Japan's Response to the Gorbachev Era, 1985–91* (Princeton, N.J.: Princeton University Press, 1992), 41.

22. Dean Acheson, quoted in Thomas G. Paterson, *Major Problems in American Foreign Policy* (Lexington, Mass.: D.C. Heath, 1984) 2: 325.

23. Robert P. Newman, *Owen Lattimore and the "Loss" of China* (Berkeley, Ca.: University of California Press, 1992), 61–63, 137, 165–66. Alexander Bevin, *The Strange Connection* (Westport, Conn.: Greenwood Press, 1992). See also, Jian Chen, "The Sino-Soviet Alliance and China's Entry into the Korean War," *Cold War International History Project*, Nº 1 (Washington, D.C.: Woodrow Wilson International Center for Scholars, June 1992).

24. See Bruce Cumings, *Origins of the Korean War* (Princeton N.J.: Princeton University Press, 1990) 2: 374–79, 381–88, 417–23, 427, 437, 441–53, 463, 515, 536–37, 555–58, 738. For view that Mao was more reluctant than Stalin, see Hao Yufan and Zhai Zhihai, "China's Decision to Enter the Korean War," *China Quarterly*, 121 (March 1990).

25. Jon Halliday, "A Secret War," *Far Eastern Economic Review*, 22 April 1993, 32–36. U.S. pilots ranged as far as Shenyang and Dalian—and Vladivostok.

26. See James Ritcher, "Reexamining Soviet Policy Towards Germany During the Berlin Interregnum." *Cold War International History Project*, Nº 3 (Washington D.C.: Woodrow Wilson International Center for Scholars, June 1992), 16.

27. Also in 1954 Kiev ceded Kouban in largely Tatar Krasnodarsk—implying a counter-claim against Moscow. Vitalij Moskalenko, First Secretary Ukrainian Embassy, Sofia, Bulgaria, interviewed by Radoslava Stefanova, 27 August 1993.

28. Rolf Steininger, *The German Question* (New York: Columbia University Press, 1990), 26.

29. Hanreider, *Germany, America, Europe*, 54, 85–88, 142.

30. Vladislav Zubok, "Khrushchev and the Berlin Crisis, 1958–62." See interview with Khrushchev in Walter Lippmann, *The Coming Tests with Russia* (Boston: Little, Brown, 1964), 26. See also James L. Richardson, *Germany and the Atlantic Alliance* (Cambridge, Mass.: Harvard University Press, 1966).

31. On East German leader Ulbricht's use of strategic leveraging against

Moscow, see Hope M. Harrison, "Ulbricht and the Concrete Rose,"*Cold War International History Project*, № 5 (Washington, D.C.: Woodrow Wilson International Center for Scholars, May 1993). See also Michael J. Sodaro, *Moscow, Germany and the West from Khrushchev to Gorbachev* (Ithaca, N.Y.: Cornell University Press, 1990), 9, 58.

32. Michael R. Beschloss, *The Crisis Years* (New York: HarperCollins, 1991), 177–78, 231–235, 242–43, 341.

33. Hanrieder, *Germany, America, Europe*, 45–50, 54, 91.

34. Stephen E. Ambrose, *Rise to Globalism* (New York: Viking Penguin Books, 1988), 163. On sterling, see Graeme P. Auton and Wolfram E. Hanrieder, *The Foreign Policies of West Germany, France, and Britain* (Englewood Cliffs, N.J.: Prentice Hall, 1980), 197.

35. David Fischer, *Stopping the Spread of Nuclear Weapons* (London: Routledge, 1992), 36; William B. Walker and Mans Lönnröth, *Nuclear Power Struggles* (London: Allen and Unwin, 1983).

36. Raymond Garthoff, *Reflections on the Cuban Missile Crisis* (Washington, D.C.: The Brookings Institution, 1989), 146. IRBMs in Cuba would have enhanced Soviet first-strike capabilities by 80 percent. (According to Moscow, Castro urged the deployment of nuclear weapons; according to Castro, he heard it on the radio. See Robert S. McNamara, "Conclusion: Thirty Years On," *IHT*, 15 October 1992. See interview with Arthur Schlesinger, Jean-Gabriel Fredet, "Castro a appris la nouvelle par la radio. . ." *Le Nouvel Observateur*, 20–26 February 1992, 47.)

37. On the Fourquet doctrine and French efforts to forge a triggering nuclear link to NATO, see Michael Harrison, *France: The Reluctant Ally* (Baltimore: Johns Hopkins University Press, 1981), 194–99. Hanrieder, *Germany, America, Europe*, 53–54. Germany's insistence upon a forward defense expressed Bonn's fear that Washington would not commit itself to a nuclear defense of Germany if NATO had a range of military options.

38. Richard deVillafranca, "Japan and the Northern Territories Dispute," *Asian Survey*, 33, 6 (June 1993).

39. On the Sino–Soviet conflict, see Adam Ulam, *The Communists* (New York: Scribner's, 1992).

40. Henry Kissinger, *White House Years* (Boston: Little, Brown, 1979), 113–14.

41. Gaddis, *Strategies of Containment*, 210n.

CHAPTER 4

1. Richard Nixon, *Memoirs* (New York: Warner, 1980), 1030. See also Henry Kissinger, *Years of Upheaval* (Boston: Little, Brown, 1982), 274–86.

2. Henry Kissinger, *White House Years* (Boston: Little, Brown, 1979), 220–23.

3. Seymour M. Hersch, *The Price of Power* (New York: Summit Books, 1983), 354–55.

4. See Karen Dawisha, "Soviet Security and the Role of the Military: The 1968 Czechoslovak Crisis," *British Journal of Political Science* 10 (1980): 343. See also,

Harry Gelman, *The Brezhnev Politburo and the Decline of Detente* (Ithaca, N.Y.: Cornell University Press, 1984), 98–99.

5. Quoted in Hersch, *The Price of Power*, 416.

6. As Andrei Gromyko put it in the summer of 1970, "We lost our last hope with the Chinese, and we must finalize the treaty with the FRG without delay . . . . It's a lever to draw Europe away from American influence." Arkady Shevchenko, *Breaking with Moscow* (New York: Knopf, 1985), 169.

7. Hersch, *The Price of Power*, 416. See also Richard J. Barnet, *The Alliance* (New York: Simon and Schuster, 1983).

8. Cited in Hanrieder, *Germany, America, Europe*, 208.

9. John W. Garver, *China's Decision for Rapprochement with the United States* (Boulder, Colo.: Westview Press, 1987), 91.

10. William J. Barnds, *The Two Koreas in East Asian Affairs* (New York: New York University Press, 1976), 175. Leonard S. Spector and Jacqueline R. Smith, "North Korea: The Next Nuclear Nightmare," *Arms Control Today* (March 1991): 8–13. Selig S. Harrison, "The Three Cornered Suspense in Northeast Asia," *IHT*, 2 November 1993, 5.

11. Joseph M. Ha, "Moscow's Policy Toward Japan," *Problems of Communism*, 26 (September–October 1977): 62.

12. Nixon, *Memoirs*, 883.

13. Ross Terrill, *800,000,000* (Boston: Little, Brown, 1972), 146; Edgar Snow, *The Long Revolution* (New York: Random House, 1972), 20.

14. Garver, *China's Decision*, 96–99.

15. Edward G. Giradet, *Afghanistan: The Soviet War* (New York: St. Martin's Press, 1985).

16. On linkage between U.S. balance of payments and burden sharing, see Hanrieder, *Germany, America, Europe*, 292.

17. See Richard J. Barnet, *The Alliance*, 354.

18. Gaddis Smith, *Morality, Reason, and Power* (New York: Hill and Wang, 1986), 67.

19. On contradictory Carter policy, see Donald Spencer, *The Carter Implosion* (New York: Praeger, 1988). UN ambassador Andrew Young predicted a massive non-violent movement in Eastern Europe; he also sought to draw "Third World" movements away from "racist" Russian grasp.

20. See Zbigniew Brzezinski, *Power and Principle* (New York: Farrar, Straus, Giroux, 1983), 178–81, 297–301, 420, 467.

21. Leslie Gelb, "Interview," *Arms Control Today*, 10, 8 (September, 1980): 6.

22. Cyrus Vance, *Hard Choices* (New York: Simon and Schuster, 1983), 120.

23. David Fischer, *Stopping the Spread of Nuclear Weapons* (London: Routledge, 1992). Jozef Goldblat, ed., *Non–Proliferation: The Why and Wherefore*, Stockholm International Peace Research Institute *SIPRI* (London: Taylor and Francis, 1985), 10–11.

24. Dieter Braun, *The Indian Ocean* (London: C. Hurst, 1983).

25. See John Lewis Gaddis, "The Reagan Administration and Soviet–American Relations," *Reagan and the World*, ed. David E. Kyvig (New York: Praeger, 1990).

26. John F. Lehman, Jr., "The Rebirth of U.S. Naval Strategy," *Strategic Review* 9, 3 (Summer 1981): 14.

27. *Far Eastern Economic Review*, 29 September 1988, 40–41.

28. On Zhao Ziyang, see Peter Jones and Sian Kevill, *China and the Soviet Union, 1949–84*, ed. Alan Day (New York: Facts on File, 1985), 173–74.

29. See Reinhard Drifte, *Japan's Foreign Policy* (London: Routledge, 1990), 57–58.

CHAPTER 5

1. "Z," "To the Stalin Mausoleum," *Daedalus* 19, 1 (Winter 1990). On the Bush administration's opposition to George Schultz and reluctance to accept Kissinger's proposal for a U.S.–Soviet deal over Eastern Europe (preferring to let events take their own course), see Michael R. Beschloss and Strobe Talbott, *At the Highest Levels* (Boston: Little, Brown, 1993), 13-17.

2. Colin L. Powell, "U.S. Forces: Challenges Ahead," *Foreign Affairs*, Winter 1992/93.

3. Hannes Adomeit, "Gorbachev and German Unification," *Problems of Communism* 39, (July–August 1990). Margaret Thatcher, *The Downing Street Years* (London: HarperCollins, 1993), 792, 813. Thatcher considered her German policy "an unambiguous failure."

4. See W.R. Snyder, "USSR-Germany—A Link Restored," *Foreign Policy*, Fall 1991.

5. "Foreign Minister Genscher," *The German Tribune*, 17 January 1992, 3.

6. On South Korean reluctance to accept burden-sharing, see *Foreign Broadcast Information Service, East Asia (FBIS EAS)*, 1 February 1990, 30.

7. On Philippine base demands and Washington's refusal to back Manilla's claims to the Spratly Islands, see *FBIS EAS*, 6 February 1990.

8. James Fallows, "Is Japan the Enemy?" *The New York Review*, 30 May 1991, 35.

9. On differing views of U.S.-Japanese technological capabilities, see Frank Langdon, ed., *Superpower Maritime Strategy in the Pacific* (London: Routledge, 1990), 18. See also Edward O. Reischauer Center, *The United States and Japan in 1992* (Washington, D.C.: SAIS, 1992), 45.

10. Shintaro Ishihara, *The Japan That Can Say No!*, trans. Ezra F. Vogel (New York: Simon and Schuster, 1991).

11. Janne E. Nolan, *Trappings of Power* (Washington, D.C.: The Brookings Institution, 1991).

12. Fallows, "Is Japan the Enemy?" For specific Japanese technological advantages, see *Japan's Choices*, ed. Masataka Kosaka (London: Pinter Publishers, 1989).

13. *FBIS Soviet Union*, 3 January 1990, 7–9.

14. Gerald Segal, "As China Grows Strong," *International Affairs*, Spring 1988, 220.

15. Mark J. Valencia, "The Spratly Islands," *The Pacific Review* 1, 4 (1988).

16. *FBIS CHINA*, 6 February 1990, 49. From the *Remin Ribao*: the U.S. "position on the Taiwan issue will constantly change in light of [the PRC's] increasing national strength and international status. It is unlikely that the United States will openly support 'Taiwan's independence' from China at the risk of its global strategic interests and relations with China." See also calls to promote "defense education." Ibid., 10. On political aspects of Chinese arms sales, see Xiaochuan Zhang, in *The Chinese View of the World*, ed., Yufan Hao and Guocang Huan (New York: Pantheon, 1989), 93–94.

17. See Hall Gardner, "China and the World After Tiananmen Square," *SAIS Review*, Winter/Spring 1991. See also, Hall Gardner, "Those Stumbling Blocks to Recognizing Vietnam Don't have to Trip US Now," *L.A. Times*, 14 March 1989.

18. *IHT*, 27 March 1991, 15. See also Roxane D. V. Sismandis, "China's International Security Policy," *Problems of Communism*, July–August 1991.

19. Alexander J. Motyl, *Sovietology, Rationality, Nationality* (New York: Columbia University Press, 1990), 103–108, 174–186.

20. See Sewerlyn Bialer, in *The Soviet Union in the 1980s*, ed. Eric P. Hoffman (New York: Academy of Political Science, 1984).

CHAPTER 6

1. *Les Nouvelles de Moscou* 24 (16 June 1992): 13. (My translation of French edition of *Moscow News*).

2. Raymond L. Garthoff, *Détente and Confrontation* (Washington, D.C.: The Brookings Institution, 1985), 90–91.

3. Banning W. Garrett and Bonnie S. Glaser, *War and Peace: The Views from Moscow and Peking* (Berkeley: Institute of International Studies, University of California Press, 1984).

4. Richard L. Sneider, *U.S.-Japanese Security Relations* (New York: Columbia University Press, 1983).

5. Jimmy Carter, *Keeping Faith* (Toronto: Bantam, 1982), 209.

6. Gary K. Bertsch, "The United States and Western Trade with the USSR," in *Trade, Technology and Soviet-American Relations*, ed. Bruce Parrott (Bloomington: Indiana University Press, 1985), 255–56.

7. Michael R. Lucas, *The Western Alliance after INF* (Boulder, Colo.: Lynne Rienner, 1990), 152–153.

8. See *China Daily*, Business Weekly, 26 March 1989. EC-PRC cooperation involved nuclear fission, space technology, energy and raw material excavation. Beijing, however, urged the EC to drop barriers to Chinese exports.

9. See Robert Cullen, "Human Rights: A Thaw Imperiled," in *Gorbachev's Russia and American Foreign Policy*, ed. Sewerlyn Bialer and Michael Mandelbaum (Boulder, Colo.: Westview Press, 1987), 146.

10. See International Institute of Strategic Studies, *IISS Strategic Survey, 1990–92*, 204. See Nolan, *Trappings*, 127. See also Joan Edelman Spero, *The Politics of*

International Economic Relations, 343.

11. Office of Technology Assessment, *Arming Our Allies* (OTA–ISC–449, Washington D.C.: GPO, May 1990).

12. On Turkish nuclear material to Pakistan, see Senator John Glenn, *IHT*, 26 June 1992, 4.

13. Edwin O. Reischauer Center, *The United States and Japan, 1989*, 37. See also Kathleen C. Bailey, *Doomsday Weapons* (Urbana, Ill.: University of Illinois Press, 1991), 17. Ivo H. Daalder, *The SDI Challenge to Europe* (Cambridge, Mass.: Ballinger, 1987): 61.5 percent of all Western technology acquired by the Soviet Union came from the United States; 10.5 percent from Germany; 8 percent from France; 7.5 percent from Britain.

14. Nathan Thayer, in Committee on Foreign Affairs, *United States-Japanese Relations* (Washington, D.C.: GPO, 1982), 218–20.

15. Carl G. Jacobsen, in *Strategic Power USA/USSR*, ed. Carl G. Jacobsen (London: Macmillan, 1990), 349.

16. Robert Campbell, "The Soviet Economic Model," in *Gorbachev's Russia*, 83.

17. Alex Nove, "The Twelfth Five Year Plan," in *The Soviet Economy Under Gorbachev*, ed. Reiner Weichhardt (Brussels: NATO Colloquium, 1991).

18. Organization of Economic Cooperation and Development, *OECD Economic Surveys: United States 1991/1992. The Economist*, 20 November 1993, 29. (The GPD of Weimar Germany declined 24 percent between 1929 and 1932.)

19. European Bank of Reconstruction and Development, *EBRD Quarterly Economic Review*, September 1992; April 1993. See also *Current Digest of the Post-Soviet Press* (CDPSP) 45, 3 (1993): 5.

20. See David Roche, in John Lloyd, "So far, so good—but so fragile," *Financial Times*, 6 April 1992.

21. On market-oriented G-7 guidelines in July 1991, see *Newsweek*, 29 July 1991, 10. On relaxed guidelines, see *Wall Street Journal*, 26–27 June 1992.

22. See *The Economist*, 28 November 1992; Andrei Shleifer, in *Wall Street Journal*, 4 June 1992.

23. *Wall Street Journal*, 15 November 1993, 2. See annual economic survey of the United Nations Economic Commission for Europe (UNECE), quoted in the *Financial Times*, 16/17 April 1992. See also Melin Fagen, former director of the UNECE, *IHT*, 12 May 1992.

24. *IHT*, 10 November 1993, 5. *Financial Times*, 12 November 1993, 16.

25. Robert Gilpin, *The Political Economy of International Relations* (Princeton N.J.: Princeton University Press, 1987), 140, 149.

26. On concerted aspects of the G-5 agreement of September 1985, see Gilpin, *The Political Economy*, 152.

27. On German burden sharing, see Hanrieder, *Germany, America, Europe*, 306; Susan Strange, *International Economic Relations of the Western World* (London: Oxford, 1976), 2: 48–49.

28. John Zysman, "U.S. Power, Trade, Technology," *International Affairs* 67, 1 (1991): 81–106.

29. Paul Kennedy, *Preparing for the 21st Century* (New York: Random House,

1993).

30. See Walter Goldstein in *Shifting into Neutral, ed.* Christopher Coker (London: Brassey's, 1990). See also David P. Calleo, *The Bankrupting of America* (New York: William Morrow, 1992), 134–37.

31. Zysman, "U.S. Power," 97–103. Trade within "blocs" is growing faster than trade between "blocs."

32. Congressman William H. Gray, in *The United States and the World Economy* (Washington, D.C.: Johns Hopkins SAIS, 1990), 13.

33. *Financial Times*, 27 October 1992. *Wall Street Journal*, 5–6 June 1992. *The German Tribune*, 8 September 1991, 7.

34. Panos Tsakaloyannis, in *The European Community and the Challenge of the Future*, ed. Juliet Lodge (London: Pinter, 1989), 253.

35. See analysis of Structural Impediments Initiative, *Wall Street Journal*, 7 January 1991, 1.

36. See Reischauer Center (1992), 60. See also Mike M. Mochizuki, "To Change or Contain: Dilemmas of American Policy toward Japan," in *Eagle in a New World*, ed. Kenneth A. Oye, Robert J. Lieber, and Donald Rothchild (New York: HarperCollins, 1992).

37. On China's growth, see Paul Bairoch, "International Industrial Levels from 1750 to 1980," *Journal of European Economic History* 11, 2 (Fall 1982). "China Survey," *The Economist*, 28 November–December 1992.

38. For concerns raised by aggressive U.S. trade policy, see *OECD Economic Surveys: United States 1991/1992*, 67–80.

CHAPTER 7

1. John Lewis Gaddis, *Strategies of Containment* (Oxford: Oxford University Press, 1982), 274, 296n, 330 and passim.

2. Raymond Garthoff, *Détente and Confrontation*, 141.

3. Richard H. Ullman, "The Covert French Connection," *Foreign Policy*, Summer 1989.

4. Franz Schurmann, *The Logic of World Power* (New York: Pantheon Books, 1974), 391.

5. On PRM 10 and Germany, see Hanrieder, *Germany, America, Europe*, 407n. On PRM 10 and China, see Banning Garret, "China Policy and the Strategic Triangle," in *Eagle Entangled*, ed. Kenneth A. Oye, Robert J. Lieber, Donald Rothschild (New York: Longman, 1979), 238–45, 259n.

6. Desmond Ball, "U.S. Strategic Policy Since 1945," in Jacobsen, *Strategic Power USA/USSR*.

7. Jacobsen, "Soviet Strategic Policy Since 1945," in Jacobsen, *Strategic Power USA/USSR*, 114.

8. Phil Williams, "The United States and NATO," in Jacobsen, *Strategic Power: USA/USSR*, 342; for Zbigniew Brzezinski's views, see *Washington Post*, 13 May 1987, A23, A26.

9. On NATO planning, see Major General John D. Robinson, in Les Aspin, Chairman, "The Fading Threat," *Report of the Defense Policy Council of the Committee on Armed Forces*, 101st Congress, 2d Session, Washington, D.C., 9 July 1990, 240.

10. See David C. Morrison, "Korean Endgame," *The National Journal*, 4 January, 1992.

11. William Walker, "Nuclear Weapons and the Former Soviet Republics," *International Affairs* 68, 2 (1992): 258. See also *Financial Times*, 27 March 1992. On leftover Soviet nuclear weapons in Czechoslovakia, Bulgaria, and former East Germany (the new Germany agreed to destroy twenty-four East German SS–23s), see *IHT*, 27–28 July 1991.

12. Jacobsen, "Soviet Naval Strategy" in *Strategic Power: USA/USSR*, 472.

13. Ibid., 474.

14. On differing views of the Trident, see Graham Spinardi, "Why the U.S. Navy Went for Hard Target Counterforce in Trident II," *International Security* 15, 2 (Fall 1990); Owen Cote, "The Trident and the Triad," *International Security*, 16, 2 (Fall 1991).

15. *Moscow News*, 24–31 May 1992, 8. To counter perceptions of Soviet naval decline, in 1994, Russian Foreign Minister Andrei Kozyrev called for an expanded naval presence "to show the world at large that Russia is not a weak power." Radio Free Europe/Radio Liberty *Daily Reports*, 51 (15 March 1994).

16. Yaacov Y. I. Vertzberger, *China's Southwestern Strategy* (New York: Praeger, 1985), 145–46.

17. The Pentagon refused to state under what conditions the AirLand Battle concept might be implemented, angering European allies. See Edward A. Corcoran, "Improving Europe's Conventional Defenses," in *Defense of the West*, ed. Robert Kennedy (Boulder, Colo.: Westview Press, 1984), 358–59.

18. Michael R. Lucas, *The Western Alliance after INF* (Boulder, Colo.: Lynne Rienner, 1990), 34.

19. On INF threat, see *Washington Post*, 30 May 1987; *Facts on File*, 22 May 1987, 364D3. See also Frank C. Langdon, "Is Japan Ready to Become a Full Western Ally," *The Pacific Review* 1, 1, (1988).

20. For details on Moscow's views of MTCR, see Martin Navias, *Ballistic Missile Proliferation in the Third World*, Adelphi Papers № 252, Summer 1990.

21. Robert S. Wang, "China's Evolving Strategic Doctrine," *Asian Survey* 24, 10 (October 1984).

22. For SDI countermeasures, see David Holloway, in *Weapons in Space*, ed. Franklyn A. Long, Donald Hafner, Jeffrey Boutwell (New York: W. W. Norton, 1986), 263, 274–75; Union of Concerned Scientists, *The Fallacy of Star Wars* (New York: Vintage, 1984), 115–28.

23. Congress authorized $4.15 billion in 1992, the highest level yet for the SDI program. The bill authorized the president to amend the ABM treaty. See IISS, *The Military Balance*, 1992–93. On change in BMD strategy, see *Defense File* (Paris: American Embassy/USIS Program Section, 7 January 1994), 7. In 1993 Congress allocated $3 billion; the Pentagon is seeking $17 billion for BMD over the 1995-99

period.

24. See comments by SDI director Henry Cooper in *Congressional Quarterly*, 6 July 1991, 1840.

25. See Sven F. Kraemer, "The Krasnoyarsk Saga," *Strategic Review*, Winter 1990. See Michael Krepon, *Washington Post*, 13 December 1986, 19. See also IISS, *The Strategic Balance*, 1986–87.

26. William Walker, "Nuclear Weapons and the Former Soviet Republics," 257–58.

27. John W. Garver, "China's Response to the Strategic Defense Initiative" *Asian Survey* 36, 11 (November 1986): 1220, 1238. China announced its SDI program in 1986. On S300 missiles, see *Far East Economic Review*, 8 April 1993, 23.

28. Leslie Gelb, in *IHT*, 22 July 1991.

29. For speculation that the Clinton administration may have dropped President Bush's promise to develop a joint U.S.-Russian BMD system that London fears could render the UK's expensive Trident system obsolete, see *Jane's Defense Weekly*, 30 October 1993, 21.

30. See Sergei Rogov in *CDPSP* 44, 14 (6 May 1992): 21.

31. See *SIPRI Yearbook* 1992 (Oxford: Oxford University, 1992), 135. Some 37 percent of the funding under the Warner–Nunn act goes into research and development for SDI itself.

CHAPTER 8

1. Andrei S. Gratchev, *L'Histoire Vraie de la Fin de l'URSS* (Paris: Editions du Rocher, 1992), 35. (My translation.)

2. Richard Nixon, in *New York Times*, 9 March 1992. In April 1992, Henry Kissinger sided with George Bush (against Richard Nixon) and cautioned against moving too fast to establish a U.S.-Russian condominium, which had been opposed by both Nixon and Kissinger in the 1970s.

3. One wonders if Washington could have better managed U.S.-Russian-Ukrainian relations by establishing a consulate in Kiev in the 1980s. See George P. Shultz, *Turmoil and Triumph* (New York: Maxwell Macmillan, 1993), 276.

4. See Stepan Kisseliov, "Où va la Russie," in *Les Nouvelles de Moscou* 42 (22 October 1991): 1–3.

5. On allied concerns, see NATO press release (91) 103 (3 December 1991).

6. *IHT*, 2 November 1992, 2. Ustina Markus, "Ukrainian-Chinese Relations," Radio Free Europe/Radio Liberty *Research Reports* 2, 45 (12 November 1993), 19–23.

7. See Edward Mortimer, *European Security after the Cold War*, Adelphi Papers Nº 271 (London: IISS, Summer 1992), 26.

8. See Andrei Kozyrev, "Partnership with the West: A Test of Strength," *Moscow News*, 43 (1992): 3.

9. The revanchist Liberal Democratic party won 70 percent of the Russian parliamentary seats in the lower house (the Duma) during the December 1993

parliamentary elections. Other anti–reformist parties, the Agrarian party and the Russian Communist Party, plus Women of Russia, won 137 seats in the lower house. The divided pro-reform groups, Russia's Choice, Russian Unity and Accord, and Movement for Democratic Reform won 131 seats. The coalition of Grigori A. Yavlinsky—a potential ally of Yeltsin—won 33 seats, whereas potential allies of the Communists won 39 seats. Boris Yeltsin then called for greater unity among reformists to check the possibility of an anti-reformist coalition. See *Bulletin de Russie*, 4 (Paris: January 1994).

10. Gratchev, *L'Histoire Vraie*, 88–94.

11. *Financial Times*, 19 June 1992.

12. See *CDPSP*, 44, 8 (25 March, 1992). See also *CDPSP*, 44, 10 (8 April 1992).

13. See Alexei K. Puskov, "Russia and America: The Honeymoon's Over," *Moscow News*, 1 (10 January 1994): 5. See also *Foreign Policy*, 93, 4 (1993/94).

14. After the Soviet withdrawal from Afghanistan, the Pakistani army revived its focus on India. See Mahwaz Ispahani, *Pakistan: Dimensions of Insecurity*, Adelphi Papers, № 246 (London, IISS: Winter 1989/90). U.S. aid was cut off in October 1990 as a result of Islamabad's nuclear weapons program. Insurgency in 1993 strengthened the efforts of *Jammat e Islam* to unify with Pakistan over the original independence movement of the *Jammu-Kashmir* Liberation Front. See *Jane's Defense Weekly*, 6 November 1993, 31. In November 1993, India accused the State Department of abandoning its "even handed" approach to Kashmir. Washington then proposed an India-Pakistan peace conference.

15. See J. Richard Walsh, "China and the New Geopolitics of Central Asia," *Asian Survey* 33, 3 (March 1993): 277. On the "plot" to undermine China's rule in Xinjiang and Inner Mongolia, see *IHT*, 30 April 1992.

16. Yevgeny Afanasyev, in *Moscow News* 40 (1992).

17. See Gerald Segal, "Northeast Asia: Common Security or à la carte," *International Affairs* 67, 4 (October 1991).

18. For Russian proposals, see Edwin O. Reischauer Center, *The United States and Japan in 1992*, 26.

19. Martin L. Lasater, "U.S. Maritime Strategy in the West Pacific in the 1990s," *Strategic Review*, Summer 1990.

20. Yitzhah Shicor, "China and the Role of the UN in the Middle East: Revised Policy," *Asian Survey* 31, 3 (March 1991).

21. In 1992, under the cover of U.S. F-16 sales to Taiwan, France sold 60 Mirage 2000-5S (more advanced than the F-16) to Taiwan despite threats that China might cut back on French trade—if not German Airbus orders.

22. Edwin O. Reischauer Center (1992), 8–10.

CHAPTER 9

1. Hall Gardner, "Past, Present, Future," *History of European Ideas* 15, 1–3 (August 1992)—written in July 1990. I first proposed a UN or CSCE presence in the former East Germany in November 1989 in an unpublished paper, "Beyond the

Multilateralization of Containment," written at Johns Hopkins SAIS. In 1991 Bosnian Vice-President Ejup Ganic asked for at least one thousand UN Blue Helmets as a preventive war force. He was told by an assistant to UN negotiator Cyrus Vance that his demand was not a function of the UN—to obtain UN protection Bosnia had to wait for the war to begin. See *Tribune de Genève*, 4 January 1993.

2. See proposal prior to Soviet breakup, Richard Ullman, *Securing Europe*, 81. Adam Daniel Rotfeld, "The CSCE: Towards a Security Organization," *SIPRI Yearbook 1993*, 179–218.

3. Eric Grove, *Maritime Strategy and European Security* (London: Brassey's, 1989), 27.

4. Paul H. Nitze, in *IHT*, 15 August 1991; Hans A. Bethe; Kurt Gottfried; Robert S. Mcnamara, "The Nuclear Threat: A Proposal," *New York Review*, 27 June 1991.

5. Charles L. Glaser and George W. Downs, "Defense Policy," *Eagle In a New World*, 90.

6. See analysis by William C. Potter, in *The Nuclear Suppliers and Nonproliferation*, ed. Rodney W. Jones (Lexington, Mass.: Lexington Books, 1985), 10.

7. *SIPRI Yearbook, 1993, 467; SIPRI Yearbook* 1992, 206. As of 1992, IAEA had not conducted a suspected site inspection.

8. William Walker, "Nuclear Weapons," *International Affairs* 68, 2 (1992): 257–58; *Moscow News* 1 (5 January, 1993).

9. See Charles Wolf, Jr., "Arms Transfers," *Wall Street Journal*, 17 March 1992.

10. *Financial Times*, 11 May 1992, 5.

11. *CDPSP* 44, 13 (29 April 1992). On Russian "privatization" of arms industry and reconversion, see *Les Nouvelles de Moscou* (17 March 1992): 9; *Les Nouvelles de Moscou*, 9 (3 March 1992): 7.

12. *SIPRI* Yearbook 1992.

13. Michael R. Lucas, *The Western Alliance after INF* (Boulder, Colo.: Lynne Riemer, 1990).

14. Martin Navias, *Ballistic Missile Proliferation in the Third World*, Adelphi Papers Nº 252 (Summer 1990), 58.

15. Steve Fetter, "Ballistic Missiles and Weapons of Mass Destruction," *America's Strategy in a Changing World*, ed. Sean M. Lynn Jones and Steven Miller (Cambridge, Mass.: MIT Press, 1992).

16. Andrei Kozyrev, in *Moscow News*, 43 (1992).

17. For these scenarios and others, see Jacques Sapir, *Feu le Système Soviétique* (Paris: Editions La Découverte, 1992).

18. See Vitaly Korotich, "The Ukraine Rising," *Foreign Policy*, Winter 1991–92. In January 1994, a classified National Intelligence Estimate stated that if the depression in Ukraine is sustained, a significant number of Ukrainian citizens would favor unification with Russia, leading Ukraine to divide along ethnic and geographic lines—possibly resulting in civil war or Russian intervention. *IHT*, 26 January 1994, 1. The pro-Russian Ukrainian Communist party and its allies won 118 out of 338 seats in the April 1994 elections; 163 seats have no party affiliation.

19. In the 1991 Russian elections, Russian presidential candidate, Vladimir Zhirinovsky, won 6 million votes. Then, in the December 1993 parliamentary elections, an estimated one–third of the military—including a purported 72 percent of the strategic rocket forces—may have voted for his revanchist liberal-democratic party (a name purposely chosen to attract "democratic" support) which won seventy seats in the Russian Duma. Zhirinovsky has demanded the reoccupation of the Baltic states and military actions against Ukraine and Kazakhstan—upon the pretense of protecting the Russian populations within those newly independent republics. In addition to threatening war with Japan if a peace treaty is not signed, he has also threatened Afghanistan, France, Germany, Iran, and Turkey. Following NATO air strikes against Bosnian Serb positions in Gorazde in April 1994, Zhirinovsky stated that NATO raids reflected German interests in the Balkans and that had he been president of Russia, he would have ordered the bombing of NATO bases in Italy in retaliation for the bombing of a "Christian and Slavic people." Yet, despite his ritual denunciation of Germany and his resurrection of Russian claims to Alaska, Zhirinovsky has concurrently called for a U.S.-German-Russian alliance. He has advocated a neo–Molotov-Ribbentrop pact that would divide Poland and return Kaliningrad to Germany—a ploy designed to draw Germany away from the EU. In addition, in a threat to partition Ukraine, Russia would seize the pro-Russian eastern sections of Ukraine plus the Crimea; Poland (under a German-Russian condominium) would obtain western sections of Ukraine. Much as higher authorities in the Weimar Republic supported Hitler as "symbolic" leverage to pressure European and American opinion into supporting German interests, Zhirinovsky may possess similar support within Russia. According to St. Petersburg Mayor Anatoli Sobtchak, Zhirinovsky was purportedly chosen by the former KGB (with Mikhail Gorbachev's blessing) and supported by revanchist military elements. (Zhirinovsky's political buffoonery is more like that of Mussolini than Hitler, however.) As he supported Yeltsin's constitution (granting the executive branch strong powers), it was rumored that Yeltsin covertly supported him to split the Communist opposition. If Zhirinovsky fails to hold his party together—another revanchist National Bolshevik or pan-Slav leader could come to power—or Zhirinovsky could use his position and media image to force a more aggressive Russian foreign policy. On the other hand, if Zhirinovsky or another revanchist leader does come to power, there is a danger that media "demonization" and political-ethical constraints may block the implementation of a realistic, but non-capitulatory, U.S.-EU-Japanese global strategy. See *Moscow News*, 1 (10 January 1994): 2; *Bulletin de Russie* 4 (January 1994).

20. Paul A. Goble, "Forget the Soviet Union," *Foreign Policy*, Spring 1992. At least 88 *oblasts* (regions) passed 14,000 regulations that directly contradicted Moscow's legislation: *The Economist*, 30 January–5 February 1993. Despite Yeltsin's efforts to bar regions from declaring sovereignty, Karelia, Sakha (Yakutia), and Chelyabinsk augmented calls for independence before the December 1993 elections. Both the August 1991 coup and the September–October 1993 suppression of the Russian parliament tended to activate fissiparous tendencies within the Russian federation itself.

Selected Bibliography

Auton, Graeme P. and Hanrieder, Wolfram F. *The Foreign Policies of West Germany, France, and Britain*. Engelwood Cliffs, N.J.: Prentice Hall, 1980.

Bailey, Thomas. *America Faces Russia*. Ithaca, N.Y.: Cornell University Press, 1950.

Beschloss, Michael R. and Talbott, Strobe. *At the Highest Levels*. Boston: Little, Brown, 1993.

Beschloss, Michael R. *The Crisis Years*. New York: HarperCollins, 1991.

Bialer, Sewerlyn and Mandelbaum, Michael, eds. *Gorbachev's Russia and American Foreign Policy*. Boulder, Colo.: Westview Press, 1987.

Blainey, Geoffrey. *The Causes of War*. London: Macmillan, 1988.

Brands, H. W. *Inside the Cold War*. New York: Oxford University Press, 1991.

Brzezinski, Zbigniew. *Power and Principle*. New York: Farrar, Straus, Giroux, 1983.

Carr, E. H. *The Twenty Years Crisis*. New York: St. Martin's Press, 1966.

Cumings, Bruce. *Origins of the Korean War*, Vol. 2. Princeton: Princeton University Press, 1990.

Fukuyama, Francis. *The End of History and the Last Man*. New York: Macmillan, 1992.

Gaddis, John Lewis. *Strategies of Containment*. Oxford: Oxford University Press, 1982.

——*The Long Peace*. New York: Oxford University Press, 1987.

——*The United States and the End of the Cold War*. New York: Oxford University Press, 1992.

Garthoff, Raymond L. *Détente and Confrontation*. Washington, D.C.: The Brookings Institution, 1985.

Garver, John W. *China's Decision for Rapprochement with the United States*. Boulder, Colo.: Westview, 1987.

Gilpin, Robert. *The Political Economy of International Relations*. Princeton, N.J.: Princeton University Press, 1987.

Gratchev, Andrei. *L'Histoire vraie de la fin de l'URSS*. Paris: Editions du Rocher, 1992.

Hanrieder, Wolfram F. *Germany, America, Europe*. New Haven, Conn.: Yale University Press, 1989.

Hersch, Seymour M. *The Price of Power*. New York: Summit Books, 1983.

Ibe, Hideo. *Japan Thrice Opened*. New York: Praeger, 1992.

Jacobsen, Carl G., ed. *Strategic Power USA/USSR*. London: Macmillan, 1990.

Jameson, J. Franklyn. *The American Revolution Considered as a Social Movement*. Gloucester, Mass.: Peter Smith, 1957, 1926.

Kennan, George. *Russia Leaves the War*. Princeton, N.J.: Princeton University Press, 1956.

Kissinger, Henry. *White House Years*. Boston: Little, Brown, 1979.

——*Years of Upheaval*. Boston: Little, Brown, 1982.

Leffler, Melvyn P. *A Preponderance of Power*. Stanford, Calif.: Stanford University Press, 1992.

Lippmann, Walter. *Public Philosopher: Selected Letters of Walter Lippmann*, ed. Blum, John Morton. New York: Ticknor and Fields, 1985.

——*U.S. War Aims*. Boston: Little, Brown, 1944.

Liska, George. *Quest for Equilibrium*. Baltimore: Johns Hopkins University Press, 1981.

——*Russia and the Road to Appeasement*. Baltimore: Johns Hopkins University Press, 1982.

Mueller, John. *Retreat From Doomsday*. New York: Basic Books, 1988.

Newman, Robert P. *Owen Lattimore and the "Loss" of China*. Berkeley, Ca.: University of California Press, 1992.

Nitze, Paul H. *From Hiroshima to Glasnost*. New York: Grove Weidenfeld, 1989.

Nixon, Richard. *Memoirs*. New York: Warner, 1980.

Paterson, Thomas G. *Soviet-American Confrontation*. Baltimore: Johns Hopkins University Press, 1973.

Polanyi, Karl. *The Great Transformation*. Boston: Beacon Hill, 1944.

Rotberg, Robert I. and Rabb, Theodore K. *The Origin and Prevention of Major Wars*. Cambridge: Cambridge University Press, 1988.

Sapir, Jacque. *Feu le Système Soviétique*. Paris: Editions La Découverte, 1992.

Saul, Norman E. *Distant Friends: The United States and Russia, 1763–1867*. Lawrence, Kan.: University of Kansas, 1991.

Shultz, George P. *Turmoil and Triumph*. New York: Maxwell Macmillan, 1993.

Snyder, Louis J. *Macro-nationalisms*. Westport, Conn.: Greenwood, 1984.

Taubman, William. *Stalin's American Policy*. New York: W. W. Norton, 1982.

Thatcher, Margaret. *The Downing Street Years*. London: HarperCollins, 1993.

Wallerstein, Immanuel. *The Politics of the World Economy*. Cambridge: Cambridge University Press, 1984.

Ulam, Adam Bruno. *The Communists*. New York: Scribner's, 1992.

Ullman, Richard. *Securing Europe*. Twickenham, UK: Adamantine, 1991.

Vance, Cyrus. *Hard Choices*. New York: Simon and Schuster, 1983.

Zubok, Vladislav M. *Khrushchev and the Berlin Crisis (1958–62)*. Cold War International History Project, Nº 6. Washington, D.C.: The Woodrow Wilson International Center for Scholars, May 1993.

Index